The Best Dressed Man in Rockaway

The Best Dressed Man in Rockaway

THE BROOKLYN PREP YEARS

Owen Loof

LUMINARE PRESS
WWW.LUMINAREPRESS.COM

The Best Dressed Man in Rockaway: The Brooklyn Prep Years
Copyright © 2022 by Owen Loof

All rights reserved. This book or any portion thereof may not be reproduced or used in any manner whatsoever without the express written permission of the publisher, except for the use of brief quotations in a book review.

Printed in the United States of America

This is a work of fiction and is the product of the author's imagination. The people, places, and things mentioned are all fictitious. Any resemblance to actual persons, living or dead, is entirely coincidental.

Luminare Press
442 Charnelton St.
Eugene, OR 97401
www.luminarepress.com

LCCN: 2022909343
ISBN: 978-1-64388-988-7

This book is dedicated to the woman without whom nothing in my life would be possible. She saved my life and pushed me to do things I never thought I could do. She may not be by my side now, but she is with me always. Her ever-present spirit was the strength and perseverance that helped me to start and complete this book. Peggy, I will love you forever.

PREFACE

I am Owen Loof, The Best Dressed Man in Rockaway. I was given that title by Katie McFadden and *The Rockaway Times* due in large part to my sartorial splendor. In my closet you will find colorful summer suits, such as the light blue with pink flamingos, the orange with yellow pineapples, and the blue with tropical sunsets. However, for occasions that dictate even more flashy attire, I don my sequined and bejeweled blazers with matching bow ties and shoes, or depending on the time of the year, the suits for every holiday and special event.

But there is more to The Best Dressed Man than the clothes. There is the dancing, performing, storytelling, and picture taking. The real essence of The Best Dressed Man is making people happy, producing smiles, and hoping that everyone has a good time. I guess you could say that The Best Dressed Man is the ultimate extrovert. However, that outgoing personality was not always present. All through elementary school, I was an introvert and a follower of both the crowd and the rules. I did not desire to get into trouble, and would never lie to the nuns or, God forbid, my mother. However, I do know when the shell was broken, a fledgling new personality emerged, and the road to The Best Dressed Man began.

In September of 1964, I began my second attempt at freshman year in the hallowed halls of Brooklyn Preparatory School. The Prep was a Jesuit high school located at 1150 Carroll Street in the Crown Heights section of Brooklyn. For

64 years the school succeeded in turning out highly educated, well-rounded young men with its discipline, religious values, classical roots (e.g., Latin and Greek), and the dress code (jackets, ties, and haircuts).

The school produced many notable graduates, such as William Peter Blatty, class of '45, author of The Exorcist; Peter King, '61, the long-serving Congressman from Long Island- and Joe Paterno, '44, the legendary head coach of the Penn State Nittany Lions. Oh, and of course The Best Dressed Man in Rockaway.

I believe it is fair to say that without Brooklyn Prep, The Best Dressed Man as we know him today might not exist. All great recipes have that one ingredient that really completes the final dish. Oh sure, there are other ingredients that contribute to whatever you are trying to concoct, but without that one key ingredient, while the dish turns out well, it is just not the way you wanted. So yes, there were other ingredients contributing to the formation of the extroverted personality, like my family, my friends, and turning fifteen in the middle of the 1960s.

However, all those ingredients would have been there wherever I went to high school. It was the uniqueness of Brooklyn Prep, from my classmates and teachers, to the administration and how I got there, that were so pivotal in laying the foundation of the extroverted personality.

In addressing how I attended Brooklyn Prep, the plan was that I would be enrolled at Bishop Loughlin High School after taking the Co-Op exam, required by Catholic school eighth-grade students intending to attend one of the Catholic Diocesan high schools. Much to everyone's dismay, whatever happened on that test day, I was denied entrance to any of those schools. Although to my complete surprise, I not only met the strict requirements to take the test for Brooklyn Technical High School, but I also did well enough on the test to be accepted to the highly-selective, prestigious school. Problem solved, right? That would be a negative. You see, Brooklyn Tech was a public school, and my mother would not allow me to attend a public school.

How she found Brooklyn Prep, one of the top prep schools in the country, and how they accepted me is still a mystery. In reflecting on the uniqueness of the school, it was not just being there, it was also the timing of when I arrived. Again, like a recipe, sometimes the ingredients must be added at the right time, and for me, starting freshman year over was a key factor.

In October of 1963, after being in Prep for the first quarter, I was hit by a car while riding my bicycle with friends. I fractured my femur, was in the hospital for three months in a body cast, then on crutches for four months after that. However, this was only the last in a series of events that put me at The Prep at the right time. I was also hit by a car in the third grade, which led me to being forced to repeat the seventh grade, notwithstanding a solid B average. It was a decision made by the nuns and my mother that I will never understand. So instead of being a thirteen-year-old freshman and one of the youngest in class, I was fifteen and one of the oldest. That is how I ended up in a freshman class that included Tom Collins, Bobby Atanasio, and Kevin Kane. They were like the pinch of salt, the whipped cream on the sundae, or the lox on the bagel. Collins was our mentor, our Daniel Boone blazing a trail with us; and when he was gone, we continued forging our own path, remembering all he taught us.

So, with the planets all aligned, and all in place in the kitchen, let the games begin!

Freshman Year

CHAPTER 1

When I got off the bus on Nostrand Avenue, I was early and there were not too many students wandering around. I headed right for Carroll Street and the entrance that would lead to the gym, where the first day's orientation would take place. Just as I approached the corner of Carroll Street and Nostrand Avenue, I noticed a short kid who looked a little bewildered. I had grown three inches, and was now five foot seven. I knew right away this boy was a freshman because I recognized myself from last year. So, I walked over and asked, "A little lost huh?"

"Yeah. I sure am. That building is a lot bigger than my old school."

"Ah don't worry! Once you get in there, you'll be fine. I'm Owen." I reached out my hand.

The boy took it and said, "Hi Owen! I'm Peter Racanelli."

"Okay Peter, no problem. Just follow me."

As we made our way up Carroll Street, I said, "This is orientation. There's speeches and stuff, then we get our homerooms and spend the rest of the day going from class to class meeting the teachers."

Peter looked up at me, trying to take in all the information he had been given, and asked, "What grade are you in, Owen?"

I cringed a little, but just answered, "I'm a freshman, Pete"

He was somewhat perplexed. "But you sure seem to know what's going on?"

"It's a long story that I'll tell you sometime."

"Thanks, man! Sure thing!"

"Come on Pete, let's get in there."

Once in the gym, we were looking for seats when I felt a tap on my shoulder and looked around to see Mr. Sullivan, the Gym teacher. "What are you doing there Loof, posing for a picture? And how's the leg?"

"Oh, hi Mr. Sullivan. I'm just lookin' for somebody. You know what happened?"

"Sure. Father Nolan let the teachers know. Bad accident. Tough break."

"In more ways than one Mr. Sullivan! But it feels fine now." And I did a little jump and dance. "See! And don't worry, I'll be ready for gym."

"Good footwork there Loof. Maybe I shouldn't tell you this, but I won't see you till January. You have pool first semester. Now hurry up and find a seat."

"Thanks Mister, see ya around."

As I stood there still scanning the bleachers, one of the guys in the first row grabbed my arm and moved over to open a seat for me, moving some other students in the process. "Sit here next to me. What'd that teacher call you? Loof?"

I sat down and looked at this new classmate, and with an extended hand answered, "Yep. Owen Loof."

The student shook my hand and said, "Hey, I'm Tom Collins. You're a freshman?"

I smiled and replied, "Yes, I'm a freshman." And then I waited for the inevitable.

"But that teacher already knew you, and that was quite a little jig you did for him. There's a story there, right?"

I looked at Collins with a sly, friendly smile, and replied, "Yes, there's a story. For now, let's just say it's not my first time here, and I'll tell you the rest later."

"I can't wait, Owney!"

I recoiled in surprise, asking, "What'd you call me?"

"Owney, right?"

"Only my cousins call me Owney! Why would you do that?"

"Well, the only Owen I ever heard of was an Irish mobster from Prohibition named Owney Madden. I thought all Owens were called Owney. Is there a problem with the name?"

"Not really, I guess. Like I said, only my cousins use it, and I only recently found out something interesting about my name."

"Okay, shoot."

"Well, you see, Owney Madden babysat my mother, while my grandmother ran a speakeasy in Hell's Kitchen during Prohibition. My uncle, who was killed at The Battle Anzio in World War ll, was also Owen. So, I guess we were both named after Mr. Madden."

My new friend patted me on the back, saying, "That's good enough for me, Owney!"

I didn't pay much attention to the orientation talks because they were almost word for word from last year, and I chatted a little with Collins, who confessed, "I'm here because my father thought the discipline would be good for me. Ya see I'm not a big rules follower." I just smiled and was not sure what to make of that, since I had been taught to follow the rules. All I knew was that Tom Collins was funny and friendly, and I hoped that we would have some classes together.

The freshman assignments for homeroom finally arrived, and we were paying more attention now. It was not until the last homeroom assignment, 1G, was announced that we heard our names. When I heard that Father Romano would be the 1G Homeroom teacher, I threw my head back and pumped both fists saying, "Yeah, all right!"

Before we rose from our seats Collins asked, "That's good?"

"Oh yeah, that's good! He was my homeroom and Latin teacher last year. A good guy, funny, and a good teacher."

On our way out of the gym, Collins put his arm on my shoulder and said, "I think we're gonna have some fun Owney."

Father Romano greeted me warmly, which surprised many of the students. Collins spread the word that I had been in the school last year, and knew a lot of the teachers. The fifteen-minute introductory session was very familiar, but I did forget the class elections. The priest announced that he would take nominations now, and then the nominees would prepare a fact sheet that would be distributed to the class before voting. There would be three nominees, and the person getting the most votes would be class president; runner-up, vice president; and finally, class secretary. As soon as Father Romano opened the nominations, Tom Collins stood up and said, "I nominate Owen Loof!"

Father Romano asked for someone to second the nomination, and Thomas Zdyrko, who was sitting next to Collins, raised his hand, and I was officially in the running. The other two candidates were Lenny Hypolite and Artie Gallagher. The bell sounded, and people got up starting for the door. I just sat there. Collins and Zdyrko looked around, and Collins said, "Come on Owney."

I looked up at Collins and uttered, "Why'd you do that?"

"You'll be great. Don't worry, leave everything to me."

I stood up and asked Zdyrko, "You don't even know me, and you seconded the nomination?"

Zdyrko pointed to Collins and said, "He told me you knew a lot about the school, and Father Romano seemed to like you."

I just shook my head in disbelief, but before I could say anything, Father Romano saw us and called out, "Hey guys, you're going to be late for the next class. Get going!"

We hurried for the door and just before exiting, Father Romano added, "Good to see you back Owen."

When we were in the hall, Zydrko looked at me and said, "See Owney! That's why!"

"OWNEY!?"

Zydrko pointed at Tom, saying, "Well, that's what he called you!"

I threw up my hands and smiled. "Okay! Fine!"

At lunch, Tom and I came off the line with our food and were looking for a seat, then I recognized a face from some classes. I said to Collins, "Hey, look right there." Collins wasn't sure where to look, and I described where to look more emphatically, pointing my tray. "Third table on the left." Collins nodded and I continued, "You see that kid next to the two empty seats? He's with us in three classes including Doolan's Math class. Let's go over there."

When we got to the table, I asked the target if the two empty seats were taken. He answered no, and we seated ourselves. I sat next to him and said, "Hey! I'm Owen Loof and this is Tom Collins. I saw you in a lot of our same classes."

"Hi! My name is Bobby Atanasio. Yeah, I remember seein' you guys."

I said, "I noticed when you walked into English that you're pretty tall."

"Wow! Can't put anything over on you, huh Owen?"

Collins piped in, "We all call him Owney!"

I burst out laughing and said, "Don't listen to anything he says. How tall are you, and do you play basketball?"

"I'm 6'1", and I play a little. You?"

"I'm gettin' better."

"I noticed that you know a lot of people, seem to know where you're goin', and how to get there."

Collins answered, "Oh, Owney here spent some time in the school last year, and he owes me the story."

They both looked at me, and I knew there was no choice but to spill the beans. In the *Readers Digest* condensed version, I related the story of the car accident, the injury, hospitalization, and recovery. I also told them I was only in school for the first quarter. Atanasio was the first to comment. "I can't imagine how that body cast felt. How's your leg now?"

"You get used to a lot of things when you have to. And my leg's as good as new."

Collins was quiet, I looked over at him, and he had his hand on his chin with a very pensive stare. I asked, "You were waitin' for the story, and now you have nothing to say?"

"I'm thinkin'."

I looked back at Atanasio and said, "Ya know Bobby. I just met this guy today. But I know when he's thinkin' like that, we should be worried."

At the end of the day, I met back up with Tom and Bobby in the gym where everyone would be dismissed for the day. Father Nolan, the Headmaster, and Father Knox, the Prefect of Discipline, made some last-minute announcements, and reminded everyone to be prepared for the start of the regular schedule tomorrow. There was a closing prayer and then dismissal, but the three of us lingered for a while to talk.

I started, "I guess you two have gym this semester, 'cause I didn't see you in the class we went to, instead of the pool."

Bobby answered, "Yeah, me and him have gym. Ya didn't go to the pool?"

"No. They're gettin' it ready. Ya know I've never seen the pool. I had gym first semester last year."

Tom asked, "Do they know when it'll be ready?"

I replied, "Yeah, Gorman said it will be ready on Monday."

It was unanimous that we were really looking forward to getting in the pool. We left the gym and were saying our goodbyes, but just before we separated, Tom said to me, "Don't worry about the campaign tomorrow, I got this."

At dinner when my parents asked how the day went, I related some of what happened, and left out a lot of what happened. Of course, I mentioned Tom Collins, and my mother, Bridget, tried not to laugh, but my father, Martin, did. I was not sure what was so funny. My father could see that I was perplexed and said, "Owen, there is a drink called a Tom Collins that is made with gin."

My mother added, "How could a parent do that to a child?"

I was almost elated, "Oh wow! That's great. I wish I had known that today. Thanks dad!"

My mother chided me, "Owen, I'm surprised at you. Don't you even think about teasing that boy."

Trying to sound sincere, I said, "Oh Mom. You know I would never do that."

My father was in the middle of taking a drink of his beer and almost choked. But before any more conversation, there was a knock on the back door. My mother opened the door, and Michael O'Connor was standing there. Michael was my best friend, and like the brother I never had. We were friends even before starting St. Camillus elementary school together in kindergarten.

"Well, hello Michael. Come right in."

"Hi Bridget. Are you all finished dinner?"

"Just about Michael. It's fine."

Michael entered the kitchen, said hello to my father and me, and sat down at the table. My mother said to Michael, "Owen was just telling us about a boy in his class named Tom Collins."

Michael's face brightened and he replied, "Wow, cool name. Like the drink."

All of us were surprised, and I asked, "How did you know that?"

"It's my mother's favorite drink."

Then Michael shared that Junior High School 180 was opening their gym on weeknights to play basketball, and tonight was the first night. He asked if I could go with him, so we could sign up. My mother asked about the time frame, and Michael told her the gym would be opened from 7 to 10 p.m. She looked over at my father, who nodded slightly, and taking a moment to think, said, "Okay. There's no homework tonight, but this can't be a regular thing once school gets going."

We were out of our seats in a blink, and I went around the table to thank my mother with a hug. When I let go and started to leave, she demanded, "I want you home by ten, Owen Loof!"

"Thanks mom, and I'll be careful!"

But as I ran out the door, I heard her say, "Sure you will Owen. Sure, you will."

I got to school early the next day, and Collins was waiting for me. I was kind of shocked and said, "Geeze, what are you doing here so early?"

"I wanted to make sure I caught you before we went in so we could go over what I wrote for you."

Collins handed me an index card. I scanned the card, looked at Collins, and said, "You're nuts! First of all, what makes you think I can actually get up in front of the class and say anything? And second, you want me to say this?"

"Look, Owney! All you want to do is get elected president so you can have more of a say in the student senate. Like any politician, you say whatever will win you votes, and when you're in office, you do what's best for you. Accept the perks of the job and have a good time."

"But this stuff? A concert with this band, The Velvet Underground, and relax the dress code. You gotta be kiddin'?" I was shaking my head and asked, "And what's this about the boat ride?"

"Like all the rest of this stuff, I was talking to some seniors on the train yesterday. They told me there used to be a senior boat ride to Rye Playland. Well, a couple of years ago, there was a band on the boat, there was a big fight, and the band got thrown overboard, piano and all. That was the end of the boat ride. So, if you start working with student government now, we'll have it when we're seniors."

"I still think you're nuts."

"Don't worry Owney. Stick with me! Come on. It's almost time. Let's go!"

Collins started walking as I delayed while holding my head in my hands, and then followed my Rasputin down the hall.

In class after the prayer, the Pledge of Allegiance, and the morning announcements, it was time for the candidate speeches. I was the last to speak, and when I got back to my seat, Collins greeted me enthusiastically saying, "That was terrific. You're a shoo-in."

"Well, it wasn't as bad as I thought it would be."

Earlier, Father Romano had handed out paper for the ballots, and everyone was busy scribbling in their votes. The first person in each row had the responsibility of collecting the votes. It only took a few minutes for all the votes to be collected and deposited on Father Romano's desk. He read each vote, and Tom McDonald recorded it on the blackboard next to each candidate's name. As the vote count was nearing the end, it was clearly a two-horse race. When the final vote was read and tabulated on the board, Collins was astounded and reacted with a loud, "What?"

The final tally was Gallagher-13, Loof-12, Hypolite-8.

The candidates all rose from their seats and went to the front of the room. Father Romano shook hands and thanked each of us. We congratulated one another, and received a round of applause from the class. The priest gave each of us a packet from student government, and said they would contact us with more information. With that, the bell sounded, and everyone started to file out. I was walking to English with Collins, and we were joined on the way by Atanasio. He asked us excitedly, "Hey! How'd the election go?"

Collins answered dejectedly, "He lost the presidency by one vote."

"Oooh. A close one. So, you're vice president, that's good."

With a questioning look and tone, Collins exclaimed, "I don't understand. I had it all worked out. Everybody I talked to voted the way they said they would." He stopped in his tracks, pointed at me, and glared. "There's only one person I didn't check with. Loof! Oh no, no Loof?"

I bowed my head sheepishly and said, "I voted for Gallagher."

Collins and Atanasio both groaned and slapped me around until we reached English class.

CHAPTER 2

On Monday, I arrived at school with only one thought on my mind. I was only thinking of last period, and my first look at and swim in the pool. After seventh period, I was almost to the pool, when I remembered, I did not go to my locker for my bathing suit. I hurried to the locker, which was on the other side of the school, and because I in was in such a hurry, my first try at the combination did not work. I finally got the locker opened and grabbed the bathing suit. As I shut the door, the bell sounded to start eighth period. I took off running as fast as I could, then when turning the last corner leading to the pool, I literally ran into Father Knox.

"Whoa there, Mr. Loof. Where are you running to?"

I explained to the priest what had happened and where I was going.

"So, Mr. Loof, the other day you were late for school, and now you are late for class. Not a good start young man. I'm not going to give you JUG, (this was the term used for detention and meant, "Judgement Under God") this time, but you better not make a habit of being late."

I replied in a respectfully quiet tone, "Thank you, Father. I'll do better, Father."

As we parted ways, and were a few steps away from each other, Father Knox turned back toward me and said, "Why did you bring a bathing suit anyway?"

I was around the corner before I could answer, and just continued to the pool. When I got to the pool's locker room, I was almost ten minutes late, and was still thinking about what Father Knox had said while quickly putting on my bathing suit.

As I got to the door leading to the pool, I knew I had to find Mr. Gorman and explain my lateness. I opened the door, stepped out onto the deck, and was astounded to see my twenty-four classmates at the other end of the pool, lined up in rows of six. Mr. Gorman was standing to one side, explaining what was going to happen. At that moment, I understood Father Knox's question. My twenty-four classmates were stark naked. The guys who were first in line jumped in the pool, and started swimming. Mr. Gorman finally spied me and yelled, "What are you doing standing there?"

He looked at his clipboard, and yelled again, "If you're Owen Loof, go take off the bathing suit and get back out here!"

That night at dinner, when my parents asked me how the day went, I told them about a joke I told in Latin class, and my mother scolded me. She reminded me that I was in school to learn and not make jokes. When I glanced at my father, he nodded, smiled, and went on reading the newspaper. I did not tell them that it was all Tom Collins' idea.

Then I told the story of what happened at the pool. My mother was starting to clear the table and was nearing the sink when I got to the part about swimming naked. She almost dropped the dishes in her hand, but miraculously nothing was broken. She gained some composure and exclaimed, "What?! The boys swim naked?"

"Yeah mom. I talked to some guys on the train home, and they said that's the way it is."

"I have never heard of such a thing. Martin, do you believe this?"

He put down the paper and looked at his wife. "My school didn't have a pool. I guess that's the way things are done in Catholic schools."

My mother was adamant in her disbelief. We attempted to calm her down, but she was still shocked by the whole thing, and said, "I'll have to look into this."

Knowing my mother, I was sorry I had mentioned the subject at all. I also learned that, like not telling her when I got smacked by the nuns because I'd only get another beating, it's best not tell her too much of what goes on in school.

A while after dinner, I came down from my room, announced that I had finished the little homework I had, and asked my mother if I could go to 180 to play basketball. She gave me the okay, and I was out the door walking down Beach 96th Street to the Boulevard. I got to the gym just in time to be included in a full-court game on the same team as Michael. Our team won that game, and then Michael, Larry McElroy, and I teamed up to split two half-court games. Later, Michael and I were sitting on the edge of the stage at one end of the gym, and I said to my friend, "I made too many mistakes in the full-court game."

Michael was sincere, and not just trying to make me feel better, when he said, "Don't worry, you really are gettin' better. And you played great in the half-court games."

"Okay whatever, but ya gotta hear this." I then told my friend the pool story.

Michael's jaw dropped, and he sat in stunned silence for a few seconds. Finally, he looked at me in disbelief. "Naked, like with no bathing suits? Like with nothing on? Everything just hanging out?"

"Yep."

Michael was incredulous, "I..I..don't believe it!"

"Well, believe it. We're gonna have swimming races, water polo, free periods. All buck naked."

Michael was still shaking his head in disbelief when I continued, "There's even a diving board."

Michael's eyes widened as he asked, "Are they gonna at least teach you how to dive?"

Bursting out laughing, I replied, "They better, because one of the Black kids, Brian Jones, did a belly flop off the board, and when he hit the water, everybody winced."

After Michael finished wincing, he said, "I still don't believe it, and I'm glad my school doesn't have a pool. But listen, I gotta go. You know I have football practice all week, and an early game on Saturday." Before leaving he added laughingly, "Be careful in the pool!"

On Thursday, with the week almost over, Tom and I got to the cafeteria and found Bobby. When we sat down, Bobby could tell something had happened. He stared at us and asked, "Okay, what's going on?"

I answered, "It was crazy." I pointed at Tom, and continued, "We're in Connolly's History class, and this guy tells me and a few other guys sittin' around us to cough every time Connolly tries to say something. So, we did it like eight times in a row. He was gettin' madder and madder. Finally, he yells and tells the whole class that we have to write on a piece of loose leaf, 'I must not cough in class' 500 times."

Bobby laughs a little and says, "Okay, that's kinda funny."

With a grin on my face and one hand raised, I said, "No, no! Wait there's more." I paused, then continued with both hands extended toward Tom, "Ya know what? You tell 'im. It's your idea."

Tom shrugs and starts, "Okay, here it is. I told some people already, and I'll get to as many as I can before I leave.

We get a piece of loose leaf, and only write on the first line, 'I must not cough in class 500 times.'"

Bobby starts laughing and says, "That's funny. But what do you think is gonna happen?"

Tom replies, "What's the difference? He's not gonna give the whole class JUG."

Bobby shoots back, "What if everybody doesn't do it?"

Without a second thought, Tom spits out, "We'll cross that bridge when we get to it. But I know I can count on Owney." And with his hand on my shoulder adds, "Right?"

The next day, the first thing Mr. Connolly did when the bell sounded to start class was to tell everyone to take out the punishment assignment and place it on their desk. Mr. Connolly was a scholastic, which meant that he wore a cassock like a priest, but was still in the process of completing his training to be ordained a Jesuit priest. As Mr. Connolly moved through the rows, it became evident that no one else had followed through with the scheme. The two holdouts were of course sitting in the last two seats in the last row. When Mr. Connolly arrived at our desks, and picked up the assignments, he was not happy. "What is this?"

Tom answered in an even tone, "We did exactly what you told us to do. You said to write, 'I must not cough in class 500 times,' and that's what we did."

The whole class laughed, which did nothing to calm down Mr. Connolly. "You two wiseacres just earned yourselves two days JUG, and on Monday I want, 'I must not cough in class,' and I want it written 1000 times not just once. Do I make myself clear?"

"Much clearer than yesterday, Mister."

When Mr. Connolly turned around to go back to the front of the room, I hit Tom with a notebook. But the teacher caught the incident out of the corner of his eye, and shouted, "Mr. Loof, are you trying for three!"

"No Mister." I then gave Tom the evil eye, and he laughed.

When we were leaving JUG that afternoon, I said, "Great plan, and we gotta do this on Monday."

Tom was nonplussed, and replied, "Did we break up the class and get a laugh? Yeah, we did. And if those other yellow bellies had gone along, it woulda been better. Look you do the crime, you do the time. It's only JUG, sometimes it's worth it."

All the way home on the train I thought about what Tom said. There was certain logic to my friend's words. While I wasn't sure if I completely agreed, I decided to pack them away for future reference.

My mother was a waitress in Curley's Diner, which was on the corner of Beach 96th Street. I stopped to see her before walking up the block to our house. The first thing she said was, "You're a little late. Where were you?"

Without hesitation, I answered, "There was a meeting for the freshman class officers, and some of the upperclassmen to get us set up for the Student Senate."

"That's very good."

"Oh yeah. There's another meeting on Monday. Should I come down here for dinner tonight?"

"Yes. It's been a while. Curley received some fresh liver today."

"Great Mom. See you in a little while." I kissed my mother's cheek, exited the diner, and walking up the block, I thought, "Well, that was pretty easy."

CHAPTER 3

I made an observation after the first quizzes in the classes I was repeating with the same teachers. A lot of the questions were the same, or similar. In Mr. Browning's English class, the first written assignment was the same. Pick a book from the summer reading list, write a two-page essay explaining the plot, and why you liked it. Since St. Camillus, I had kept track of my grades by saving things like tests and written assignments. So, I was able to find the essay I had written last year on George Orwell's *Animal Farm*. The grade on the paper was a B, and Mr. Browning had made a few comments. So, I retyped the essay and followed the teacher's suggestions to make some minor changes. The day Mr. Browning returned the papers, because of the seating arrangement, Tom and I were the last to receive our essays. As Mr. Browning was handing me my paper, he said, "That was well written, Loof. Some good insights on Animal Farm."

I looked at the grade, and it was an A. "Thank you, Mister."

Tom got his paper, for which he received a C, and once outside the room he asked me my grade. When I told him the grade, he reacted with a mixture of excitement and teasing, "An A. Very good you nerd."

"Well, there is a story. I'll tell you at lunch."

At lunch, Tom and I were already at a table when Bobby arrived. Before he even sat down, Tom exclaimed, "Glad you're here. You know this nerd got an A on Browning's essay. But wait, he says there's a story."

After Bobby was finally seated, I explained how I had written the essay. Tom was almost beside himself, and with a somewhat raised voice asked, "Wait, you're telling me that you have all your tests, quizzes, and basically all your assignments from last year?"

"Maybe not all of them, but a lot of them."

Tom looked at me with a sly little grin, and challenged, "And when exactly were you going to tell your best friends about this? Or were you?"

I was somewhat flustered, stammering, "I really wasn't sure till we got Browning's assignment, and I wasn't sure how much I actually had till I looked."

Tom kept up the pressure. "And now that you know, what are you going to do?"

I smiled, put my arms on their shoulders, and declared, "How could I not share my good fortune with my best buddies!"

Tom was happy, and warned, "But look, we gotta be smart about this and not do too good. Oh, and on quizzes and tests, we can't have the same answers or get the same marks. So, all we do is change one or two answers we know are correct, and we work out a signal, so I know which one you changed, and I'll change different ones." After a slight pause, Tom held up his index finger, and continued, "Oh yeah, and let's be really careful on copying homework and written assignments!"

Just before we parted company, I made sure my friends took note of something. "Now remember, I was only here for the first marking period. So, I got no notes or anything after that, and have no idea what went on the rest of the year. After this, we're on our own."

Tom smiled and added, "Well, there's still the three of us and we'll be working together, right?"

We came together like in a football huddle, put our hands on top of one another, and spelled out in a yell, "T-E-A-M!" Then we released our hands, pumping fists in the air, and completed the chant, "YEAH!"

The rest of the marking period went smoothly. The day grades arrived, I was the first one home and was able to retrieve the mail. I brought the mail into the kitchen, and looking at the envelope that said Brooklyn Prep, I thought about my options. I could get rid of them completely without opening the envelope, but then I wouldn't know the grades. So, better to open the envelope, and then destroy the evidence. Standing there looking at the envelope, I thought, "Wait, these grades are going to be pretty good." I took the envelope and placed it right on top of the mail. I wanted my parents to see it first. I smiled, and went to my room to get a little homework done, so I could go play basketball later.

When I heard the gate, then the back door, and voices, I knew that my parents were home. I decided to bide my time, and not be too overanxious. Instead, I would just let them open the envelope, look at the grades, then call me down. Normally the waiting would be nerve-wracking, but in this instance, I was confident that my parents would be pleased with the report. Finally, the parent conference ended, and I was summoned to the kitchen.

When I got to the kitchen, both my parents were sitting at the table, and my father was holding the grade sheet. He was smiling and said, "This is a very good report son."

"Thanks dad. You know, I didn't even look at it yet."

He handed the report to me, and I saw pretty much what I expected. The overall average was 89, with a grade of 90 or better in four subjects. I also earned one of the highest math grades ever, an 85, but it was still the lowest grade on the report.

I was still going over the report when my mother added, "The grades are very nice Owen, but you must really try harder to do better in math. If you had a higher grade there, your overall average would have been over 90, which would have been an A."

I tried not to show what I was really feeling, and said, "Okay mom. I'll try and do better."

She was continuing to look over the report, and seemed about to say something, but my father spoke first. "It's okay Owen. Why don't you go back to your room and finish your assignment? We'll call you when dinner's ready."

He got a dirty look from his wife, and a look of relief from me, as I hurried out of the kitchen, and up the stairs. Once safely in my room, it seemed that my father knew what I knew. The words that would certainly be on my mother's lips. "You know you could do better if you just apply yourself."

I thought, "Thanks dad."

Tom Collins and Bobby Atanasio also pleased their parents with good grades. Bobby's average was a little better than mine because he had a better science grade. Tom's average was a tad lower than mine because he did not do as well in history. It seemed to me that Tom Collins was just not that concerned with his grades one way or another. For when I reminded both of my friends that we were now in unchartered territory with our grades, Tom responded with a shrug saying, "Grades are not the best factor in determining who's learning better. The 'A' student is not necessarily learning more than the 'C' student. The 'A' student is just rememberin' the stuff better that day."

Throughout the second marking period, we continued to keep track of our grades. By the middle of November, it was apparent that our grades were in the decline, and something had to be done to remedy the situation. The first thing we did was approach two or three of the really smart people in each class, and offer inducements for their help during exams and quizzes. These inducements could include buying them lunch and providing protection from the jocks, during gym or pool especially. Sometimes the suggestion would be that if the help was not forthcoming, it would be a shame if one of their books turned up missing.

There were two steps next in the process. First, one of the smart students would make a cheat sheet for us, and second, there was the sign system. This was similar to the signs a third-base coach would give to a batter in baseball. The system was most effective in multiple-choice exams. Tom Collins would indicate what question an answer was for by using his fingers. The answer would be transmitted by coded gestures, such as: A=scratch the nose, B=pull left ear, C=pull right ear, D=brush your hand across your forehead. The signs would be changed periodically, and sometimes they would switch to the desk tap method. Tap once for A, twice for B, and so on. The cheat sheets were used to good advantage for fill-in-the-blank and short-answer questions. Collins was the expert at hiding cheat sheets, and Bobby and I were learning fast and well. In the first exams and quizzes after implementing the system, there was an improvement in grades, especially in Latin, history, and English.

The Tuesday after Thanksgiving, Tom and I sat down with Bobby at lunch, and I blurted out before anyone else could say anything, "Oh, did I tell you guys that at the student senate meeting yesterday, they announced that the plans for a dance to be held here were finalized?"

Tom reacted with some surprise. "Whoa! How long has this been in the works?"

"I don't know, maybe a month or so."

Waving his hand between himself and Bobby, Tom continued, "And you didn't say anything to us?"

I got flustered and said, "I don't know. I guess I forgot."

Bobby started to laugh, and Tom said somewhat exasperatedly with his hand raised, "You forgot?" After a short pause and with a shake of his head, he kept going, "A dance with girls. And you forgot to keep us abreast of the situation?"

Bobby almost choked on his food, and I was also laughing, but still was able to counter, "Who said anything about girls?"

After the three of us stopped laughing, Tom threw a French fry at me and said, "Okay, okay! Tell us what the deal is."

"Well, the dance committee has been in touch with the girls from St. Brendan's."

Tom interrupted with his best Groucho Marx impression, "And how much touching did they do?"

"All I know is I wish I had been on the committee. But seriously folks, it's going to be for freshmen, and the idea is that since St. Brendan's is our sister school, the two freshman classes should get to know one another."

Tom asked, "So Owney, when is this shindig supposed to happen?"

"Not this Saturday. The following Saturday, December 12th. Oh yeah, it's supposed to be like a holiday thing. Ya can wear some kind of Christmassy stuff."

Bobby added, "That sounds good. At least we can't throw the band overboard."

Tom pondered aloud, "But imagine what we could do to Santa Claus."

CHAPTER 4

At dinner on Friday, December 11th, there was a discussion of some news items of the day. I really was not listening closely to the conversation. All I wanted to do was get to 180 and play basketball. Tonight was going to be a big night. Some white guys from St. Francis, a local Catholic parish and elementary school where basketball was part of the religion, were going to play a team of Black players from The Hammels housing project. The game grew out of a friendly argument between a guy from St. Francis and two guys from Hammels. I played some half-court games with the Hammels' guys, and they were really good to me, even though I wasn't as good as they were. The two teams were going to put their best players on the court, so I definitely did not want to miss this game.

As everyone at the table was finishing up, my mother asked about school. "So, Owen, we haven't talked about school in a while, is everything okay?"

"Sure, mom it's going fine."

"I know you usually keep pretty good track of your grades. How do you think you're doing?"

"Everything looks okay so far. Today in pool I scored two goals, and our team is in first place in our class tournament."

"Thank you for reminding me about your pool class. I still want to find out from the headmaster why they have you boys swimming without any bathing suits."

I cringed, regretting bringing up pool, but recovered enough to look at my mother and say, "Oh, me and a couple of the guys were talking to Father Swanson, the student counselor, and Father Romano, and that came up in the conversation."

She looked at me with surprise, and remarked, "Really, Owen!"

My father put down the newspaper, and made sure his hearing aid was turned on as I continued, "Yeah, they said that it was a tradition that started when they first got the pool. Yeah, ya see in Ancient Greece all the athletes competed naked, especially in the Olympic Games. So, they wanted to instill the discipline and study of that time to go hand in hand with the classical languages of Greek and Latin that are the hallmarks of the school."

My parents sat there a little stunned, and glanced at one another before my mom spoke. "That's what the two priests said?"

I shook my head, saying, "Well, maybe not word for word, but pretty much."

My father added, "It is true about the Olympics in Ancient Greece."

My mother looked at her husband, and then her son. She stood up and announced, "Okay Owen. Well, I am going to the bathroom. Could you two please clear the table, and I'll be back to do the dishes." Then she pushed her chair back, and walked out of the kitchen.

I got up and began picking up my plate and glass. As I started walking to the sink, my father said, "That was quite a story there son."

"You think she bought it?"

"I would have to say no. But you really don't want her talking to the school, right?"

"Yep."

"I'll see what I can do. Now get out of here and go play basketball."

"Thanks dad!" Then I was out the door in a flash.

At the gym, Michael was already involved in a game when I got there. We talked briefly between games, as I was included in one or two. Then it was time for the big game of the night. It was St. Francis vs. Hammels in a five-on-five full-court game.

Of the ten players lined up to play, there were five players that would go on to play college, ball and one, Denis Winters, who made it to the NBA. While the two teams were warming up, one of the Hammels players took a wrong step on his lay-up and twisted an ankle. He got, up limping badly, and tried to walk it off. He was in a lot of pain, and finally conceded there was no way he was going to be able to play.

The Hammels team now only had four players. They were standing around discussing their options and looking around the gym to see if anyone would volunteer to help them out. Everyone seemed to be walking away, so I walked toward the Hammels huddle, and called to one of the players I knew, Curtis Brooks. "Hey Curtis, I'll play with you guys."

The other four players turned their heads, and before Brooks could say anything, the leader of the Hammels team, Ray Alford, said, "Who is this guy, and can he play at all?"

Brooks looked at Alford and said, "Ray, I've played on the same team as him a couple of times, and while he's not the best player out here, he can play defense. He can run all day, and for a white boy, he can jump. He's a good guy, too. Besides, it doesn't look like anybody else wants to help us out."

Alford said, "You sure we wouldn't be better off just the four of us? I really want to win this game."

I looked sternly at Alford and said, "Ray, those St. Francis guys are a bunch of snobby knuckleheads, and I wanna beat them even more than you do."

The Hammels players chuckled, and Alford thrust his index finger hard to my chest, and said, "Okay, but don't fuck this up!"

Before I got ready to take the court, Michael caught up with me, asking, "What are you doing?"

"I'm gonna play a basketball game."

"With the guys from Hammels?"

"Yeah, with the guys from Hammels. It's no big deal, and we're gonna stick it to those schmucks from St. Francis."

"You do notice that you are a white guy on a Black team playing a White team?"

"Oh my God! You're right. They are Black! And I wouldn't care if they were purple. I'm playing basketball. I'll talk to you after me and my team finish celebratin' our victory."

The game started slowly with the two teams feeling each other out. Each side had good scoring runs, which led to many lead changes. As for me, I did what I did best by running, jumping, and playing defense. I did not dribble or shoot when it was not the right thing to do, but I did make some good plays. There were excellent passes that led to easy buckets for teammates, and I surprised Winters by blocking his shot from behind after an offensive rebound.

I was also instrumental in restoring order when Alford was driving for a basket and he beat Winters, but one of the other St. Francis players just barreled into him, knocking Alford to the floor. The refs did blow the whistle for a foul. But when Alford got up, he started toward the offending player, who had turned his back and was walking away. Another St. Francis player grabbed Alford from behind, then the player who committed the foul turned, and was about to throw a punch. I was the closest Hammels player, and gave the guy just enough of a shove to prevent any such occurrence, and Brooks wrapped him up. I then turned around to ensure no other St. Francis players would get involved.

The game ended in a 52-48 victory for Hammels, and we got together at mid-court congratulating one another with back slaps, handshakes, and a hug or two. After that short celebration, we walked over to our opponents, and all ten players exchanged handshakes, saying, "Thanks for a good game." Winters hugged Alford, smiled, and said, "I think a rematch is necessary."

Alford returned the smile and responded, "Sure thing. It'll be a pleasure."

When Winters shook hands with me, he had a few words. "What's your name again?"

"Owen Loof."

"That was a cool thing you did replacin' their guy like that. There are some fools around here."

"Yeah well, there are fools everywhere, and they come in all colors. I won't treat you like one until you prove to me you are one."

"Sounds good to me. And by the way, that was some play knocking the ball out of my hands under the boards. You weren't perfect out there, but you helped your team by knowing your role."

"Thanks man. I appreciate that, and if you make it to the NBA, I'll always be able to say, I made a great play on that guy once."

"You sure can!" Then we both laughed, shaking hands one more time.

But just before Winters turned to leave, I added, "I really wanted to beat you guys tonight!"

"And you did. But you better be here for the rematch.!" We both laughed again, and parted ways.

I was surprised to find Michael standing right behind me when I turned around. He handed me a towel and said, "Good game, pal. But you know some people are not happy with what you did."

"Well, some people can kiss my butt. Can you just grab my stuff for me? I'm going to say so long to the guys. Meet me over there, okay?"

I started over to where my teammates were gathered, and as I got closer, Alford saw me coming. With outstretched hands, he announced, "And here's our honorary Black man for the night."

He hugged me as the other four players backslapped and mussed my hair. When Alford let me go, he continued, "You listened very well to what I told you before the game." There was a slight pause for effect, and with everyone waiting, gave his last shot of the night, "You didn't fuck it up!"

Michael caught up with me as we exited the gym, and said, "Why don't you come over for a little while before you go home. It's early."

"Thanks, but I gotta take a shower, and I gotta meet Tom Collins and Bobby Atanasio at Bobby's house early tomorrow. We're gonna go to the dance from there. Then we're going back to Bobby's after the dance and stay over."

"Tom Collins. I love that name. Imagine if his parents' name was Daniels, and they named him Jack?"

I laughed and said, "Oh God. That would definitely be worse than Tom Collins, and he'd be an alcoholic for sure."

"Okay look, if you're going home, I'm going up to my house now. I guess I'll talk to you Sunday and you can tell me what happened."

"Collins has got somethin' up his sleeve. I just know it."

"He's probably gonna spike the juice with some gin. Don't drink too much my friend, and be careful walking home."

"Thanks for the warning, man, I will."

I entered the house using the back door, and then stopped at the refrigerator for some milk and a snack. When I got to the living room, my father was reading with the news on in the background. I told him about the game, and he said, "Sounds like an exciting game, and I'm happy you stepped in for the fellas like you did. Luckily, your mother went to bed, she's working at the diner early tomorrow." He paused and continued, "Oh yeah, tomorrow. The dance is tomorrow night, and I'll be driving you to your friend's house."

"Thanks dad. That's great."

"One more thing Owen, your mother and I spoke about our dinner conversation."

"Really?" I closed my eyes, and waited for the other shoe to drop.

"Yes. She was, let's say, somewhat skeptical of your story. But I asked her if she really thought you could make up a story like that. She did not want to believe that. Then I reminded her that she was the Catholic, it was a Catholic school, and she had to believe they had a good reason."

I opened my eyes and asked, "So, she's cool with it?"

"Well, I wouldn't go that far. She doesn't completely understand, but she is not going to the school about it. She trusts her religion."

"Wow, thanks Dad! I'll talk to you in the morning."

He stood up and hugged me, "Good night, Owen."

I went to my room, read a little while finishing a snack, and fell asleep thinking what a great dad I had.

CHAPTER 5

The next night, since I was part of student government, I had been instructed to be at the school an hour and a half before the dance to assist with setting up the gym. When I arrived with Tom and Bobby, Charlie Russo was in the process of detailing the events of the evening and assigning responsibilities. "As you all know, we will be giving out gifts at the end of the night. Santa and his elves will be giving the boys St. Brendan's key chains, and the girls will get Prep key chains. And before you ask, yes, I will be Santa, so have your fun now."

After the laughter and applause died down, he gave everyone their assignments. When that was finished, Russo walked over to me, Tom, and Bobby. "Listen Owney, Vic Martella was supposed to be one of the elves, but he's sick. You and him are about the same size, so we need you to take his place, okay?"

"Sure Charlie, I can do that."

"Thanks, but just to be sure, why not go check out the costume."

Then before he walked away, Russo thanked Tom and Bobby for showing up to help. Tom then smiled at me and said, "Okay go, you know what you have to do!"

The dance began with the introductions of the dance committees and student government officers from both schools, who had worked so hard to make the night possible.

Then there were announcements about general rules and where the bathrooms were located. The band was introduced, and most of the Prep students knew them. They were seniors at the school who called themselves The Hilltoppers. They started playing a few fast songs and the student government people started dancing, as did a lot of other people. Some of the boys moved quickly off the floor, but if you were standing near a person of the opposite gender, some people just started dancing together. Though, it did seem that there were always more girl-girl couples on the floor.

Bobby and I were one of the first who got off the dance floor as quickly as possible. Tom however was a different story. He danced with three different girls to the first three songs before rejoining us. I was the first to address the issue with him. "That was pretty amazing. You looked good out there. You can really dance."

"Listen you sputniks, girls love it when a guy can dance, so my advice is to learn. And all Irishmen can dance."

I said, "Well maybe there's hope for me, I'm half Irish." I pointed at Bobby and continued, "Is there any hope for the Italian here?"

"Nah, especially big gawky ones."

While attempting to playfully swat Tom, who ducked, Bobby said, "I resent that you leprechaun!"

Our attention was diverted to the stage as the band started to play the first slow song of the evening. It was the very romantic, "I Only Have Eyes for You" by The Flamingos, which they announced was a lady's choice. The ladies began the search, and right away there more than were a few couples on the dance floor. I did not notice the auburn-haired, hazel-eyed girl in the gray pleated mini skirt and long-sleeved gray knit top approaching. Tom did however and was readying himself to accept her request. The girl ignored both Tom and Bobby, asking me, "Hello, may I have this dance?"

To say I was surprised would be the understatement of all time. I was frozen, but Tom snapped his fingers in my face, gave me a nudge, and said, "You're not allowed to refuse. That's the rules."

The girl nodded, took my hand, and added, "Your friend is right!" She then led me out to the dance floor.

She was an inch shorter than I was, and while not a skinny little thing, was well-proportioned, and the tight knit top accentuated her blossoming development. We had taken the first tentative steps, and before I could tell her that I was not a dancer, the girl spoke first, "You're Owen Loof."

I was again surprised, but kept my composure this time, and responded, "Yes, that's right. Wait I know. You're Joanie Miller." Before she could answer, I stepped on her foot and said, "Oops, sorry."

"That's okay, yes I'm Joanie Miller. I remember you from St. Camillus, and the sixth grade Christmas play when Mary kissed you."

"You really remember that?" I was trying to think of a way to say I remembered Joanie without saying she looked different than the short chubby girl, who played Mary in her sixth-grade play. So, I just ignored any mention of her appearance, and added, "I can't believe you remember that."

When the music stopped, Joanie took my arm and practically dragged me away with her, saying, "Come with me and meet some of my friends, Owen."

It wasn't like I had any choice at this point, and before I knew it, I was standing with five girls. I looked back once to my two cronies for help, but they were laughing and waving me to keep going. Joanie said to her friends, "This is one of my friends from Rockaway, Owen Loof. Owen, I'd like you to meet Nancy, Pamela, Diane and Carol."

I took the hand of each girl as they were introduced. They were all different with varied hair colors, sizes, and shapes. But each one was as pretty as the other, and my eyes were twitching like Raymond Shaw, looking at multiple Queen of Diamonds in the *Manchurian Candidate*. Introductions complete, Joanie continued, "Owen and I went to St. Camillus together."

Nancy asked, "You were always in the same class?"

"No, no. Owen was a year or two ahead of me."

This answer led to Nancy's next question, which was asked somewhat derisively. "So, he got left back a lot, right?"

The other girls started to laugh, and Joanie cut them off saying, "Nope, Owen just likes getting hit by cars and landing in the hospital."

The girls thought that was even funnier and were laughing again. I smiled and said, "Yeah, it's an exhilarating feeling flying through the air, and sometimes I don't even try. I'll just be standing there minding my own business, and boom! A car comes out of nowhere and I'm flying."

Tom and Bobby wandered over as the band returned from one of their breaks, and they played a couple of fast songs, and then "Under the Boardwalk" by The Drifters. Joanie asked excitedly, "Who can Cha Cha?"

Tom wasted no time in taking Joanie's hand and whisking her off to the dance floor. Diane looked at Bobby, who nodded, and they also set off to dance. Nancy and Carol were standing there, and Nancy held her hand out for me. I hesitated, then two guys brushed past me, and the two girls were gone with them to Cha Cha, leaving me alone.

After "Under the Boardwalk" was finished, the band went right into "Twist and Shout," a song that was a hit for The Isley Brothers in 1962, and covered by The Beatles in '64. Almost everyone was on the dance floor, and as I watched, I felt even I could pull this one off.

I glanced around and saw a short girl. She was maybe five feet tall, with dark hair and thick black horn-rimmed glasses, standing all by herself. I had seen her with friends at various times during the night, but was pretty sure she had not danced at all. So, I approached her and said, "Hi! I'm Owen. Would you like to dance?"

The girl seemed taken aback, and replied, "Oh, I don't know. I really can't dance."

I looked at her and smiled, "Well that makes two of us." I took her hand and added, "Come on, this is an easy one. You'll be fine."

As we headed out to the dance floor, she looked up at me, and said, "Thanks Owen, I'm Cheryl."

We both did fine and stayed on the dance floor together for another fast song that was easy to dance to, and after all that twisting and jumping around, the band announced that they were going to slow it down and began, "In the Still of the Night" by The Five Satins. We did not move as the first notes of the song were played. Cheryl looked up at me, and said, "You don't have to do this if you don't want to." Then she began to turn away.

I held both her hands, turned her around, and said, "Well, if you don't mind getting your toes stepped on a couple of more times." Cheryl smiled, I took her in my arms, and we were dancing. I did step on her toes a couple of times during the first few steps, but we kept the movement simple, and got into a slight rhythm.

Tom Collins took notice of what was happening, and together with Joanie and her friends, friends of Cheryl, and some of the other guys, they started to form a circle around us. We were at first oblivious to what was happening, but I finally realized what was going on as the circle grew larger. I didn't want to say anything to Cheryl, but she also became aware of the situation. When she did, I could see and feel her start to panic. I was also not feeling too comfortable, but I knew I couldn't panic for Cheryl's sake. Plus, I also knew that was exactly what Collins expected would happen. So, I held onto Cheryl a little tighter, and lowered my head to whisper in her ear, "It'll be okay Cheryl. Just stay with me and be calm. We can do this."

I was not as sure as I sounded, or exactly what I was going to do, but when Cheryl looked up at me, she was still slightly terrified. I smiled at her, and in a low voice said, "Smile. You're doing great. It's almost over."

She smiled back, and I felt that she was actually somewhat less tense. Then an idea popped into my head. I had seen my mother and father finish a dance with a certain move many times. While I wasn't too sure I could pull it off, the song was ending and there was no time to think. I looked at Cheryl and said, "Just trust me, okay?"

She smiled and nodded. I took her right hand, and spun her out to full extension. Then I gave her one twirl, let go with my right hand, but grabbed her hand with my left, put my right hand around her waist, and tilted her back slightly against my arm. With the dip complete, and the applause building, we stood together. I raised our arms, and said to Cheryl, "We have to bow a couple of times."

It seemed like the entire gym was watching, and we did three bows around the circle to a louder applause each time.

The gym was still abuzz as we left the floor hand in hand. There was a smattering of applause with congratulating handshakes and hugs. People kept saying things like, "Great job," and "Terrific dance," and the band even acknowledged, "The best dance of the night."

The excitement finally died down, the band went on playing, and we sat down on the first row of bleachers. Bobby, Tom, Joanie, and Nancy were with us, and Cheryl's friends were still fussing over her. Tom looked at me and remarked, "That was some fancy finish out there man."

Then Joanie added, "That was amazing Owen! Simply amazing! I can't wait to tell the people in Rockaway."

I put my arm around Cheryl's shoulder, and announced for everyone to hear, "It was amazing because I had an amazing partner."

Cheryl was smiling broadly and blushing a little, but just then, Nick Sama appeared and said, "Okay Loof, it's time to go change."

I kept my arm where it was, and answered, "Right Nick, I'm coming."

With a confused look, Cheryl asked, "Change? Change for what?"

Before I could say anything, Tom answered the question. "Fred Astaire here is going to be one of Santa's elves, and help give out the presents."

While holding up my hands, and covering Cheryl's ears, I said, "But you never heard anything about presents from me."

I took my arm off Cheryl's shoulder, and prepared to stand up, but before I did Cheryl reached over, threw her arms around my neck, and gave me a kiss on the cheek. After the oohs and ahhs of the assembled friends, she said, "Thank you Owen. That was simply wonderful. You got me to do something I never thought I would, or could do. I really can't believe it."

As I stood up, there were a couple of more oohs and ahhs. I reached for Cheryl's hand, kissed it and said, "I really can't believe it myself. We did it together."

A little while later, the band began playing, "Santa Claus is Coming to Town." The gym doors opened, with the elves bounding through, followed closely by the jolly fat man in the red suit. The elves went right to work, reaching into the bag, and giving gift boxes to the girls. The elves would take as many boxes as they could handle, and find girls to receive them. Some of the girls were not waiting for the elves to reach them, and things did get somewhat disorderly. A little more than halfway down what was no longer a line of girls, as I had just finished pulling four boxes out of the bag, I saw one of the other elves hand Joanie and Nancy their boxes. Without trying to make a big deal, and ensuring no one noticed, I walked over to the two girls, and said, "Here, take these boxes and give me those back."

Joanie hesitated, and asked, "What's the difference?"

"Just trust me and don't ask questions. Just take these, okay?"

The two girls looked at each other, and complied with my request. Once the switch was complete, I said, "Thanks girls, I'll see ya later."

While I was assisting in handing out the boys' gifts, I looked for Cheryl. Finally, I spied her and a friend entering the gym. I ran over and asked, "Hey, where were ya? It looks like ya didn't get a gift box."

Cheryl responded with a slight smile, "Oh Owen, your elf costume is adorable. Rita had a little problem…" She hesitated as her friend blushed, and gave Cheryl a soft slap on the arm. Then she continued, "But no, we weren't here when the gifts were given out."

I was happy, and smiled broadly saying, "Well you're in luck because you are a friend of the elves. Stay right here, and I'll be right back."

I returned quickly saying, "It is my pleasure to present your gifts personally, but remember, don't open them until everybody else does."

The girls both smiled gleefully, and said in unison, "Thank you, thank you!"

I responded happily, "No problem, but right now I got some things to do, including gettin' out of this suit. I'll see ya before we leave."

Before I turned away, Cheryl beckoned me with her index finger to indicate she wanted me to bend down. When I did, she kissed me on the cheek and gave me a hug adding, "Okay Owen, see you later."

When the gift boxes were all distributed, Santa and the elves then paraded down the center of the floor, waving to the crowd as the band played a medley of Christmas songs. The entourage stopped in front of the stage, and spread out in a single line as Charlie Russo and Susan Grasso, the freshman student council president at St. Brendan's, were on the stage with the band. The music stopped, and Russo announced, "Okay! Everybody open your boxes!"

It took a few seconds, but then the screaming started. Boxes and spiders were being thrown in the air, and girls were running all around. It was quite chaotic to say the least. Girls were stomping on the spiders, trying to kick them away. Boys ran across the gym, but were not really sure what to do. Then one of the girls bent down and picked up one of the spiders. There were two boys standing next to her and she threw the spider at them yelling, "They're rubber you assholes!"

It took another few minutes for the word to spread around, and calm was somewhat restored. The spiders were captured and disposed of, and any key chains that fell to the floor were returned to their boxes. The girls were upset, the dance committees were upset, and Father Knox was upset. After much discussion it was decided that the dance was over. Many of the girls had already left before the announcement was made. It was promised that some sort of arrangements would be made to make up for the debacle, and a complete investigation would be conducted to find out how it happened. It was further stressed that anyone found to be responsible would be dealt with swiftly and severely.

The boys were ordered to take seats in the bleachers, and watched as the girls collected their belongings and filed out of the gym. In all the confusion after the opening of the gifts, I lost my friends, but there they were already seated in the top row of the bleachers. As I neared them, they made room for me, and Tom could see from the expression on my face that I was about to talk about what had happened. He put his finger to his lips to let me know that I should keep my mouth shut. I nodded my head, covertly understanding the message.

The girls were all gone, and it was just the boys who paid to attend the dance, the dance committee, the student council officers, Santa, and the elves. Father Knox stood in front of the bleachers and addressed the prisoners. "Would any one like to tell me how this happened?"

There was silence, so he continued, "One person, or more than one person, took a very joyous occasion, a special opportunity for the two schools, and ruined it completely. I did not find this prank the least bit funny."

There were a couple of bowed heads, and other attempts at hiding smiles and snickers. The clearly agitated priest continued, "Some of you do think it was funny. Well, listen to me my young friends, I am not amused at all. I will do all I can to find those responsible, and God help them when I do. Now get off those bleachers, and get this gym cleaned and straightened up before anyone leaves."

The investigation concluded after a week. There were threats to punish the whole freshman class if no one confessed or turned in the perpetrators. It was an idle threat that was never carried out, and no one was ever found to be responsible for the crime. The school authorities concluded that the spiders were not inserted at the school. There were only three or four people who had access to the gifts before the dance. However, Father Knox felt they were beyond reproach, and the evidence was circumstantial at best. Since it was so close to the Christmas holidays, it was finally decided that each of the two hundred and sixty freshmen were to donate two dollars, and the five hundred and twenty dollars would be given to the freshman class at St. Brendan's.

From the Monday after the incident, through the weeklong investigation, and until the Christmas break, the spiders were a topic of discussion throughout the school, and there was very little gray area in the opinions. People either believed those responsible should confess and be expelled, or given a medal, and some hoped they would come forward for congratulations.

Christmas came and went uneventfully, but pleasantly, with the added bonus of being a little warmer than normal.

As it happened, I was going to spend my first midnight on New Year's Eve away from my family. There was a party at Maryanne Lawlor's house. Maryanne was Michael's girlfriend, and her parents would be there to chaperone, along with other members of the Lawlor family and some of their friends. The adults would be upstairs while the young people would be downstairs in the beautifully finished basement.

It was a great party, with good music, dancing, teenage talk, and of course smuggled in alcohol. Michael was busy helping Maryanne organize everything, but he spotted me standing by myself, so he walked over and handed me a refreshment saying, "Here you go my friend."

I replied, "Thank you," and proceeded to take a drink. I coughed a little, while shaking my head and said, "That's beer!"

"You're a genius Loof. A genius!"

"You're giving people beer?"

"Not everybody, but some people brought their own. I think we got a handle on it though."

"Famous last words." We touched cups, and after taking a drink, I noticed a familiar face and gushed, "Geeze, it's good to see Joanie. I haven't seen her since the dance. I wonder how she's doin'?"

"Well, it looks like you'll get to ask, 'cause here she comes." As he started to leave, Michael pointed at my cup and said, "Let me know when you need another one."

Joanie surprised me with a hug as we exchanged holiday greetings. She then asked, "So Owen, why haven't I seen you out there dancing tonight?"

"Because I'm not really a good dancer, and don't like it."

"Well after seeing you at the dance with Cheryl Landy, I would beg to differ. Oh, and speaking of the dance, thank you. We received the money, part of which was given to the nuns for Christmas gifts they distributed to kids in struggling families."

"Well, you should really thank our entire freshman class."

"Something tells me I should be thanking you, and whoever helped you put those spiders in the boxes."

I looked Joanie straight in the eye and calmly responded, "Gee Joanie, they did a thorough investigation and can't figure it out. It's a complete mystery."

Joanie smiled, gave me a peck on the cheek, and said, "Sure Owen! A complete mystery."

CHAPTER 6

The first week back after Christmas break, there were still a few people talking about the spider dance, and the school authorities had not completely given up hope of finding the people responsible for the act. On Friday, Bobby and I were waiting for Tom, who was being kept after class by Mr. Stone, the Science teacher. We did not know what he did, so besides the fact that we always hung out for a little while on Friday, we were anxious to find out what he had done. A little past three thirty Tom showed up in our usual meeting place, a good a pizza place three blocks from the school on Rogers Avenue. Tom sat down with his slice and drink, and I opened the conversation. "Well Stone didn't keep you too long. So, what'd you do?"

Tom took a swig of his drink, and began, "So we were discussing hormones in class, and I just wanted to contribute something."

Bobby rolled his eyes exclaiming, "Oh no!"

"All I said was I know how to make a hormone. So, Stone asked, 'Okay, Mr. Collins, how do you make a hormone?'"

"I answered, don't pay her."

Our response was two blank stares for a couple seconds before it finally registered, and there were groans, laughter, and head holding. I recovered enough and asked, "Why would you do that?"

Tom's reply was, "Come on Owney, school's boring. Ya gotta break the monotony with a laugh once in a while."

"But there's detention and demerits?"

With a shrug of his shoulders, Tom responded, "A small price to pay. Just pick your spots. It's all about the laugh."

Bobby then asked, "But with the spiders nobody knows who produced the laugh."

Tom's answer was, "Sometimes that's even better. Like I said, pick your spots, and sometimes discretion is the better part of valor."

The remainder of January and February was cold and uneventful. There were a couple of big snowstorms which closed the school. Tom missed quite a few days of school when he got a case of mononucleosis, and even when he was in school, he was not himself. Without Tom's leadership, a lot of the shenanigans were muted, but not eliminated. Then on his return he was able to hide Mr. Browning's grade book for two days. He was also able to "borrow" Mr. Doolan's teacher's edition math book during a lunch period, and we were able to write out the answers for the next four chapters and sold the answers for two dollars apiece.

The snow finally melted, and with the month of March came thoughts of baseball. I heard the call for junior varsity baseball tryouts during the morning announcements. There were going to be three days of tryouts, and I thought about going out for the team, but I got JUG on the tryouts' first two days. I received the two-days' JUG for handing in an English essay late. I had finished the assignment two days early and then gave it to Tom to take home the night before the essay was due. He then failed to show up for school the next two days, and I did a JUG for each day the essay was missing. When he returned to school on the third day, he found me even before homeroom, and started with an apology, "Owney I am really, really sorry. But ya gotta hear what happened."

I responded a little upset, "Oh, I wanna hear what happened, okay! And this oughta be good!"

"Owney wait, listen. This is the truth. My dog died."

I started to turn away while throwing up my hands and shaking my head. I turned back and said, "I can't believe you're using the dog died story. Did you run out of grandfathers?"

Tom chuckled a little and answered, "I'll have you know both my grandfathers are still very much alive. Seriously Owney, my dog got hit by a car, and we took him to the dog hospital. We were there like all night, but he didn't make it." He opened his book bag, pulled out some papers, and went on, "Look I got receipts and a note from the vet. I'm really legit this time."

I leaned over to read the papers, and said with a certain bit of astonishment, "Geeze, your dog really did get hit by a car. I don't believe it, Tom Collins actually telling the truth. Will wonders ever cease! But I'm sure you can understand my doubt."

"Sure, why do you think I brought in all this proof." Then reaching in the book bag again he produced my essay, and while handing it over said, "Here's your essay. But don't worry I'm not gonna hand in mine today because it would be too suspicious."

"But you know you'll get JUG."

"Maybe I can get out of it with all this proof of my dog dying. And Owney, this is a teachable moment here. The JUG will be worth it in order to do all we can to protect us from suspicion. If Browning is as smart as I think he is, just handing in your essay on the same day I come back will put a question in his head. So, handing in my essay one or two days later will maybe throw him off a little."

I nodded my head while saying, "Okay, and look, I am really sorry about your dog."

Tom not only did not get JUG, but he also got an extra day to hand in the essay. At our lockers after school, I said to him, "I can't believe you got that extra day and I got two days JUG. If it was anybody else, I'd be really pissed."

"You know how sorry I am about that. But my…"

"Yeah, yeah, your dog died. But I was gonna tryout for the JV baseball team."

"So go out there today."

"It's the last day of tryouts. There'd be no point now."

"Oh, I didn't know that. You're probably right. Sorry, man."

"Ahhh, it's all right. But I'm gonna take a walk out there and check it out. I'll talk to you tomorrow."

The next day I overheard two guys talking about the baseball team, and I waited for the right moment before approaching them. Jerry Clifford and Billy Ward were both in my math class and I began, "Hey guys! That's great that you both made the team."

The two boys replied together while giving me a playful punch on each shoulder. "Owney how's it going!"

Then Ward said, "Hey, thanks for those Math answers. They really helped and were well worth the price. Remember your two good customers the next time."

Jerry Clifford was nodding his agreement and I said, "We're always looking for repeat business and customer service is very important to us. We're looking for some new products right now. You'll be the first to know."

The two baseball players laughed, and were thanking

me when I continued, "But listen, guys. I couldn't help overhearing, what exactly is a team manger?"

Clifford responded, "Well you kinda help with a lot of things around the team. Like the equipment, water, keeping score, just helping the coach with stuff. Plus, you're part of the team, you even get a letter."

That last bit of information was really an eye-opener. Receiving a letter to put on your sweater or school jacket for being on a sports ream was a pretty big deal. So, I would not be a player, but most people (especially girls) would not know that.

I tried not to sound too excited, and said as calmly as possible, "Thanks guys. I think I'll try to catch Coach now."

I found my way to Coach Sullivan's office, and the door was opened. The Coach was sitting at his desk, which was strewn with papers, looking at his grade book. He was a balding, stocky, middle-aged man with a rather gruff personality, and a strict disciplinarian. He rubbed a lot of people the wrong way, but it did not seem to bother him in the least. The Coach always said that he wasn't there to be our friend. He was our teacher and coach. Mr. Sullivan loved his job at school, and was a well-respected, well-remembered figure at Prep.

When I knocked on the door, Mr. Sullivan looked up to see who it was and said, "Loof, come on in, I don't have a lot of time, but what can I do for you? Your gym grade is fine. You're doing good work."

"Hi Coach. No, it's not about my grade. I heard you talking to a couple of the guys about a baseball team manager. They told me some of what it's about and I'm interested."

"Well Loof, it's not an easy job and you'll be working with one of my guys from last year, Louie Doyle.

"Really! I remember him from last year. He was in my homeroom."

"That's good that you know one another. It'll make it easier. Can you go out there today?"

"Oh no. I can't today."

"It's okay. You be out there tomorrow, and Louie will give you the breakdown."

"Thanks Coach. I'll be there tomorrow."

One Friday night toward the end of the season, I was at 180 with Michael. We had not seen a lot of each other lately due to the time constraints with our baseball teams. Michael attended Bishop Loughlin. They were having a better season than us, and he let me know it. I told a few stories of the razzing I had to endure as the new guy. There was the usual name calling, and water seemed a big thing for baseball players. They would pour water on me during the game and throw me in the shower with my clothes on after. Leaving bats to trip over, hot foots, and shaving cream showers were also very popular. Michael of course understood because some of the same things were happening on his team.

On our way out of the gym, I stopped and said, "Oh wait! I forgot to tell you. Remember how I said that I wanted Sullivan to remember me because he coaches all the JV teams, and that'll help when I try out for basketball next year?"

"Sure. What happened?"

"So, Louie missed a couple of games early in the season and I had to do the scorebook when he wasn't there. But when he comes back, Sullivan says he wants me to keep doing the book. Louie wasn't happy but that's what the Coach wanted."

"Did he say why?"

"Nope, I guess he just liked the way I did it better. But wait, there's more. Usually somebody who's not playing gets to coach first base. So, one game we were a little short-handed, and Sullivan let me coach there. Some of the guys from last year told me he never let Louie do that."

"It sure does sound like you're making an impression."

We ended the baseball season with a losing record, and it was only a few weeks till the end of the school year. Between managing the baseball team and basketball at 180, talking to my parents was kept to a minimum. I had deftly avoided much discussion of the third marking period grades in which my overall average had dipped another two points to 85.

On Saturday morning the week before finals, my mother was working an extra shift at the Diner. After breakfast and completing a few little chores around the house, my father was taking a rest in the backyard with an adult beverage and a book. I approached him, and announced, "I'm goin' up to the Cottages to see who's there and then probably meet Michael on the boardwalk later. We may hit the waves."

My father looked up from the book saying, "Okay, be careful son."

"Thanks dad. See ya later."

But before I had taken two steps, my father called. "Owen wait. Come back and sit for a minute."

I turned around, retrieved a chair, sat next to my father, and announced, "It was accident, I didn't mean to do it, and I'm sorry I said it." Then I started to stand up.

"Very funny. Just sit." When I was back in the chair, he continued, "I know finals are starting soon and your mother is getting concerned. With your tracking system, how do you think you're doing?"

"You know I've been busy with baseball and stuff, but I really think I'm doin' okay."

"Owen, you know just okay is not going to sit well with your mother."

"Yeah, yeah, I know mom well enough by now. But dad, it's all good. I'm really doing fine. I can deal with mom."

His eyes widened while tilting his head and nodding, then said, "Oh really! Well one of these days, my wise son, you must sit down and enlighten me. Because I certainly haven't figured it out and I've been trying for twenty years.

"That's crazy dad. Where do ya think I learned! See ya later." I stood up, gave my father a hug, and was gone in a flash.

As finals approached some of the regular customers were clamoring to know if the answer-selling business would be providing product for the upcoming exams. The Collins-Loof-Atanasio brain trust was trying to find a way to satisfy the needs of their clientele. Finals were scheduled to start on Wednesday, June 17. On Friday, June 12, Bobby came to school with the answer. When Tom and I arrived at lunch, Bobby looked like he was positively going to burst. Tom noticed right away and demanded, "Okay Atanasio you got something to tell us. Spit it out."

"Okay, Okay! Last week my brother, Anthony, got home from school, and my father asked him to clean out some stuff in the basement. So, I get home from school one day and Anthony calls me from the basement."

Tom interrupts saying, "Is this gonna be a long story, or what?"

Bobby gets a little annoyed and says, "Shut up, ya really wanna hear this. So, I go to the basement and my brother has a whole pile of papers. It turns out they're old tests from when he went here. For the next few days, he helped me sort them by grade, subject, and teacher. I'm pretty sure we got stuff we can use."

Tom clapped his hands, pumped his fists, and said, "Great, wonderful! We can come to your house this weekend, right?"

Bobby nodded and answering, "I just have to clear it with my mom, but it shouldn't be a problem."

It was agreed that after everyone checked with parents, phone calls would be made to complete the arrangements. Everyone got the green light, and the three businessmen spent the weekend getting their product line together. There were four subjects in which the teachers were still at the school from Anthony Atanasio's time. The subjects were religion, Latin, math, and science.

It was hard work, but the cheat sheets were ready to go on sale Monday after school. The answers sold for four dollars, but you could get a partial refund depending on the number of answers that were the same or similar. The science exam was the only one that was problematic with only a small number of answers that were really helpful. However, very few people asked for any of their money back since the sheets were extremely helpful in the other subjects.

The plan for the last day of testing was to meet at our office, the pizza place on Rogers Avenue, to hand out any possible refunds and split up the money. Bobby and I arrived early and took care of the returns. Much to our surprise, some of the refund money was offset by people offering their thanks monetarily. After a while, we began to worry about what had happened to our mentor. Finally, Tom arrived, we took one look at his forlorn expression, and realized right away that something was wrong. This time it was Bobby's turn to ask the obvious question. "Oh crap, something's up. Spit it out Collins."

Tom slumped in his seat and started, "Well, I was at my locker gettin' stuff to leave. When I pulled out my history book, almost everything fell out of my locker including some of the leftover sheets. Papers went flying across the hall. Don't you know Sullivan was walking by right at that moment."

Atanasio broke in, "Let me guess. He picked up some of the sheets and guessed what they were, right?"

"Well, no. He picked up a couple, looked at them, and yeah he was a little suspicious."

I said, "So, he wouldn't have known what they were anyway!"

"Maybe, but the key was that I did not panic, hurry, or act nervous. I just nonchalantly picked up the rest of the books and papers, made small talk, and answered his questions. Like I said, he was helping me, and I put the stuff back in the locker. He reminded me I had to clean out my locker by next week, then he told me to be careful and have a nice summer. I wished him the same, and he left."

Bobby said, "Boy, that was pretty close."

Tom chuckled and answered, "It was, but the key was not acting guilty and raising his suspicions. Remember, the man's been teaching a long time. He's not stupid. You see, that's the mistake a lot of people make. They believe that the teacher, the boss, the supervisor is stupid. Never underestimate your opponent."

Bobby and I nodded our understanding of the lesson we had just received, and we had some pizza and cokes, with a little rum added to the sodas. Then we divvied up the profits and began to say our goodbyes. There were hugs all around, wishing each other well for the summer, and I reminded them about my birthday party in August. Tom started down Rogers Avenue. Bobby and I watched our mentor walk away. We did not know it at the time, but he would not be with us for sophomore year.

Sophomore Year

CHAPTER 7

When I got off the bus on Nostrand Avenue, I paused for a minute before making my way to Carrol Street and into the gym lobby. Knowing that Tom Collins was not going to be there caused me such mixed emotions. Tom did help me celebrate my birthday, but he did give me the bad news that he would not be returning to Prep. He told me that there were family matters involved that made continuing at the school very difficult. His parents tried to find a way to make staying at the school work, and It was a painful decision for all of them, but in the end, it was just impossible. Of course, Bobby Atanasio was still there, as were a lot of people that knew me through Tom's presence, but everything was going to be different.

As I entered the gym and walked down the aisle between the floor seats and the bleachers looking for Bobby, there were a lot of familiar faces, but no one said anything or acknowledged my greeting. Bobby yelled down to me from the top row of the bleachers. I saw him, waved, and looked for a way to get up there. Before I could even start the ascent, I heard my name being called and looked to see Mr. Sullivan standing by the stage. "Loof, hey Loof! Come down here!"

I hurried to him, and said, "Hey Coach. How was your summer?"

"Fine Loof, fine. I didn't call you over here for small talk. Are you interested in being the JV Football manager? You did a good job for the baseball team. I can use you."

"Sure Coach, thanks!"

"Don't thank me. You're gonna work your butt off! Come to the field today and we'll get everything set."

"Okay, sure thing Coach. See you on the field."

"Right, now hurry up and find a seat."

The Coach walked away, and I maneuvered my way rather roughly through the bleachers to reach Bobby. When I was finally seated, Bobby asked about the chat with Sullivan. I told him what was going on and he asked, "You really want to do that?"

"Why not? The guy asked me. And I tell ya, it's gonna help me when I try out for the basketball team."

"Whatever you say, Owney."

Our conversation was interrupted by a guy in the row in front of us who turned around and said, "Owney Loof, right?" I nodded and the questioner continued, "Kevin Kane. Your business helped me a lot last year. I'm looking forward to still being a good customer."

Bobby and I looked at one another, and I replied, "Well unfortunately the CEO accepted a more lucrative position, and the business filed for bankruptcy. So, it is not certain at this time if the company can restructure itself into a viable enterprise."

"That's very bad news. I hope you will keep me apprised of the situation."

Before I could respond, Kane's name was called for homeroom 2B, and he said so long as he bounded down the bleachers. Bobby looked at me and asked adamantly, "What the hell was that all about?"

Before I could say anything, Bobby heard his name called for homeroom 2C. He jumped up and hurried down the bleachers to join the rest of the students following their teacher, a scholastic, Mr. McGuire. I had to wait a while longer before I would find out where I was going and who my homeroom teacher would be. Finally, my name was called for the next to last homeroom, 2G, and my homeroom teacher was another new scholastic, Mr. Delasalvo.

Everything was like normal at homeroom, and then I received my schedule. Scanning the paper, nothing stood out until I got to the foreign language. According to what was in front of me, I had French and Mr. Delasalvo.

When the bell sounded ending homeroom, I waited, and then stopped at Mr. Delasalvo's desk. The scholastic looked up from some papers and said, "Yes Mr..., no, no don't tell me, um, Loof. Owen Loof."

"That's right, Mister."

"So, Mr. Loof, what can I do for you?"

"I'm going over my schedule, and I was just wondering how I got French as my foreign language."

"Well, that is the language you must have chosen on the elective form you received."

"You see, that's the thing, Mister. I'm pretty sure I picked Spanish."

The teacher opened another folder on his desk, pulled out a sheet of paper, and while showing it to me said, "But if you look right here, Mr. Loof, the form you filled out has French as the foreign language you selected."

I stared at the form in disbelief, which the scholastic noticed and asked, "Is there a problem Mr. Loof?"

Shaking my head and gently pushing the form away, I replied smiling, "No, ahh no! Everything's okay Mister, I'll see you in class later."

"Tres bien, Monsieur! Au revoir."

"Something in there means goodbye."

"Tres bien, very good, and you're right au revoir is goodbye. You're a natural, Mr. Loof. Now hurry up before you're late for the next class."

"Okay Mister, au revoir." I waved and as I went through the door, I could hear Mr. Delasalvo laughing.

I liked Mr. Delasalvo, and enjoyed the exchange with the new teacher. However, I was not laughing and was definitely not happy. When I looked at the elective form, I could clearly see that the language boxes to check your choice had been altered. There was only one person who could be responsible for the alteration. Why my mother wanted me to take French, I just could not figure out. It would be useless to say anything about it at this point, for arguing with her was pointless. So, all I could do was say tres bien, and make the best of it.

Kevin Kane and Bobby were both in Mr. Delasalvo's French class, and the class was right before lunch, so we went to the cafeteria together. Once settled in and eating, Kevin again asked about the business. Since there was no one else at the table or within earshot, I felt I could be more open about what happened than I was in the gym. I also could tell from the way Kevin had approached the question that he was trustworthy. "Look Kevin, you remember Tom Collins, right?"

"Sure, and from your answer in the gym this morning, something happened and he's no longer at the school."

"Correct, and I'm not going into the gory details, but suffice it to say that he received an offer he could not refuse, and while he hated to leave, it was a move that had to be made. He was the boss, and we just have to figure out what we can do on our own." I looked at Bobby and asked, "Do you understand this morning now?" Bobby nodded, and while turning back to Kevin, I put my hand on Bobby's shoulder and said, "Geeze, you think an Italian would understand these things."

Bobby replied, "Be careful there, Paddy!"

I laughed and retorted, "Actually I'm a Cloggy. My father's people are from Holland. I'm only half a Paddy."

After the laughter and playful slapping stopped, I said to Kevin, "Seriously though, we'll see what happens. But I want to ask you something else, Kev. I'm going to be a manager of the JV football team and I was wondering if you wanted to come to practice later, and see if Sullivan could use another hand."

"What does the manger do exactly?"

"Really just anything Sullivan tells you to do. You know, taking care of the uniforms and equipment. Making sure there's water and towels. You help the team get ready for games and help Sullivan after. It's not easy, but it's fun. And you get a letter."

Kevin replied, "I don't know. Maybe!"

"Okay, think about it. I'm with this lug all afternoon. We all have Berry last period for history, and we'll talk then."

"Sounds good. I'll let you know then."

The afternoon classes went by quickly, and Mr. Berry dismissed his class after the bell because of a mistake made in his syllabus. Once outside the classroom, I asked Kevin if he had made a decision.

"Yeah sure, why not. If it's all right with Sullivan, I'll do it."

"Cool. It'll be fun. Go put your stuff in your locker for today. But after this, bring your stuff to the locker room."

Kevin looked at Bobby and asked, "You wouldn't do it?"

Bobby opened his mouth to answer, but I beat him to it, "No, no. He's a real athlete. He couldn't lower himself. A big-time basketball player."

As Bobby took a step toward me, I jumped behind Kevin, laughed, stuck out my tongue, and started running down the hall, shouting, "I'll meet you here in ten minutes, Kev."

Coach Sullivan was happy to have Kevin join the team. After the first week of practice, and the first game of the season, which was a shutout win over Xavier High School, Kevin and I had a talk. He asked, "Are these guys always like this?"

"Yeah, pretty much. It's just really good-natured pranks. They're kinda like the ten-year-old boy who only teases the girls he secretly likes."

"But some of the things are a bit over the top."

"Yeah, I guess. But I think I got a plan. We gotta give it back and be funny. Are you with me?"

"Sure, let's go for it."

So, over the next few weeks, Kevin and I gave as good as we got. We put Ben Gay in jock straps, shaving cream in helmets, and added insects or foul-tasting ingredients to water bottles. Pranks were also answered with insults. Timmy Delaney was one of the best jokers on the team and had gotten me a couple times. Delaney and some teammates were discussing grades on a bus ride back from another shutout win. I overheard the conversation, popped my head over the seat, and chipped in, "Delaney, if your I.Q. was any lower, you'd trip over it."

Delaney tried to slap at me, but I ducked. Then he said, "Really Loof!"

I popped up again saying, "You know guys, for Delaney, bubblegum cards are part of the great books series."

A bunch of the guys started chanting, "Go Loof Go!"

Frankie Muto, a very large offensive lineman, said, "Hey Delaney, the manager's got your number."

Owen Loof

Like a turtle popping his head out of his shell, my head appeared just over the seat back, and I said, "Muto, it's okay to go home later. They cleaned your cage."

The "Go Loof Go" chant started again. Muto rose from his seat and was trying to get at me, but the bus braked hard, and he was sent sprawling backwards along the floor. This sight caused a roar of laughter, and Coach Sullivan turned to see what had happened and yelled, "Muto, what the hell are you doing back there? Get up off the floor you idiot. That's going to cost you laps on Monday."

Muto picked himself up off the floor and as he was finding his seat, was throwing daggers at me with his eyes, and I was sticking out my tongue.

There were also stupid dances with jockstraps on our heads, and Coach Sullivan was not immune from being a target of the pranksters. We would hide things like the playbook and his whistle. Once we called the school and left a message from his wife to call immediately.

When he got back, he was so mad he cancelled the rest of practice. The team came to expect something crazy from their two mangers, and was never let down. The season ended with the team winning its conference championship.

The JV season ended before the varsity's. However, the varsity managers had failed a couple of subjects in the first marking period, and were academically ineligible to perform their duties. So, Kevin and I became the Varsity football managers. This meant that we were collecting the pads and uniforms after practice on November 9, 1965.

That day, there was the usual banter between the players, but these were upperclassmen, and as underclassmen we knew this was not the time to fool around. We were almost finished, and beside the last few Varsity players, there were two players who had been promoted from JV. It was a little past 5p.m., and the only players left were senior, Bill Larkin, and two JV players, Pat Santisi, and Ronnie Hickey. As Larkin was handing in his equipment, Santisi and Hickey started horsing around, and at one point, Hickey said that Santisi was too short to jump high enough to reach some hooks on the wall from a standing start. When Santisi was able to complete the task, he challenged Hickey by saying, "Okay, smart ass. I bet you can't jump up and touch the top of the overhanging lights."

"You're on pal. This'll be easy."

He positioned himself under the light and launched upward. He got as high as the light but couldn't get the over the top. When he landed, he let out a yell and shouted, "Ahh shit. Wait, one more shot. I can do this."

Larkin left, I looked at Kevin and said, "Oh God! He's nuts, and I know he'll keep trying till he does it."

Hickey got into position once more, howled, and took off with his hand stretched as far as he could. This time his hand went over the edge of the fixture, and he slammed it hard. Immediately all the lights in the room went out. I yelled, "Jesus Christ, Hickey! You killed the whole freakin' room!"

"I didn't do anything. But you owe me Santisi." Then he pointed toward me and Kevin saying, "And you guys didn't see nothin'."

I responded, "Oh sure you nut job. Whatever!" Then I said to Kevin, "He's never gonna be too old to find new ways to be stupid."

We finished putting everything away and locked up the equipment closet. Then made our way through the darkened room until we found the door. Once we exited the room, we expected the hallway to be illuminated. We discovered that was not the case. Continuing our journey, it became apparent that it wasn't just the equipment room that was dark. I peered at Kevin through the dark, and said, "That idiot knocked out the whole school."

We made our way to the locker room, and then up the stairs into the gym. There were about seventy-five students, Coach Sullivan, Father Knox, and a few other scholastics. The students were in groups on the bleachers, and there were some candles and lanterns providing some light.

I looked around, and asked Kevin, "Do you see that stupid Hickey?"

"No, I don't see him."

"Yeah sure! He hightailed it out of here as quick as he could. And now, they're keeping everyone here to find out who's responsible for taking out all the lights."

Charlie Russo, one of the stars of the JV football team, and a sophomore senator on the student council, turned around and said, "Owney, what are you talking about. The whole city's blacked out."

Before I could answer, Father Knox announced, "It seems that there is a major blackout affecting all of the New England states except Maine, along with New York, New Jersey, and Pennsylvania."

He went on to say that students would be taken to a phone to call their parents. If parents were able to reach the school, a pickup point would be arranged. Any student whose parents had no way of getting to the school would stay on the premises until they could be picked up by a family member.

I started to tell Russo about what happened in the equipment room, and as I told more of the story most of the guys sitting nearby tuned into the conversation. When I reached the end of the tale, Russo asked, "Are you saying what I think you're saying?"

I retorted defiantly, "I'm just tellin' you all what happened."

Everybody started laughing, and some people were throwing scraps of paper at me. Russo and Dickie Cummings, who I knew from my first freshman year, began slapping me around. Father Knox became aware of the commotion and shouted, "What's going on up there? Who is that standing up?"

I looked down through the dim light, and waved saying, "It's me Father, Owen Loof."

"What are you doing, Loof?"

"I'm tellin' them who caused the big Blackout."

"You know who is responsible for this massive Blackout Loof?"

"Sure Father. It was Ronnie Hickey."

There was a brief silence, and then Father Knox started laughing. Everyone in the bleachers joined in and Father Knox added, "Thank you Loof. I'll pass that information on to the authorities. Now have a seat son." The Priest was still chuckling to himself and shaking his head as he led the next group of students to make their phone calls.

There were about fifteen students, including Kevin and me that were stranded at the school all night. The lights in the school and most of the city came back on about 4a.m., and there was obviously no school. When the school was back in session, the story going around was that I had made Father Knox laugh. No one had ever seen Father Knox laugh. Seniors I did not know, juniors I knew from first freshman year, and present classmates were stopping me in the hall and coming to my table at lunch to talk about what happened. Even some of the other priests were saying what a great thing it was.

The Friday after the blackout I was at 180, and during a break in the games, I was talking to Michael. I related the story of what had gone on before, during, and after the blackout. When I was finished Michael said, "That's pretty funny, O. It looks like you're making a name for yourself."

"You know I was kinda surprised at that. But ya know, it felt pretty good not to be invisible."

CHAPTER 8

On Monday, JV basketball tryouts were scheduled to begin, and I got increasingly excited as the big day neared. Bobby, who was going to be a starter on the team, finally said, "Ya gotta calm down, Owney. You won't be able to do anything right if you stay keyed up like this."

"Yeah, yeah! Okay, okay!

Mr. Berry's history class ended, and I was out the door and on my way to the gym like the Road Runner escaping Wile E. Coyote. I was the first one in the gym, suited up and shooting around. Slowly but surely, more players drifted in until there were fourteen prospective candidates on the floor.

Coach Sullivan appeared, and announced that there would be two days of tryouts, and everyone would know their team status tomorrow. Then the work started. There were the warm-up drills to get the heart rate going. We took our lay-ups. Then came the dribbling and passing drills, the footwork drills, and finally the 3-on-2-s and the 2-on-1-s. The last twenty minutes of day one consisted of a scrimmage game with everybody getting time on the court.

After showering and while we were changing, I asked Bobby, "So, what'd ya think?"

"You looked all right out there. You know the game, and did a lot of things right. There are parts of your game that need improvement, but you look like a basketball player."

"Yeah, I know I don't dribble that well, and my shooting is inconsistent, but I've gotten a lot better at both."

"Don't worry Owney, you're doing great."

The next day, practice went along the same lines as the day before except the scrimmage was a little longer. I actually made a couple of good jump shots. I got good position under the boards, and twice out rebounded John Alleva and Brian Cox, two of the team's taller and better players. I played good defense and never got tired.

Bobby and I were on the same team, and during a time-out he said to me, "You're playing real good out there today Owney."

Timmy Delaney, who was sitting next to me and added, "He's right, Owney, you look like you really belong out there."

When the scrimmage ended, Coach Sullivan sat everyone down in the bleachers, and let the players cool down before making the announcement. Inside I was ready to explode with anticipation, but I was hiding it well. Finally, Coach Sullivan was standing in front of his players with clipboard in hand, and began his speech, "That was as fine a two-day tryout I have ever run. You all played very well. So, for the first time I can remember, I am not making any cuts."

All around, there were smiles and handshakes with pats on the back. I was elated to say the least. Then the Coach delivered the unkindest cut of all. Looking right at me he announced, "And Loof, you'll be my right-hand man. I really need someone dependable for the book and the clock. I know I can count on you." After a short pause he asked, "You think you could get that Kane kid? You two work well together. Okay men, hit the showers. Practice tomorrow at 5."

Everybody jumped up and started making their way to the locker room stairwell. I just sat there expressionless.

Bobby did his best to console me. "I'm really sorry Owney. That's just not right." I sat stock still staring right past Bobby, who continued, "But the Coach really does trust you. He thinks you're the best guy for the job."

I still would not be moved. Bobby, getting a little exasperated asked, "So you're just gonna sit there. You're not gonna say anything."

I just gave him a blank stare, and Bobby finally had enough. He threw up his hands saying, "Well then sit there if that's what you want. See you tomorrow." He waited a second or two, and getting no reaction from me, walked away.

I made it home, and had time to think on the train. It was bowling night for my mother and father, and they were gone when I got there. There was dinner to heat up, and when I finished eating, the choice was do some homework or go play basketball. The fact was that neither option was very appealing at the time, but maybe Michael would be at 180. Michael was there and I was sitting on the edge of the stage when he joined me and asked, "Hey man, ya not playin' tonight?"

I answered dejectedly, "Nah, not in the mood."

"Okay, what's a matter?"

With my head down but in an angry tone, I responded, "You are not going to believe this. Fourteen freakin' people try out for the team and thirteen freakin' people make the team."

"You were the only person he cut. You're right, I don't believe it."

"Wait, wait, there's more. I am the team manager. I get to keep the clock, do the book, and pick up all their shit. Why? Because he can count me." I jumped up flailing my arms in the air, and continued. "I needed to be Jerry West, Oscar Robertson, and Wilt Chamberlain combined to make the team. And you know what, even then he still woulda made me the manager. That was my job as soon as I walked in the gym." Then I sat back down still seething.

"Calm down O, calm down!"

"'Calm down,' he says!" I jumped up again, and said, "All that work on the baseball team and the football team. And this is what I get."

Michael slapped me on the arm saying, "Listen, all that work paid off. Maybe not the way you wanted, but it paid off. And you know why? Because you made yourself invaluable. He trusts you, and knows you're the best person for the job. He coulda put you on the team and you woulda sat on the bench just gettin' some garbage time minutes. But he wanted you to help the team the best way you could by doing what you do best."

"But I was good enough to be on the bench. This was my only chance to be a player, and he had no intention of giving me that chance. That's what really bothers me. But fine, you're right, I am part of the team, and I'll be the best freakin' manager ever."

"All right O! That's the spirit!"

I looked at my best friend, and we shook hands. Before I released his grip, I said, "I feel a little better, but I'm still not real happy."

I decided to walk home on the Boardwalk. It was a typical November night, a little chilly but there was not much of a breeze, which made it almost comfortable. There were no clouds, and even though there was a last quarter moon, it was pretty bright. For me, the ocean was calming, and I believed I would always have to live near the ocean.

I could hear the waves breaking and watched the moonlight shimmering on the water, which helped bring the events of the day, and the words of my friend into a new perspective. When I got home, my parents were not yet back from bowling. There was a homework assignment to work on, but I decided to blow it off. I just turned off the light, jumped into bed with my clothes on, and fell asleep with many thoughts racing through my head.

I walked into school the next morning with a much different attitude, and on my way to homeroom made a point to stop and see if Bobby was in his homeroom. We arrived at the same time, and Bobby asked, "Hey man, how are you doin'?"

I waved my hand and said, "Yeah, yeah, I'm fine. Don't worry."

"That's good I'm glad. And you are a…."

I cut him off abruptly, "Please, don't give that 'part of the team shit,' okay! Sure, you guys know that, and Coach knows that, but people remember the players, not the ones doing the clock or the book. I'll do the job for you guys and Sullivan, but I think I've learned where my niche is."

Slightly tilting his head, Bobby looked at me with a skeptical expression, saying, "I don't think I like the look in your eyes. It's the Tom Collins look."

I smiled and replied, "The bell's gonna ring. I'll see ya in French."

Mr. Delasalvo's French class was on the third floor, but the classroom was on the same side of the building as the pool. So instead of a three-story drop, it was only two stories down to the top of the pool building. When I reached the classroom, there was no one else around, but as usual, Mr. Delasalvo had opened the door, and would not be back until the bell sounded. The classroom had unusual but classic windows. There was a ledge at floor level with an indentation so you could step onto the ledge and stand in the window. There were three windows in the room with one directly opposite the teacher's desk.

I hurried over to that window, and opened it just a crack. Then I went to the back window, opened it, slipped out onto the narrow ledge of the building, and closed the window. I made my way quickly but carefully along the ledge and stopped just short of the front window. I watched as Mr. Delasalvo entered the classroom and the students drifted in behind him.

When the bell sounded, I waited for a brief moment then, instead of bending down, I placed my foot in the opening, raised the window high enough to grab with my hand, opened it all the way, and stepped into the classroom. Kevin stood up applauding, and was joined by most of the class. Everybody was laughing except for Mr. Delasalvo, who said excitedly, "Loof, what are you doing?"

I calmly replied, "Bonjour, Monsieur. Je suis ici pour la classe." (Hello, Mister. I am here for class.)

There was a smattering of laughter again and a still somewhat flustered Mr. Delasalvo replied, "I am glad you're here, Loof…" He paused, raised his finger, and continued in French, "C'est bien que vous soyez ici, mais s'il vous plait utilisez la porte a partir de maintenant et asseyez-vous."

I stood there and the rest of the class was silent. The French teacher was clearly exasperated and explained, "I told him it was nice that he was here, but to use the door from now on, and sit down."

I found my seat, the class laughed, and Mr. Delasalvo was shaking his head trying to hide the smile on his face.

At lunch when I entered the cafeteria, there was a section of the room that was populated by mostly sophomores, and they gave me a round of applause. Some people patted me on the back and tried to shake my hand. There were words of encouragement and compliments like "Classic, Loof, classic!" and "Hey Loof, wish I coulda seen it!" and "I did, Delasalvo's face was priceless!" and "keep it up Loof."

I finally made my way over to the usual table with Kevin and Bobby. Then I sat down with a satisfied sigh and a wide smile. Bobby looked at me and said, "Well here he is ladies and gentlemen, the star of the show, your friend and mine, Owen Loof."

I bowed my head saying, "Thank, thank you!"

Kevin added, "That was crazy, man. What were you thinking?"

"Ya know what Tom Collins would say. 'Too much thinkin's not good for ya.'" Kevin and Bobby shook their heads and laughed as I continued. "And I talked with Michael last night. He said I gotta do what I do best. Well, today convinced me that's what I'm gonna do, so are you guys with me?"

The three friends joined hands, and raised their arms together while letting out a howl that had the whole cafeteria looking.

CHAPTER 9

The JV basketball team was having an uneven season. They would lose one, then win a couple and then lose a couple. In the games leading up to Christmas break, Bobby was the team's leading scorer, with Danny McHale and John Alleva also providing outstanding talent. True to my word, I was performing my duties on the clock, the book, and the needs of the team flawlessly. After one game, Coach Sullivan pulled me aside and said, "That was very good you noticed that weakness in the Bishop Ford defense. It really helped us tonight." He smiled and added, "Maybe I should make you an assistant coach."

In the locker room after a 62-59 home-court victory over Xaverian, Bobby, Timmy Delaney, and Brian Duffy approached me as I was working on the final statistics. Bobby started the conversation, "Owney, some of the guys were talking, and they think you were playing games with the clock at the end of the game."

I looked up at the three players and asked, "What'd ya talking about?"

"Well, they think you didn't turn the clock on for us a couple of times at the end of the game."

"Do you really think that I would cheat to help you guys out? You know I'm not smart enough to do that."

Delaney glanced at the other two players, and with a turned-up palm pointed at me, said, "Of course guys, Kane might be able to pull it off, but we're talkin' 'bout Loof here." Everybody laughed, Delaney gave me a wink, and the three players left to change clothes.

I did not give up trying to become a better basketball player, and played as much as I could. I was at 180 just about every night, and the intramural games at school accorded me more court time. Basketball became almost an obsession. But this obsession did not interfere with my other plans. I had a reputation now, but knew I could not overplay my hand. I would not be predicable, and always leave them wanting more.

There were the normal things like stupid questions and stupid answers just to get under the teacher's skin. In two different classes, I started a small fire on my desk, and told the teachers I was only trying to keep warm. I did the window entrance once more, and then for one class, roller skated in wearing a pink tutu.

Just before Christmas break, I walked into Latin class wearing a trench coat. I took my seat, and right after the bell sounded, Mr. Kusick noticed the outfit and asked me to take it off. I shook my head and just sat there. Mr. Kusick was not happy and said angrily, "Loof, did you hear me! I said, take that coat off!" I again said nothing, and did not move.

Kevin interceded saying, "Mister really. You don't want him to take the coat off."

Mr. Kusick was extremely irritated at this point and shouted, "Shut up Kane. Loof, I demand that you take that coat off right now."

I did as I was told, and rose from my seat. I unbuttoned the garment slowly, flung it open, and dropped it to the floor. The class was filled with hysterical laughter, but a shocked, and clearly furious Mr. Kusick, yelled, "Loof you idiot, where are your clothes? Put the coat back on and go get your clothes."

Before I left the classroom I said, "Geeze Mister, I'm just gettin' ready for pool next period!"

One week after school resumed in January, I arrived home to an empty house. It was Tuesday bowling night, and the instructions for this night were to pick up dinner at Curley's. It was a little past 7 p.m. when I entered the kitchen, put the food on the table, and started to remove my coat. In the process, I noticed the mail stuck in the napkin holder. Without really thinking and doing something I rarely did, I picked up the mail and looked through it. I did not know, or for that matter care about what I was looking at until I saw the envelope from Brooklyn Prep. I had completely forgotten about grades being due. I put the other mail back in the napkin holder, put my coat on the back of the chair, sat down, and stared at the envelope. After a little more than a minute of contemplation, I opened the envelope.

After scanning over the document, I carefully returned it to the envelope, and set it back down on the table. I then removed dinner from the bag, and went into the living room to watch a little of *Combat*. After eating, I cleaned up everything, put on my coat, stuffed the envelope with the grades in my pocket, and rushed out to find Michael.

I checked the gym first, and was not too surprised that he was not there. He was playing varsity basketball and was getting home late from practice and games, so he was not at 180 a lot. I ran over to Michael's house. His father let me in, and when we were settled in Michael's room he asked, "What's up, man? Something happen?"

I reached in my pocket, and handed him the envelope. "Your grades, huh?"

"That's right!"

"So, how'd you do?"

"You got 'em, go head and look."

Michael looked the paper up and down, saying, "Well ya passed everything."

"That is true. But except for History, every mark is lower than last time. In fact, they're the lowest grades I've gotten at Prep, and I only passed geometry and science by the skin of my teeth. And you know just passing is not gonna sit well with my mother."

Michael held up the envelope and said, "Wait a minute. The envelope's opened, but your mother hasn't seen it, which means you opened it."

"Elementary my dear Watson!"

"So, you're gonna try and get away with her not seeing them?"

"Yeah, that's right, and I want you to hold 'em here until I figure out if they saw the envelope or not. Then I'll decide what to do."

"Okay pal, gotcha covered, and good luck." As I stood up to leave Michael added, "Oh listen, in a couple of weeks we come to your school for a varsity game."

"Really? That's cool. It'll be fun to watch us kick your ass." We both laughed, and Michael threw a pillow at me. Then just before exiting the room I added, "I hope you score fifty points, and we win the game." Then I picked up the pillow and threw it back at him.

The JV basketball team started the second half of the season with three straight victories. There was a thirty-point rout of St. Augustine. Then they positively demolished archrival, St. John's, scoring one hundred and five points while giving up only sixty-seven. Everybody on the team got to play and everyone scored at least one point. I was of course very happy for the win, but I still believed I should have been out there. Finally, there was a sweet 75-67 win over Holy Trinity with players on both teams being old CYO rivals

After the JV game, the Varsity was also playing Holy Trinity, and I was sitting by the clock table finishing up compiling the stats. The Varsity coach, Mr. Lang, sat down beside me and asked, "You're Loof, right?"

"Yes sir, that's me. Did I do something wrong?"

Mr. Lang smiled and said, "I don't think so. But is there something you want to tell me?"

I stammered out a reply. "Um, Um, n-n-no sir. Um, uhh, what do you need me for?"

"To tell you the truth, Loof, I do need you. Coach Sullivan tells me you are doing a great job for the JV, and it seems one of my managers is academically ineligible for the rest of the season. So, I need somebody to do the clock at the home games. Can you help me out?"

"Sure Coach, I can do that."

The coach shook my hand saying, "Good, you start tonight!"

When he walked away, I felt really terrific about being noticed for doing a good job, but I still wanted to be playing.

Before the Varsity game, I called home to let them know I would be later than normal. It was almost 8:30 p.m. when I finally got home, and my parents were watching *The Man from Uncle*. After taking off my coat and hanging it up, my father asked, "You said something about the varsity team on the phone. So, what happened?"

I explained about the Varsity managers, Coach Lang, and doing the clock for the varsity games. When I was finished talking, my mother interjected herself into the conversation by saying, "So, if the varsity managers are not able to do their duties because of their grades, they must have received their grades."

My father nodded, and I shifted my feet saying, "I guess so."

Now my mother was sitting straight up and looking from her husband to her son, and asked pointedly, "Well then, why haven't we seen your grades?"

My father was now studying me carefully, and I replied calmly, "You didn't get them yet?"

Glancing over at her husband, my mother asked, "Have you seen any mail from Prep?"

My father was smart enough to just shake his head, and she continued in a decidedly accusatory tone, "I have not either, and we certainly should have received them by now. I think…"

I interrupted my mother by saying explicitly, "You're right mom. We should have gotten them by now, and I'll go to the office on Monday and find out what happened." Then before either of my parents could say anything, I added, "I have a history report due Monday and it's been a busy week. I have it almost halfway done and I wanna free up the weekend by gettin' a lot done tonight." I went over and kissed both my parents, and peacefully ascended the stairs to my room.

When I got to my room, I shut the door quietly, walked over to the bed, picked up one of the pillows and fired it across the room. Then I threw myself on the bed and thought, "Damn it, why did I hafta tell them about the varsity managers. STUPIDE!"

The last Friday in January was the day Michael and Bishop Loughlin visited Prep. The JV would be playing first, and just as I had finished setting up the clock table, I heard a familiar voice from behind. "Hey there O! Ya got your office all set up, huh?"

"Michael, me lad! Yep, this is what I do. Hope you're ready for two defeats."

"No way that's gonna happen O. You're gonna be crying in the car on the way home."

"What car on the way home?"

"Oh yeah. Look, my Pop's gonna be here tonight. Ya got a ride home. I gotta go find the team. Talk to you later."

"Thanks man." And as Michael hurried away, I shouted after him, "Bring a lot of tissues for the ride."

In the JV game Bobby Atanasio was a dominating force and was almost scoring at will. Midway through the second quarter, he picked up his second foul, which forced him to the bench. Delany, McHale, and Alleva picked up the slack, and Prep was ahead by four points at halftime. With the game still close in the last quarter, Atanasio was charged with an offensive foul, his fourth, and had to sit down again. Once more, players came off the bench and did their jobs, which resulted in a 58-45 victory for the Brooklyn Prep Blue Eagles. I could see the Bishop Loughlin varsity sitting in the bleachers behind the JV bench. I walked across the court, and waited a few feet from the bench, and when I saw Michael I said with a laugh, "One down and one to go!"

The game started and Michael was not a starter, but he was the second player off the bench. The Loughlin team was bigger than Prep, but that had been the case for most of the season, so they knew how to handle the situation. The first quarter was a see-saw affair that would carry over for the rest of the game. I almost got caught playing with the clock, and then at halftime I took advantage of another opportunity.

Louie Doyle, who was keeping our scorebook, said to me, "Owney I gotta go down to the locker room, total up the first half stats for me, okay?"

"Sure Louie."

As Louie left the table, the Loughlin scorer also left the table leaving his scorebook open. I glanced at the Loughlin scorebook, and noticed that the scorer had not yet closed the first half fouls with a line for differentiation. I quickly picked up the other scorer's pen, and added a foul to each of Loughlin's best players. Then in our scorebook, I duplicated the additions, so the books would match. I nonchalantly took the Prep scorebook, and finished the work for Louie. The Loughlin scorer returned to the table and completed his job without noticing anything amiss.

In the final minute of the fourth quarter with both players on the bench with foul trouble, Loughlin was back up by a single point. Michael was back in the game and his team was attempting to hold the ball and run out the clock. They were doing a good job, but there was an attempted pass to Michael, and he mishandled the catch. Prep's Pete McGrath pounced on the mistake, took off down the court, and made the lay-up, giving us a one-point victory.

In the locker room after the game, I made sure to congratulate the varsity guys and tell them how they had provided me with a sweet win. I went to the coach's office and said goodnight to Coach Lang, then added, "Sorry about the clock thing coach. You know I wouldn't do anything on purpose."

The coach answered, "I know, Loof, I know. Don't worry, you're doing a fine job. Have a good weekend. Oh, and there's only one home game next week."

"Thanks coach, enjoy your weekend too." But before

I turned to leave, I noticed a small box of tissues on the coach's desk and asked, "Um, uh, Coach, do you think I could have that box of tissues?"

The coach looked up a little puzzled and replied, "What, the tissues? Sure Loof, take 'em and go."

When I got to the foyer in front of the gym, Michael was standing there with his father. As I walked up to them, I greeted Mr. O'Connor, "Hi Mike! Thanks for the ride home." Then I took the box of tissues from behind my back, and with a broad grin, presented them to my friend. Michael accepted the gift, took the towel that was draped over his shoulder, and tried to swat me. I ducked, and then started running for the door with Michael in hot pursuit.

On the Monday after the Bishop Loughlin basketball games, it was snowing on the way to school and there was between two to three inches of snow already on the ground. By lunch period, another two inches fell. I started a snowball fight in the cafeteria and accidently hit a teacher, which got me two days JUG. I was able to negotiate with Father Knox, who agreed to schedule the JUG around the basketball games.

The next night, my mother was working late at the Diner, and I went to 180 to avoid her. I was hoping that she would be asleep by the time I returned, but that was not the case. She was alone in the living room watching the end of *Peyton Place*. I attempted to it make through the room, and up the stairs before she could react, but was not successful.

She looked up from the TV screen and called to me, "Oh Owen, I'm glad I caught you. Did you go to the registrar's office to get some information about the grades?"

I was disappointed, but kept my composure and answered, "I did mom, but Mr. Wood was not in the office today. I'll try again tomorrow."

She was obviously miffed and said, "Okay Owen, but this is not going to be acceptable for too much longer. I want to get to the bottom of this."

In a somewhat forceful tone I stated, "That's what I want too Mom!"

She nodded, and changed the channel on the TV. I noticed the channel she had tuned to, and asked, "You're gonna watch *I Spy Mom*?"

"Yes, I think so. I like the show." She picked up her glass and handed it to me saying, "Do your mother a favor and get me fresh ice so I can make another drink out here."

"Sure Mom." Then I went to the kitchen, filled the glass with ice, and returned to the living room. I gave my mother the glass and she proceeded to mix her drink. Then mother and son settled in to watch the program.

CHAPTER 10

The Friday after the storm was the first Friday of the month, which meant the whole school would be attending Mass. The Mass was celebrated in the gym, and on this day, it would be taking place immediately before lunch. I talked Kevin into skipping Mass, and instead going to get pizza. We got caught, and received three days JUG. Father Knox looked at me and said, "Loof, you still have one day left to serve from the snowball fight and now these three. You're getting to be a permanent fixture at JUG young man."

As we were walking to class Kevin said, "Man, three days JUG! What about basketball?"

I wrapped my arm around my friend's shoulders and said, "Don't worry, we'll work it out. And wasn't the pizza worth it?"

That night when I got back from 180, my mother wasted no time in hitting me with the bad news. "I spoke with Mr. Wood yesterday, Owen."

I knew this day would arrive sooner or later, but hoped to have more control over the situation. In a very calm and nonchalant voice, I responded, "Really, that's good Mom. I got a little busy and forgot to stop at his office. So, what'd he say?"

She gave me 'the look,' which meant trouble. "We'll talk about you being busy later, but what he told me about your grades was not very good."

She went through the grades revealing nothing I did not already know, but tried to look as surprised as possible.

When she finally got to the end of describing how bad my marks were, I interjected, "Mom, I can't believe they're that bad. I kind of figured the math and science grades were gonna take a hit, but I'm shocked at the other marks. Maybe they made a mistake."

'The look' became more intense, and her voice began to raise a few decibels. "Don't you try to get cute with me, young man. There's no mistake. Your grades are a disaster."

I attempted to present a defense by saying, "But Mom, I passed everything."

As soon as the words were out of my mouth, I realized I had made a mistake. Now the shouting began. "And you think just passing is good enough! Well, it's not! And that business about being busy, it's that basketball. Between the school team and 180, all you think about is basketball. It's become an obsession with you. What am I going to do with you? Things are going to have to change."

She paused and took a deep breath just as my father entered the kitchen. She put her hands on her hips, looked at her husband, then pointed at me saying, "He's impossible. Talk to your son. I'll be right back." She brushed past a none- too-shocked Martin Loof and huffed her way out of the room.

He sat down at the table across from me and said, "Look you know we only want what's best for you. If you really don't want to hear her, just try harder and do better."

"You're right Dad and I will do better. I just wish I could turn my hearing aid off like you do when you don't wanna hear her."

My father rose from his chair with a laugh. He walked to me and began mussing up my hair, while gently slapping me upside the head a few times.

A week after basketball season ended, the three Musketeers were talking at lunch and Kevin said, "Owney, Sullivan asked me about working the baseball season and I said I would. What about you?

"You can do it if you want, but I'm done." Kevin and Bobby gave me a surprised and questioning look, and I continued, "Don't look at me like that. I worked for Sullivan three times now and it was fine. I had fun and I'm happy he likes the job I did. I just don't wanna do it anymore."

Bobby interjected, "And the whole thing with not makin' the basketball team has nothin' to do with it?"

"Absolutely nothing! Read my lips, I-just-don't-want-to-do-it-anymore! And besides, I wanna concentrate on my grades." The look of puzzlement on the faces of my friends from earlier turned to shock, and I added with emphasis, "Really!"

The first Monday in April, Bobby, Kevin, and I arrived at the biology lab with the rest of the class to find cages filled with live frogs. Everybody was huddled around the cages when Mr. Harrison entered the classroom, and the bell sounded. He banged on his desk to get everyone's attention and raised his voice saying, "Okay, okay, come on take your seats." When all were seated, he continued. "As you can see, we have received the frogs that will be used for our dissection lab at the end of the week."

I raised my hand, Mr. Harrison acknowledged me, and I said, "Mr. Harrison, the frogs are alive."

"Yes, they are Loof."

"So, we're gonna dissect them while they're still alive?"

Mr. Harrison replied matter of factly, "Yes that is correct Loof."

I was not letting it go. "So, you mean we're gonna kill the frogs while we're dissecting them?"

Mr. Harrison was getting a little annoyed, and you could hear it in his voice when he responded, "Well yes Loof, that is unfortunately true, but we do our best to make it as humane as possible."

I slumped in my seat with my head in my hands, then stood up with my hands together as in prayer, and moaned, "Oh Mr. Harrison! As humane as possible! We're gonna kill the poor little frogs! They've been ripped away from their parents and now their little bodies are gonna be cut to pieces, dying in agony, just so we can look at their internal organs."

The teacher was clearly not amused at the performance and shouted, "You stop that, Loof! Now sit down and be quiet! The frogs are not going to feel any pain."

I took my seat holding my head muttering, "How do you know? Have you ever been dissected alive?"

Mr. Harrison was now at my desk with his finger in my face. "I am warning you Loof, you stop this right now."

When I looked up at the teacher, with a tear running down my face, I exclaimed, "Ohhh, Mr. Harrison! I don't know if I can do this. You want me to kill the little frog."

"That's going to cost you a JUG Loof! Now shut up!"

I sat there with my hands over my eyes sobbing. Everybody was looking at me in silence. Mr. Harrison began the lesson for the day and was able to divert attention away from me. Kevin was sitting in the seat directly opposite me and glanced over as I slowly moved my hands from in front of my face, just enough to expose a broad grin.

I did my JUG on Tuesday, and three days later, on Friday, was the frog dissection lab. That morning, Kevin, Bobby, and I arrived at school together. We entered through the Carroll Street doors, and as we passed in front of the gym, the hallway leading to the pool was abuzz with activity. Students and teachers were coming and going with some in more of a hurry than others, but all were extremely animated. We stopped right in front of the trophy case, and just breathed in the excitement of the feverish activity unfolding before our eyes.

Then we spied Jack Fredreck, who was in every class with me, and our lockers were side by side, coming down the hall. He saw his three classmates and said, "Hey Owney ain't this amazing!"

"Uh, I guess so Jack. What happened?"

Jack seemed surprised and asked, "Really? You guys didn't hear?"

Bobby answered this time, "No, we just got here. What happened?"

Very excitedly, Jack explained, "Well, all the frogs from the bio lab are in the pool. Boy, they're havin' some time trying to catch them all. Father Nolan is really pissed. If they catch the people who did this, they'll probably get expelled. But boy I wish I had done it."

I looked at my compatriots and said to Jack, "Thanks for the info, Jack, and you're right. Those guys are in big trouble."

On my way to my locker some of the classmates I knew, and quite a few I did not, were giving me the "okay" sign, or a thumbs up, or laughing and saying, "Good one Owney." When I got to my locker, Sam Vanacort and Jimmy Linden from biology class were waiting. Vanacort started by saying, "This was terrific Owney. How'd you do it?"

"Do what? I don't know what…. Oh, you mean the frogs. I had nothin' to do with that."

Linden added, "Come on Owney, you can tell us. Everybody knows you did it."

My calm reply was, "Well you can tell everybody that they're wrong. 'Cause I didn't do it and I have no idea who did."

Vanacort and Linden smiled at me, and both patted me on each shoulder with Vanacort saying, "Sure Owney, sure. We understand why you don't want to say anything. That's cool. But ya did good!"

Every class that morning, and everywhere I went, it was the same story. A couple of seniors even stopped me on my way to biology to offer congratulations. There was no sense in trying to protest my innocence, so I just remained silent. When I got to Biology, Mr. Harrison was not there yet, and on my entrance the class gave me a standing ovation.

Trying my best Elvis impersonation, I said, "Thank you. Thank you very much." After some additional applause I continued, "But I want to state this publicly. I did not put the frogs from the bio lab in the pool, and I have no idea who did."

Some of the guys were just shaking their heads and there was a smattering of laughter as Mr. Harrison entered the room. He saw me standing in front of the room, and in a decidedly angry tone said, "You went over the line with this one Loof. Those are expensive frogs, and you disrupted the pool schedule and this class."

"Mister, I was just explaining to the class that I did not…"

Mr. Harrison interrupted, "Stop right there Loof. Don't say another word. Father Knox wants to see you in his office right now. So go, just go."

I threw my hands up in the air and declared, "Fine I'll go. But I don't know what you people are talking about." As I left the room, there were waves and a few thumbs up from classmates. Then when just outside in the hall, I heard Mr.

Harrison saying, "Don't you people encourage him. He'll get what's coming to him."

I knocked on Father Knox's door, and the voice from within told me to enter. I was about halfway to the desk, when the priest looked up and said, "You have really done it this time Loof. This stunt is beyond the pale. What were you thinking?"

I looked at the priest in stunned disbelief and said, "Father I swear, I did not do this."

"Loof come on now. After that scene you put on in biology the other day, for which you paid the price, you are the absolute number one and only suspect. Also, if you confess now, it will be much easier for you."

I fell heavily into the chair in front of Father Knox's desk, and with my hand on my forehead began to cry. Through my tears I stammered out, "This is just not fair. Why doesn't anyone believe me? I do feel bad for the frogs, that's true. But who would be dumb enough to try this stunt after what happened in class?" I paused, and continued sobbing, then added, "I don't know why everyone thinks I could of pulled this off. It's crazy!"

"Of course, I don't believe you did this by yourself. So just tell us who helped you."

I grabbed some tissues from a box on the desk, blew my nose hard, and with tears running down my cheeks, I put my hand on the Bible, which was always on the desk and stated, "I swear Father! I had nothing to do with taking the frogs from the bio lab and placing them in the pool. But I promise that if I get any information about who did, you will be the first to know." I removed my hand from the Bible, seemed to regain my composure, and standing up straight, looked right at Father Knox awaiting the priest's response.

I definitely noted the skepticism in the Priest's face. He just stared at me. Finally, he walked around his desk and put his hand on my shoulder saying, "Okay son, you go back to your class now." I turned toward the door and was trying to hold my smile until safely out of range. But just as I reached the office door, I heard the voice of the priest say, "This matter is not over by any means, Mr. Loof."

There was not much time left in Biology, so I did not return to class. Instead, I opted to wait in the cafeteria for Kevin and Bobby. When they arrived, they of course wanted to know how the meeting with Father Knox had gone. I did not want to discuss the matter with all the people around to eavesdrop. We found a quiet spot in the courtyard just outside the cafeteria doors. After sitting down on a bench, Bobby was the first to ask, "So come on, don't beat around the bush, tell us already!"

I explained exactly what happened in the meeting, not leaving out any details. Bobby sat there with his mouth agape, and Kevin was not sure whether he should laugh or not. Then Kevin looked askance at me and finally said, "Okay, let's say that's exactly what happened. The question is, did he buy it?"

"First of all, that is exactly what happened. Would I lie to you guys?"

Both boys replied resoundingly, "YES!"

I jumped back in my seat, and said through a chuckle, "Geeze, you didn't have to bite my head off. But I am not lying about what happened with Father Knox. Now to address your question, maybe, maybe not. I thought I had him, but the way he said he was going to keep investigating, I thought he was talking right to me."

Kevin interjected, "I'm tellin' ya Owney, Mr. Harrison is really angry, and from what you said, Father Knox was pretty mad too. But everybody's talkin' about it, and says you did great."

"Well, that's cool that everyone's talkin' about what happened. I'm just hopin' that when the investigation is over, they don't actually find out who really put those frogs in the pool."

Kevin and Bobby froze for a moment, then burst out in hysterics while pushing me off the bench and slapping me playfully about the head and body.

CHAPTER 11

A little less than two weeks later, I got to school early, found Bobby and said, "Listen, where's Kevin?"

"I don't know, haven't seen him."

"Okay, I'll catch him in French. I got a great idea, but I wanna tell you both at the same time. At lunch, you're gonna love this."

Bobby rolled his eyes and said, "Oh God no. I'm already nervous."

"Will you stop. Would I ever lead you wrong?"

"You don't really want me to answer that, do you?"

I smiled and pushed my friend's shoulder, saying, "I'll see you in French and we'll talk at lunch."

In French and biology, I only told Kevin I had a plan to make some money, and would provide details later. At the end of biology when the three of us left the classroom, Kevin and Bobby immediately began pressing me for information on this great idea. I just said, "Wait till we get to my office."

We skipped the cafeteria completely, and I led them to the set of benches in the courtyard between the pool and the main office wing of the school building. Finally, when we were all seated, Bobby gritted his teeth, and asked very impatiently, "Okay Owney, enough, right now! What is this plan?"

"Okay, okay! Do you two know what important sports event takes place on the first Saturday in May?" Kevin and

Bobby glanced at one another, and then to me shaking their heads. I continued, "Well I'll tell you. It's the day the Kentucky Derby is run at Churchill Downs."

Kevin snapped his fingers and said, "Wait, wait, it's a horse race, right?"

I replied somewhat indignantly, "It's not just a horse race. It's the most historically famous horse race in America."

Bobby asked, "Fine, it's a big horse race. Is there a point here? What does it have to do with your plan?"

I responded, "Calm down big guy, I'm gettin' there. I went to my cousin's house over the weekend, we were in my uncle's bar, and he was doing this thing with the Derby."

I went on to explain that you paid twenty dollars to pick one of the fifteen horses in the race. You do not choose your own horse. It's just the luck of the draw. He sells as many fifteen-horse tickets as he can, takes twenty bucks from each ticket, and gives out the rest of the money. There are prizes if your horse finished first, second, third, or fourth.

Kevin looked at me like I had two heads and said, "You're crazy. Nobody's gonna give us twenty dollars."

With a wave of my hand and distinctly miffed, I replied, "Of course I know that. We're not gonna charge twenty bucks. It'll only be five bucks, which is seventy-five dollars. We take five on each ticket, which leaves seventy, and we give twenty-five to the winner, twenty for second, fifteen for third, and ten for fourth." I pointed at Bobby and asked, "Hey math whiz, those numbers all add up, right?"

Bobby took a minute to process the numbers, and then nodded his affirmation. "Okay boys, we're in business. I'll get started on the lists tonight, and you guys can start makin' them up tomorrow. Listen, we gotta get on this. There's only a week to sell tickets. I'll take some to Rockaway and you guys sell 'em too."

In two days, we had one hundred tickets ready, and Friday, a week and a day before the race, there were twenty-five tickets sold. Over the weekend, another one hundred tickets were produced. Between all of us distributing tickets, brisk business on Monday and Tuesday in school, and even Michael chipping in with some sales, the tickets were selling like hotcakes. By the time I left in the afternoon, the ticket sales totaled one hundred and twenty. On the train ride home, I was actually considering making up a few more tickets just in case.

I arrived at school the next morning with a spring in my step, prepared for another good sales day. I was running a little late, and decided to use the President Street entrance, which was closer to my locker. There was a long hallway that led to a short corridor that forced you to walk past Father Knox's office. When I turned into that short corridor, Father Knox was coming out of his office. He spied me and said, "Oh good Loof, you saved me some steps. You are just the person I'm looking for. Come in here."

I knew there was only one reason that Father Knox would be looking for me, and as I walked toward the priest and entered the office, I was preparing myself. I started to take a seat, but Father Knox said, "It's okay Loof, you don't have to sit down." This turn of events puzzled me, but I did not let it show and I remained ready. Then the priest asked, "Loof, what are you trying to pull here?"

"What d'ya mean, Father? I'm not doin' anything."

"So, you call taking money for a horse racing scheme, doing nothing?"

"Horse racing? I don't know anything about horse racing Father."

"That's very interesting Loof." He then proceeded to pull one of the betting tickets out of his pocket and showed it to me saying, "So I guess you know nothing about this then?"

"Not a clue Father, what is that?"

"Look closely at the names that are written on the piece of paper."

I did take a good look, and there it was staring me right in the face, Mr. Corning, the new Science teacher. I was not going to give in until the last possible moment and said, "I see Mr. Corning's name, but some of the other names look kinda funny."

"Loof, Mr. Corning explained the whole thing to me after he showed the ticket in the teachers' lounge." I started to say something, but the priest cut me off saying, "It's okay Loof, you're not in trouble. The Kentucky Derby is an American tradition. I remember listening to Gallant Fox win in 1930, and he went on to win the Triple Crown. Then in 1938 there was the Seabiscuit-War Admiral match race that was a national event. So, first I want a chance to pick a horse, and here's the five dollars for that, and then let's talk about the money raised."

The priest went on to say that the five dollar per ticket profit would be donated to the school. I negotiated by saying that it was a lot of work writing up the slips, and there were expenses associated with the sale and distribution. We finally agreed on $1.50 per ticket for the workers and $3.50 for the school. After shaking hands on the deal, I said, "Nice doing business with you, Father. I'll be right back so you can make your pick."

"Very good Loof, now get out there and sell those tickets."

When I told Kevin and Bobby what had transpired, to say they were flabbergasted would be an understatement. Kevin asked, "So who did Father pick?"

"Well, when I went back to his office, he pulled out the horse who everybody thinks will be the favorite, Kauai King."

Bobby said, "I guess God was looking out for him."

I added, "Well, of course the favorite doesn't always win. And I don't know if God was watchin', but Kauai King was the only horse's name in the bowl."

We all had a good laugh, and then Kevin brought up the notion that we were giving up a lot of money to the school. I have an explanation for that. "That is true, but now that we have raising money for the school behind us, we'll probably sell more tickets, which means we'll make more money 'cause of the volume."

I was proved right, when between every place we were selling, the remainder of the original two hundred tickets were sold. This fact necessitated producing fifty more tickets that also sold out.

On the Friday before the race, I discovered another bonus to having the backing of the school for this endeavor. When I was leaving for the day, I was able to leave money with Father Knox, which meant I would not have to worry about it over the weekend. I knocked on the priest's door, and when called in I said, "Hey Father, here's the money and the tickets. We'll bring in the rest of the money on Monday."

"Very good Loof, I hear we did exceptionally well."

"Yep, we did great Father. But I'm trusting you not to take that money and put on Kauai King's nose."

The priest smiled and said, "And I'm trusting you boys to bring in the correct amount on Monday. Now, get out of here Loof before I give you JUG for the rest of the year."

"Touché, Father! Enjoy the weekend and good luck tomorrow."

The next day we gathered at Bobby's house to watch the race. None of us had told our parents about the fundraising for the school, and Bobby's mother was intrigued by her son's sudden interest in a horse race. I took credit for being the bad influence that introduced her son to the evils of the sport of kings. The excitement was building throughout the day, and finally it was time for the race. The final odds did make Kauai King the favorite.

When the gate opened, it was like a Calvary charge with fifteen horses jockeying for position. By the time they passed the grandstand for the first time, Kauai King had raced to the lead. I said, "Wire to wire in the Derby is not easy."

Down the back stretch, the favorite was stubbornly maintaining the lead. I noted, "It looks like he's doing it pretty easy."

Turning for home, the King was still in front and holding the lead through the stretch run with jockey, Don Brumfield, tapping the horse a few times left-handed. There were three or four horses making a run, and I was on my feet jumping up and down yelling, "Come on King! Go King! Hold on baby!"

My friends were sitting there as much watching my antics as the race. But even they were standing up as the horses approached the finish line. At the wire, Kauai King was in front by a length, and I left my feet, pumping my fist in the air, shouting, "Yes, yes! That a boy King!"

Bobby asked, "Geeze Owney, you always get this excited?"

"Yep! I love watching the horses run, and how the jockey and the horse work together. And with a great finish like that, it's exhilarating! Oh, and in a race like this on TV, it's cool to see rich people goin' just as crazy as a two-dollar bettor."

Then Kevin inquired, "Even if you didn't bet?"

"Yeah, even without betting. It's still exciting." I took a breath and continued, "But today, my father called my uncle, and we both bet fifty dollars to win on the King."

Kevin and Bobby started calling me names and throwing couch cushions at me.

May went by in a blur, and included a few days JUG, but Father Knox let me off with just warnings. There was an assembly in June, where the Kentucky Derby trio were introduced, and we were congratulated for our fundraising efforts. There was a milestone for Michael when graduated from Bishop Loughlin, and decided not to go away for college. The final exams were taken, and everything was set for the summer. Then, the letter arrived from Prep with all the bad news.

One week after the last exam, I went surfing with Michael. After returning home and taking a shower, I went downstairs to the kitchen, where I found my mother reading the mail. Without looking up from her reading she said, "I have a letter here from school, Owen."

I had no idea what the contents of the letter said, but the tone of her voice could only mean that it was not good. She glared at me, and demanded, "Come over here and sit down."

From experience, I thought it would be a better idea to stay out of range, just in case, and answered, "That's okay mom. I'll stand right here."

My Mother's face told me that the answer might have made things worse. But she began talking in a fairly calm tone. "First, they are thanking us for the excellent job you did last month in raising a sizeable amount of money for the school. What exactly did you do?"

I had hoped this day would not arrive, but thought, "I did a good thing. I can tell most of the truth." So, I explained everything that had transpired with a few omissions. The biggest one being the monetary advantage we had worked out with Father Knox. She was aghast and exclaimed loudly, "Gambling on horses to raise money! It was your idea, and they went along with it!"

I knew that this was another place where I should shave the truth a little, and answered, "Yep, I presented the idea, they liked it. The school made money, and everybody had a great time."

My mother raised her hand to her forehead, and was clearly still shocked. "But gambling? I don't believe it!"

I had a quick response, "Come on mom. You go to the track with Uncle Jimmy and Aunt Mary all the time. It's not like we were bookies or something really taking bets. And what about the St. Camillus Bazaar and all the chance books we had to sell? We did the same thing. People bought a chance, and a lot of people won money."

She did not expect that kind of a response from me. I was not being disrespectful, and on one hand she had to think about what I said. But she was flustered by the answer nonetheless, and spat out a reply, "I don't know, I don't know. It's just not the same."

I knew well enough not to press the issue and asked, "Is that all mom? I'm going up to the Cottages for a while before dinner, okay?

She declared adamantly, "No Owen! That's not all! It says here that you failed geometry and English so you will have to attend Summer school."

I was well aware that the less I said the better, and replied, "Really, I'm a little surprised."

With this, she really raised her voice, and I took a few steps back. "That's all you have to say? This is totally unacceptable Owen. And I am not surprised, you spent too much time on frivolous outside activities like playing basketball."

At that moment, my father entered the kitchen through the back door. Taking a look at his wife and son, he realized he was walking into a perilous situation. Before he could say a word, my mother handed him the Prep letter and emptied both barrels. "Just take a look at this. Look at your son's grades, and do you want to know what he did in that school? Really, I don't know what we are going to do with your son."

So, he knew that I was in very hot water, and while he had no desire to join me in the pot, he was going to try and take a little heat off me, "So what has MY SON done now?"

She glowered at her husband. "Don't you get sarcastic with me Martin Loof." She then proceeded to relate the particulars of what she had learned from the letter and from me.

I looked straight passed my mother and right at my father, answering, "I'm really sorry. You know how I am with math, and geometry was really confusing. Besides, when am I gonna use it anyway. I tried the best I could."

My mother jumped back into the conversation, "You obviously did not try hard enough or do your best."

My father interrupted, "Your mother's right Owen. We all know you can do better, and you really must."

She pointed her finger at me, I took another step back, and she vociferated, "That's right mister, you better, and there will be consequences for you if you don't. Do you hear me?"

I shifted my feet, moved my head back and forth, and sighed saying, "Well I kinda ruined my summer and I don't wanna do that again. I also don't wanna disappoint either of you. I promise that starting with the summer classes, I will do better, and carry that on to next year."

My mother stood up and said to her husband, "You better talk some sense into your son." Then as she passed me, I moved to my left, since my mother always led with her right, and she said forcefully, "I don't want to see another report like this again, understand?"

Knowing I would never say what I really thinking, I coyly replied, "I will do everything I can to make sure you don't."

With my mother out of the room, my father and I sat down at the kitchen table, and I started, "I really will try my best dad, I promise. Junior year will be different."

He reached across the table, touched my hand, and said, "I know you will try to make that happen, son." Then he paused, straightened up, and looked at me saying, "So you copied your Uncle Jimmy's Kentucky Derby Pool and made some money for the school."

"Yeah, it was really cool Dad."

"And you told your mother everything?"

"Well maybe not everything."

"You didn't tell her about our fifty-dollar bet, did you?"

I smiled at my father, and answered, "Of course not! Why would I do that? Don't worry dad."

Junior Year

CHAPTER 12

When I got off the bus on Nostrand Avenue, I was running late, but was in no particular hurry. I stopped to look through the fence surrounding the field with the school in the background. It didn't look as big and imposing as it did three years ago. I realized I was almost seven inches taller, and reflected on how different things were this time and how much I had changed. As the walk toward Carroll Street began, I had no idea what my third year plus in high school would bring, but I was ready for whatever it was. When I reached the doors, I paused and said to myself, "Bring it on junior year. I'm ready."

Entering the foyer, I saw no one, and the gym doors were closed. I knew this meant the Orientation Assembly had already begun. I stopped to think, and then walked over to the water fountain, and moistened my shirt and forehead. Then I loosened my tie and let my blazer fall off one shoulder. When I got to the gym door, I opened my book bag, and mussed my hair a little more. I picked the right-side doors because I knew freshman and sophomores would be in the bleachers on that side.

I smiled, took a deep breath, and noisily pushed open the double doors. I staggered between a couple of teachers, heading toward the bottom row of the bleachers. The sophomores sitting at the end of the row quickly rose to give me room as I collapsed into the empty space. Father

Nolan stopped his address in mid-sentence. Mr. Sullivan and Mr. Berry rushed over, and everyone turned to see what the commotion was.

While the two teachers were attending to me, Father Nolan asked from the stage, "Is everything all right back there?"

With a wave of his hand, Mr. Sullivan gave the priest the indication all was well, and Father Nolan continued his speech. I was assisted out of the gym and down to the coach's office, where I was placed on a couch.

Mr. Berry had to leave because he had a homeroom assignment, and when he was gone Coach Sullivan asked, "How you feeling there, Loof?"

"Better, Coach, much better."

The coach then asked the obvious question. "So, Loof, what happened?"

I knew that the question was coming and was prepared. I looked at the coach, sighing deeply and said, "Well, it's like this coach. I was walking up the steps from the train at Nostrand Avenue, and these three guys came up behind me, and one of them grabbed my book bag. I didn't want to give it up, so there was a struggle. I kicked the guy holding my bag in the knee, and he fell down and let go. One of the other guys threw a punch, which I ducked, and I pushed him out of the way. When the third guy tried to grab me, I made like Billy Ward sidestepping a Xavier tackler, and ran for the bus. They caught up to me just as I got on the bus, and I kicked the first guy into the other two, and when they cleared the door, the driver closed it quick."

Coach Sullivan inspected me closely and said suspiciously, "That's quite a story Loof."

I stared right at the coach saying, "And it's the absolute truth Coach!"

"Okay Loof, okay. You stay put, and I'll be back."

I was not sure how long he was gone, and when he returned, he was accompanied by Father Nolan and another priest. Father Nolan spoke first, "How are you feeling now Owen?"

"I'm really feeling okay, thanks Father."

Father Nolan continued, "Coach Sullivan has explained what happened. You had quite an experience."

With an air of confidence I stated, "It's not the worst fight I ever had Father."

The three adults laughed, and Father Nolan said, "That's good to know Owen. I think we should call your…"

I interrupted the priest, "No, no Father. Don't do that. It's no big deal. There's no harm done. I'm fine. They're both workin'. Just let me get myself fixed up and I'll get to my classes."

Father Nolan glanced at the other priest and the coach who both gestured that they were in agreement with my assessment of the situation, then he said to me, "Okay, as long as you say everything's all right. When you are ready, report to Father Richards's office, and he will give you your schedule." He paused and added, "Oh yes, you were not at the assembly. This is Father Richards, the new Prefect of Discipline. We all know you are aware of where his office is."

I stood up to shake hands with the new priest saying, "Nice to meet you Father. Welcome to the school. I'll be in your office as soon as I can."

He responded sternly, "Thank you Loof, but don't take too long!"

"Don't worry Father, I'll be quick." Then I thanked the coach and Father Nolan, and left the office to find a bathroom.

After leaving Father Richards's office and checking the schedule, I saw that it was time for third period French with Mr. Garell, who was a new teacher. The classroom was on the second floor at the end of the hallway. The bell had not sounded yet, but it was very close, and there were only a few stragglers in the hall. Sam Vanacort, who was in my homeroom the last two years, ran up to me from behind and asked, "Hey Owney, what the hell happened to you this morning? You okay?"

"Yeah, yeah, I'm fine. Just had a little incident on the way to school this morning, but it's cool now."

"That's good, man. Everybody's talking about it ya know?"

"Whatever, I'm trying to get to French. I'll talk to you later."

Vanacort smiled, patted me on the back, and walked into the nearest classroom. I continued down the hall, arriving at the assigned room as the bell sounded. I shuffled my feet around and rolled my shoulders, then opened the door. All eyes were on me, and as I moved forward, I caught my back foot on the door. I fell forward tucking my head in, and as I hit the floor, transitioned into a front somersault. After one roll, I sprang to my feet directly in front of Mr. Garell's desk, and put the note from Father Richards on his desk. Then I extended my hand and said, "Hi! Mr. Garell, right? I'm Owen Loof. I am in your class. C'est un plaisir de vous recontrer."

The teacher was surprised, but he did shake my hand. He then answered in English, "It's nice to meet you also Mr. Loof, I think. So that was you this morning in the gym. It appears you have a habit of making grand entrances. Will this be an everyday occurrence?"

"Oh, I'm sorry Mister. I'm a little clumsy and was in a hurry to get here. But if you want a special entrance every day....?"

"No, no Loof, that's quite unnecessary. Now go sit down."

When I turned around to face my classmates, I took a bow to the applause and laughter I was receiving, and found a seat in the back of the room between Kevin and Bobby as Mr. Garell was shouting, "All right, all right, enough of that noise! Settle down and be quiet! We have work to do."

The three compatriots left the class together on the way to lunch. The first thing I said was, "Doesn't that guy look like Soupy Sales?"

Kevin and Bobby desperately wanted to get their friend alone to find out what had actually happened. They whisked me out of the cafeteria for the private talk. Once we were all settled, I related the story exactly the way I told it in Coach Sullivan's office. When I was finished, my two friends just stared very questioningly. They turned to one another, and then back to me. After a long pause Kevin said, "They actually bought that story? Come on Owney, this is us you're talking to here. You can tell us the truth."

I put one hand on Kevin's shoulder, and my other hand on Bobby's, and said, "You are exactly right. I can tell you the truth. And I just did. What I told you is exactly what happened to me this morning."

Kevin and Bobby again glanced at one another, and Bobby said to Kevin sarcastically, "If that wasn't the real story, he would tell us, right?"

Kevin nodded, and said even more sarcastically, "Oh yeah, sure."

I declared dejectedly, "Wow, my best friends questioning my veracity. I am hurt."

They both started playfully roughing me up, and Bobby said, "Oh shut up you idiot. Ya know Kev, we'll get the story when he's ready, but I guess we gotta be careful around this beast, huh?"

Sliding away, feigning fright, and laughing, Kevin said, "Please don't hurt us."

When the laughing ended, I said, "All right, all right enough. But seriously, can we please keep the wraps on this story. I'd like to keep it quiet, okay?"

Bobby asked, "So what should we say?"

"Just say what I'm gonna say. There was a problem on the train that is being looked into."

Both of my friends agreed not to say anything, but as the day went on it was obvious the story had spread throughout the school. On the way to gym class with them, I asked, "Ya sure you guys didn't say anything?" When they assured me they had not, I said, "This is crazy. I swear I don't how this happened. How could it get around so quick? There are seniors that know. There are freshman that know for God's sake."

Kevin and Bobby shrugged their shoulders as we entered the gym and found seats in the bleachers. Since it was only orientation day, Coach Sullivan was only going to go over the basics of what we were going to do and the class rules. When the class was almost over, he pointed to me and announced, "I have been telling all my classes about what happened to Loof this morning." He then gave a shortened version of the story that kept in enough details to make me sound heroic. Then he ended the speech by smiling and saying, "We may incorporate some self-defense tactics that Loof will show us."

People were applauding, and I stood up taking a bow. Sullivan was about to admonish the celebrity when the bell sounded, and he said, "Okay you slackers. Get out of here and be ready to work tomorrow." Then he called out to me. "Be careful on the train there, Loof. Don't hurt anybody."

Before I could leave the gym, I was besieged by classmates wanting more information on the story. I embellished the story a little, and when it was all over leaving just me with my two amigos, Bobby said, "Umm, there were some things you told them that you didn't tell us."

Without skipping a beat, I said, "You know it was a pretty upsetting experience that kinda shook me up a little. Now that there's been time to calm down, I'm gettin' a much clearer picture."

Bobby looked at Kevin saying, "He's gettin' a much clearer picture. Ya got that?"

Kevin nodded, I knew what was coming, and started running as fast as I could.

After my escape, I was on my way to the hallway leading to the President Street exit when I saw Mr. Delasalvo approaching. I stopped and said, "Hey Mister, how's it goin'?"

"Fine Loof, very good." Then he asked, "Who do you have for French?"

"It's a new teacher, Mr. Garell."

"That's good. I've spoken with him and he's a good man. You'll do fine."

"Thanks Mister, but he can't be as good as you were. I'll keep you posted." I turned to leave, and Mr. Delasalvo smiled saying, "That was quite an entrance this morning." Then he gave me a wink and a smile saying, "And be careful on the train in the morning."

CHAPTER 13

The third week of school, Coach Sullivan announced in Gym that the intramural basketball games would begin the following week. Each class had until Friday to turn in their rosters of seven players and one alternate. Anyone who played on the school basketball teams were ineligible for intramurals. Kevin, Bobby, and I were in homeroom 3F, and at the meeting to put the team together, Bobby was asked to serve as coach. After the roster was set and as the meeting was ending, Bobby announced, "Listen guys, I have heard that John Alleva is gonna be coachin' 3D. Me and him played against one another all through elementary school and I could only beat him a couple of times. If there's one game I wanna win, it's that game."

I grabbed Kevin's hand, and the others joined in standing up and shouting in unison, "We got this Coach!"

The games were going well for both 3F and 3D as both teams had identical 4-0 records when it was time to square off. Jimmy Linden and Richie Walters were leading the team in scoring. I was not too far behind, and also doing a good job rebounding. However, it was a total team effort with Kevin, Jack Fredreck, and Pat Santisi all contributing to the victories. The 3D team was obviously playing well, and their best players were two new students, Charlie Westbrook, and Benny Giordano. But they also had three other really good players in Johnny Killbride, Bobby Rovegno, and Mike Hoffman.

Just before the game started, Alleva and Atanasio met at half-court to shake hands, and Alleva said to his longtime rival, "You're gonna need more than luck Atanasio. These new guys, Westbrook and Giordano are really good. They could be playing varsity this year. Why don't you just give up now? You're going down just like in CYO." Then he started to walk away laughing.

Bobby called out after him, "Yeah, we'll see who's laughing at the end of the game, big man!"

With the tip off, 3D's top players lived up to their reputation as their team jumped out to a 10-0 lead. Coaches were only allowed two timeouts, but Bobby used one right away to calm things down. The time out helped as Walters and Linden started scoring, Jack Fredreck hit a couple of bombs from outside, and the team defense was much better. At halftime, 3F was in front, but by only four points, 22-18.

The third quarter saw the lead change hands as both teams had good scoring runs, and heading into the last minute of the third quarter, 3F was leading 34-32. Then disaster struck, as Walters and Linden each picked up their fourth fouls. Then, in the first two minutes of the final quarter, with 3F still ahead by two points, both players were forced to the bench with their fifth fouls. When Linden was assessed his last foul and joined Walters on the bench, Atanasio was livid at the questionable nature of the foul and was almost ejected from the gym. The game remained close right to the end as Pat Santisi and I did a commendable job on Westbrook and Giordano, and the rest of the team also played well. But 3D had too many weapons, and they pulled away in the last minute and a half to win by eight points.

After the final buzzer, the two teams exchanged handshakes and congratulations for a hard fought, well-played game. When it was time for the coaches to speak, Alleva said, "That was a lot closer than I thought it would be. I was actually a little worried for a while."

With a deadpanned expression, Atanasio challenged, "Not for nothin', but I did play the last four minutes with my best players on the bench, thanks to the refs."

Alleva started laughing saying, "Wah, wah, wah! Blame the refs! Just accept it, man. I got your number, and I always will."

Atanasio smiled back declaring, "Yeah, we'll see! They'll be another game, my friend!" After a quick hug, they left to join their respective teams.

The seven 3F players were sitting on the bottom row of bleachers when their coach approached and he said, "You guys all played great. We'll get 'em next time." The bell sounded ending Lunch, and Bobby shook hands one more time with all his players and we started to leave the gym. When Bobby and Kevin reached the door, they noticed that I was not with them, and they turned to find me. I was hurrying toward them, obviously upset at something. As I neared Kevin asked, "What's a matter, man?"

Angrily I exclaimed, "Do you fuckin' believe this? It's only the fifth week of school and it's startin', already."

Kevin was trying to calm me down, and asked again, "What are you talkin' about?"

I proclaimed loudly, "During the game somebody stole my fuckin' History book!"

Bobby was correct about meeting 3D on the court again. It happened ten days later in the championship game for the juniors. 3D was undefeated, and the only loss on the slate of 3F was the game against 3D.

The Saturday before the big game, Michael and I had petitioned Father Murray, the St. Camillus CYO coach, to open the gym for us. The whole 3F team showed up to go over a few things and work on a new defense. Ed Breen, and a few other guys from the neighborhood, agreed to help out in a scrimmage. On Monday, when Bobby, Kevin, and I left French for the walk to the gym and the championship game, Bobby said, "I hope I thanked your friends enough for helping us out on Saturday. I really think it could make a difference. But do you guys' drink like that all the time, and where did you get the beer on a Saturday afternoon?"

"We only do it on special occasions. Was the sun out on Saturday?" Bobby nodded, and I answered my own question. "See, a special occasion. And as for obtaining the brew, that's top secret, and if I told you I'd have to kill you."

We got to the gym, met the rest of the team, and warmed up for the contest ahead. Alleva made a point of stopping in front of the 3F bench, doing a little dance while pointing his fingers in a pumping motion saying, "Going down, Atanasio, going down!"

Bobby just smiled at his rival, turned to his team, and said, "This could be the biggest game of your lives. You'll always remember how we beat their pants off." Then looking straight at me admonished, "Now that doesn't mean trying to take their pants off, Owney. Play hard, play clean, and let's not give the refs a chance to take it away from us!"

Everybody laughed, and I said, "I hear ya coach. I got this." Then I put my hand in the middle of the circle, and when the entire team joined hands, I started, "Saint Ignatius of Loyola." The whole team raised their hands in the air while shouting, "Pray for us!"

Right from the opening tap everyone could see that this game was going to be different. I was playing like a man possessed at both ends of the court. I made two steals that led to easy lay-ups by Jack Fredreck and Richie Walters. I hit two straight jump shots, one from each corner, and put back a Jimmy Linden miss. On top of this offense, I was covering Westbrook like a blanket. First denying him the ball, and when he did handle it, giving him no room to take a shot. I even drew two offensive fouls on his drives to the basket, which forced him to take seat on the bench for the last three minutes of the first quarter. When the quarter ended, the scoreboard read, 3F-16/3D-4.

For all intents and purposes, the game was over right there. The team rallied around me, and everyone elevated their game. But I played the game of my life scoring 26 of the team's 42 points and securing more rebounds than anyone on either team. On the defensive end of the court, I held 3D leading scorer Charlie Westbrook to only six points before he fouled out midway through the last quarter.

But the game ended on a disappointing note for 3F and me. On the last play of the game, Kevin took a jump shot from the right side of the foul line that hit the front of the rim and bounced in the air. I jumped and got my right hand over the rim, trying to grab the ball. I could not get both hands on the ball and tipped it with my right hand. When I came down, my left foot landed half on the floor and half on Jimmy Linden's foot. My ankle twisted in an unnatural position, and I crumpled to the floor in a lot of pain just as the final buzzer sounded.

I rolled over, stayed in a prone position for a few seconds, then sat up grabbing my ankle. Jimmy Linden looked down at me and asked, "Owney you all right?"

I looked up replying somewhat sarcastically, "Oh yeah, I'm just fine. Except for the pain in my freakin' ankle, sure everything's great."

Players from both teams were crowded around with Bobby and Kevin kneeling next to their friend. Kevin said, "I'm not asking how it feels, but you think you can walk?"

"Well, there's only one way to find out. Help me up."

They got me to the nearest bleacher, sat me down, and started to unlace my sneakers. Just then, Coach Sullivan appeared through the crowd shouting, "Leave the sneakers tied for now. It'll keep the swelling down." Then he looked at me saying, "Stay right there Loof. I'm going to get some ice packs."

As the Coach walked away, the bell sounded ending Lunch. Everybody was getting their stuff together and starting to leave. Players from both teams stopped to shake hands and compliment me on the game I had played. Charlie Westbrook was more than complimentary when he exclaimed, "I can't remember the last time somebody shut me down like that. That was one great game. See ya man."

Kevin and Bobby were the last to talk with me, and sat down on either side. Bobby began, "Unbelievable game, dude! I'll never forget this. I didn't just beat Alleva, I killed 'im. Thanks, man."

Kevin added, "Terrific, just terrific! I didn't think you had it in ya!"

I responded with a smile, "Neither did I, as a matter of fact!"

As we were sitting there, Alleva walked over and inquired, "Yo Owney, what the hell did these guys feed you today? You were outa your head today."

Bobby replied, "I don't know what he ate, but I'm sure as hell gonna find out. And I'm gonna look for the pile of shit he stepped in too."

CHAPTER 14

My ankle was very badly sprained, so I was out of school for two weeks. I was welcomed back by everyone in homeroom, but it was noted that I was wearing the long black trench coat again. Some people in the class had witnessed the earlier wearing of the trench coat and knew something was going to happen. Even Mr. Quinn questioned why I was wearing the trench coat. Kevin finally asked, "Okay, what's the deal?"

With a blank look on my face, I replied, "I have no idea what you mean."

Kevin reached for the coat saying, "Do you have any clothes on under there?"

I pulled away and bumped into Bobby, who also started pulling at the coat exclaiming, "Come Owney, open up!"

I again eluded the grasp, and shouted, "Mister, they're trying to kill me!"

Mr. Quinn yelled, "Enough you three. Calm down and sit down! You hear me!"

I raised my chin, brushed myself off, and found a seat saying, "Geeze, what's wrong with you guys, attacking me on my first day back at school."

Kevin declared in a somewhat forceful tone, "We know you, Owney. There's something going on, or off, under that coat."

I shook my head and sighed, while saying, "Wow, a guy can't even wear a coat to school without being attacked and accused of having ulterior motives. I am positively shocked and hurt."

Before anything else could be said, the bell sounded to end homeroom. Kevin and Bobby rose from their seats to leave, but I remained seated with my arms folded against my chest and frowning noticeably. My friends looked back at me, and Bobby asked, "Well, you comin'?"

"Yeah, I'll be there. I gotta pee."

Kevin looked at Bobby and said, "I'm tellin' ya somethin's coming. Be ready!" Just before they left the room, I called to them. Then I stood up and flung open the trench coat. I was wearing tan khaki pants with a white shirt and pink tie, and a blue sport jacket. I exclaimed forcefully, "There, ya happy! Can I go pee now?"

Both of my friends wore surprised looks, and Kevin raised his hands palm up saying, "Okay, okay, Owney, relax. Sorry man, see you in trig."

The bell sounded to begin Mr. Benny's trigonometry class, and I was not in my seat. Mr. Benny noted the empty seat, and Kevin said, "He was in homeroom, Mister. He said he had to use the bathroom."

This was satisfactory for Mr. Benny, and he began the class. A few minutes passed, the door opened, and I entered the room, saying to the teacher, "Sorry Mister, my stomach was a little funny and I had to go."

"Fine, Loof, fine, just take a seat. Oh, and take that coat off."

I stopped in front of the teacher's desk and asked, "You want me to take the coat off right now?"

A perturbed Mr. Benny said, "I don't care when you do it, Loof! Just do it and let the class get back to work!"

I started to slowly unbutton the trench coat, while making a three-hundred-and-sixty-degree turn. Students were on the edge of their seats, and Mr. Benny was definitely not being entertained. When all the buttons were undone, I slid the coat off my shoulders and then dropped it to the floor. The whole class went into hysterics, and Mr. Benny was speechless.

I was wearing clothes this time. I was resplendent in a green plaid girl's school uniform skirt, that hit a good two inches above the knee, with a white blouse and a green snap-on cross tie. To cap off the outfit, on my feet were a pair of saddle shoes and green knee socks. I turned to the class, curtseyed, bent down very ladylike to pick up the coat, and sashayed to my seat to the delight of my classmates. Before I was halfway down the row, Mr. Benny called my name and said calmly, "Loof, go change your clothes, please."

When I got to Mr. Starkey's second period Latin class, Bobby was waiting and had already heard what I had done, as had some of the other guys. Jimmy Linden said, "Way to make a comeback, Owney." There were handshakes and laughs with words of encouragement. I finally made it to Bobby, who stated stridently, "You bum!"

"What's wrong with you?"

"What's wrong with me is… I didn't get to see the outfit. So, I repeat, you bum!"

Later, Bobby and I joined Kevin, and as we were entering French class, I pointed to Mr. Garell and said, "I'm tellin' you guys, he looks like Soupy Sales."

Five minutes into the class Mr. Garell was showing a slide and asked, "Que se passé-t-il sur la photo?" (What is happening in the picture?)

I raised my hand, which everyone in the class knew, except for Mr. Garell, that I was not going to give a serious answer. Any student who had also raised his hand quickly returned it to their desk, which left the teacher one option for an answer. So, he said, "Ahh, Monsieur Loof?"

I got up from my seat, stuck my arm out with my fingers bent in a semi closed fist, and in a deep gravelly voice replied, "RRUFF A RUFF/ A RRUFF A RUFF/ RRUFF A RRUFF A RUFFF!"

Most of the class was laughing, but there were some who did not understand what was going on except for Owney being Owney. Since Mr. Garell was new in the school and not very familiar with Owen Loof, he just got annoyed and flustered. He started out yelling in French, "Ce n'est –pas-pas drole, euh-Loof…" He stopped and was trying to find the words and finished in English, "Sit down, Loof, and watch yourself."

I sat down and waited ten minutes, when Mr. Garell again asked what was going on in the slide that was being projected on the screen. I skipped the formality of raising my hand and instead leapt to my feet, assumed the same position as before, and with a high-pitched gravelly voice responded, "RRUFF A RUFF/ A RRUFF A RUFF/ RRUFF A RRUFF A RUFFF!"

Mr. Garell pointed to the door and shouted, "C'est tout, Loof! Sortez et attendez dans le couloir!"

No translation was necessary, I rose from my seat, and walked to the door giving my classmates a smile and a wave as I left the room.

When class ended, I went in to see Mr. Garell, who informed me I was receiving JUG for disrupting the class. I apologized, took the JUG slip, and said thank you, which I could see annoyed and puzzled the teacher. As I left the room, Alex Avitabile and Kevin O'Rourke were waiting in the hallway. O'Rourke said, "I know there was a joke there, but I'm sorry, I missed it." Avitabile indicated he was in the same boat.

I chuckled and said, "Okay, it's all right. Do either of you watch *Soupy Sales*?"

O'Rourke indicated that he did not, and Avitabile responded, "Wait, isn't that the guy with the kid's show who told kids to take money from their parents and send it to him?"

My face brightened saying, "Yeah, yeah that's the Soupman. It was New Year's Day he and he was joking around, but he got money in the mail. Some of it was like Monopoly money, but he got suspended. People made a big thing out of it."

O'Rourke asked a little impatiently, "What's that got to do with the joke in class?"

"Yeah, yeah sorry, Kev! Ya see I think Mr. Garell is a dead ringer for Soupy. So, on the show there are these hand puppets, and you only see one shaggy paw when they're talking. They're supposed to be dogs. One is a male, the biggest, meanest dog in the United States, called White Fang. He talks in short grunts and growls that Soupy interprets. The other is female, the biggest, sweetest dog in the United States, called Black Tooth, whose grunts and growls are high pitched and feminine."

O'Rourke grinned broadly, and pointed his finger at me saying, "Got it! White Fang and Black Tooth in Soupy Sales' French class. You're nuts, but do you think Garell got it?"

I shrugged and said, "I don't think so. But that's not important. I knew what I was doing, and there were other people like you guys who didn't get it. But the guys who got it laughed, Garell was upset, and it broke up the class a little. It was a success!"

By this time, we had reached the cafeteria, O'Rourke and Avitabile said so long and went to get lunch, while I went to find Bobby and Kevin. They were at the regular table, and when I arrived, I put my books on the table. As I did this, Bobby took notice of one particular book, and mentioned to me, "I see you got a new History book. How much did it cost?"

"What are you talkin' about, it didn't cost anything. You think I was gonna tell my mother she had to pay for a new book?"

At first Bobby looked puzzled, but then the realization hit him, "You didn't?"

As I sat down, I looked at my friend and said, "Well somebody stole my book, so I stole somebody else's!"

CHAPTER 15

*O*n the Tuesday before Thanksgiving, in the middle of a Latin quiz, I fell out of my seat and landed on the floor unconscious. Mr. Starkey yelled, "Get up Loof! You get up right now!"

Bobby and Danny McHale got to me and knelt beside me trying to determine if this was the real thing. Bobby looked up at Mr. Starkey, who was now standing over his three students, and said, "I don't think he's kidding, Mister."

Mr. Starkey had the students in the rows closest to me move to the other side of the room. They dampened some napkins, and dabbed my face and forehead. After a few minutes, I slowly opened my eyes to see the faces of all the people standing around me. I blinked and coughed, then opened my eyes without saying a word. Mr. Starkey was the first to speak, "Are you awake down there, Loof?"

"W-whaat ha-ppen-ed?"

Mr. Starkey replied questioningly, "That's what we would like to know?"

Bobby and Danny helped me to a sitting position, and I said groggily, "I don't know Mister, I just got real dizzy."

Then just as they got me into a seat, Father Richards and Coach Sullivan entered the room. The Coach took my pulse and told me to follow his finger as he moved it back and forth in front of my face. Father Richards asked, "How are you feeling, son?"

With slurry speech, I answered, "Not great, but a lot better than five minutes ago, Father."

The priest looked at the Coach, then at me, and said, "Okay Loof, come with us for now." The two adults helped me to my feet, and taking an arm each, walked me out of the classroom.

I was out of my classes the rest of the day, and then Kevin found me at my locker after last period. I was closing my locker when he got to me and I said, "Hey Kev."

The tone of his voice gave every indication of being perturbed when he said, "'Hi Kev', that's all I get is a 'Hi Kev!' What the hell happened?"

"Whoa, whoa, relax. I'll get there, don't worry." I went on to explain that after leaving class, they took me to the coach's office where Sullivan took my blood pressure and temperature, and he gave me some water and a candy bar. Then just before seventh period, he took me to Father Richards's office where he said my uncle was driving my mother to the school.

"Yeah! Yeah! but what happened to **YOU?**"

I looked right at him saying, "I don't know, man. I was takin' the quiz and the paper got a little blurry, I got dizzy, and the next thing I knew I was lookin' up at people from the floor." He looked at me with a tilt to his head and a funny look, but I continued quickly, "You know I fractured my skull and I've had a couple of concussions, but I don't know, this was weird."

"Okay man, I hope you feel better. You think you'll be here tomorrow?"

"I really don't think so, and I'll probably miss the St. John's game on Thursday. You have a good Thanksgiving."

"I got ya, you too. See ya next week."

We were going in opposite directions, and once I went through the doorway leading to the stairwell, I stopped before heading down the stairs. I leaned against the wall, closed my eyes, and smiled broadly. Then with my eyes stilled closed, I lowered my head, brought it back up quickly, and shaking my hands hanging by my side I thought, "I promise I'll tell 'im next week. I couldn't break character, there's still a lot of people I gotta fool."

The day I returned to school, I met Bobby in Mr. Quinn's History class, and he could tell that something was wrong. I walked in without saying a word to anyone. I threw my book bag on the floor and sat down with my arms folded staring straight ahead. Bobby was trying not to laugh, and some of the other guys were looking, expecting something to happen. Not able to take it anymore Bobby said, "And a good morning to you Mr. Loof."

I began tapping on the desk, glanced at my friend, and then quickly jerked my head back facing forward. Bobby was now a little annoyed, and asked, "Okay, enough bullshit! What's goin' on?"

Without moving my head, I announced, "What's goin' on? What's goin' on you ask? I'll tell you what's goin' on!" I reached down, picked up my book bag, and removed three textbooks and a notebook, placing them down heavily on the desk. Then I asked, "What class is this?"

I did not give my classmate a chance to answer and exclaimed, "This is History class! Do you see a history book on my desk?" I again did not give him a chance to answer, but just kept on talking. "No, you do not see a history book, and I did not forget it. I didn't leave it home, or anything like that. Do you know what happened?" Bobby just sat there waiting for an answer. "Well, somebody took it. It was practically brand new. I only had it a little longer than the first one."

Bobby waited to make sure he could speak and said, "But it was a book you stole."

"That is immaterial to the case. People wanna play! Okay, I'll play!"

At lunch time, Kevin, Bobby, and I headed to the gym after eating. Bobby went over to talk with some guys from the basketball team, and Kevin said he had to find Louie Stathis and Johnny Killbride to work on a history project. As I passed by a couple of guys from the football team, I heard them talking about wrestling and some of the matches that had been on television recently.

I was familiar with the names they were tossing around, like Bruno Sammartino, who was the heavyweight champ, BoBo Brazil, and Smasher Sloan. The matches were entertaining enough, but I really enjoyed the way they used the interviews to set up the match. I watched and listened for a few minutes, and then had an idea.

Timmy Delaney was in the wrestling discussion group with Charlie Russo, Richie Walters, and Jimmy Linden. I walked over and pulled Delaney aside, and he asked, "Owney, what'd ya doin'? What's goin' on man?"

"I was listening to you guys talkin' about wrestling. Ya wanna help me have some fun and be the wrestling interviewer?"

Delaney was always up for a laugh, and with me he knew it would be a good one. He answered, "Sure Owney, what'd we do?"

"Okay, I need Russo, so just tell him we're gonna do a wrestling interview. When I walk over, just introduce me as The Purple Plague. I'll have a response and we'll go from there."

"I like it, Owney. Gimme a minute to let Russo know what's goin' on."

I waited and watched as Delaney talked to Russo, and they both gave me the thumbs up that they were on board. Delaney maneuvered Russo in front of the rolled-up bleachers, and a small group of people gathered around. As soon as they were situated, I approached them shouting, "Wait a minute, Mr. Madden, I have something to say."

Delaney and Russo turned toward the shouting, with Delaney saying, "Ladies and gentlemen, we are being joined by The Purple Plague, who really seems upset at something."

"You are damned right I'm upset, Mr. Madden!" I pointed my finger at Russo and continued, "This overstuffed has-been punk, Mongolian Mool, ambushed my friend, Chief Hungry Owl, during his match with The Masher. I don't like it when my friends get hurt and taken advantage of. You have unleashed the deadly wrath of The Plague, Mool! You have no idea what you are up against, brother!"

The Mongolian Mool answered back in a funky accent, "Listen little man, Hungry Turkey deserved everything he got, and you better not stick your tiny purple nose in the middle of this. You might be the disease, but I have the cure!"

The Plague stepped around Mr. Madden, got nose to nose with the Mool, and said, "The Plague has chopped down bigger men than you, Mool. When the Plague is finished with you, you'll be heading back to the Khangai Mountains in a box.

The bell sounded ending the period, and Mr. Madden stepped between the wrestlers, separating them saying, "Well, there you have it ladies and gentlemen. Could this be the start of something big? Only time will tell."

The crowd had grown since the beginning of the interview, and there was applause and laughter as everyone was leaving the gym. I hung back with Delaney and Russo, and Delaney declared, "That was great! By the end, we had half the gym watching, and they loved it."

Russo was smiling and shaking his head, and asked, "I think we were all great and everybody was into it, but I have one question, Owney. What the hell is a Mongolian Mool, and are those mountains really in Mongolia?"

Through my laughter, I replied, "I was trying to come up with a funny way to say mule and that's how it came it. Exactly what it is, I haven't figured out yet, but yes, those are real mountains in Mongolia."

We were out of the gym and set to go in different directions, when I stopped and asked, "Hey wait, are you guys down with seein' where we can take this?"

They both indicated that they were all in and agreed to the next installment the next day at lunch.

In the gym the next day, Delaney positioned himself in front of the stage, and made an announcement welcoming everyone to Mr. Madden's All-Star Wrestling Show. He waited for a crowd to gather, and started, "Thank you all for joining us here tonight. We have a great card featuring two main events. Before we get to those matches though, The Mongolian Mool is back with us to speak about what went on between him and The Purple Plague."

Charlie Russo walked up to Delaney from the left, and immediately launched a verbal assault, "Listen Madden, I don't know what you were trying to pull with bringing that pencil-necked geek, the purple something or other, on and taking up my time."

A frightened Mr. Madden replied, "I can assure you Mr. Mool, that I had no idea The Purple Plague was going to be there."

The Mool was still angry and said, "That better be true, Madden. And if that little pipsqueak has anything else to say, I will stamp him out with these vaccines!" Then he faced the crowd with a scowl while holding up his fists.

At that moment, I entered the gym from the stairway on the right side of the stage. As I walked toward Madden and the Mool, Kevin and Bobby were in the middle of the crowd, and right on cue began chanting, "Purple Plague, Purple Plague!" The chant was picked up by others in the crowd, and The Plague waved to acknowledge his fans.

When the Mool saw and heard what was happening, he became almost apoplectic. He was jumping up and down and pounding his fists against his chest, while grunting and growling.

When The Plague reached Mr. Madden, he pointed with an outstretched, palms up hand saying, "Look at this Mr. Madden. The Mongolian Mool is acting exactly as you would expect from a fierce, bearlike animal from the remote regions of the Mongolian Mountains."

The Mool stopped some of his antics, but was still furious, and in an almost mournful wail shouted, "I am not an animal!"

The Plague looked at the crowd, shrugged, and said, "A picture is worth a thousand words." At which point the crowd began chanting, "Purple Plague, Purple Plague!" This again sent the Mool into a rage.

The Plague said calmly, "Mr. Madden, do his handlers have a tranquilizer gun for this animal?"

The Mool became even more enraged, and started yelling, "I am not an animal, I am not an animal!"

The chanting continued, and The Plague signaled for the crowd to quiet down, and when they did, Mool also quieted down and relaxed a little. The Plague then declared, "Mr. Madden, I came here tonight to officially challenge The Mongolian Mool to a revenge match." The crowd cheered, and The Plague continued, "But I don't think a Mongolian mool is a fierce bear. A Mongolian mool is really a chicken."

This caused Mool to throw his head back, spin around, and growl saying, "Listen you disease carried by rats, you think you're ready for me! I am the best of the best and you have no idea what you are getting yourself into." Then he tried to get around Mr. Madden, who was trying to hold him at bay, and said threateningly slow, "The bear will eat you alive."

Richie Walters was standing in the first row of the crowd and gave Mr. Madden a sign that the period was about to end, so he announced, "There you have it ladies and gentlemen. You heard it here. Two days from now, right here on our show, a revenge match pitting The Purple Plague against The Mongolian Mool!"

The crowd cheered, the two wrestlers stood nose to nose, and The Mool said, "You can run, but you can't hide. I'll be on your tail."

The Plague countered, "I can see it in your eyes how afraid you really are. If fear were snow, you would be a walking blizzard right now."

As the crowd cheered, the bell sounded, and Mr. Madden stepped between the two wrestlers, who continued taunting one another as they were being led away by their handlers. The crowd was still cheering as Mr. Madden announced, "Thank you for tuning in tonight and we will be sure to keep you updated on the match details.

The gym was buzzing as it emptied out, and the three main characters were standing together. I was smiling, looked at Delaney, and asked, "Two days from now. A wrestling match?"

"Well, you're the one who mentioned it first. Everyone seemed to be eatin' it up, and when Richie let me know the period was ending, I had to say something. And that's what popped out."

We all laughed, and I looked at Russo asking, "What'd ya think Charlie?"

"Sure, why not? We can't let the fans down, right?"

The next day, as soon as Delaney entered the gym and started walking toward the stage, most of the gym followed him. When he got to his spot, he wasted no time in starting the show. "Good evening ladies and gentlemen, and wrestling fans everywhere. Thank you for joining us tonight on Mr. Madden's All-Star Wrestling Show. We have a great show tonight, and as you have probably heard, tomorrow our feature match will be the Revenge Match between The Purple Plague and The Mongolian Mool."

With that announcement, half the crowd began chanting, "Purple Plague! Purple Plague!"

Another segment of the crowd voiced their support for The Mool in their own way, "MOOOOOOOOL! MOOOOOOOOL!"

In the middle of the noise and before anything else could be said, The Purple Plague and his two handlers emerged from the stairway door on the right side of the stage. As soon as he appeared, the crowd cheered, and the chant got louder. The Plague responded by waving and throwing a thumbs up sign all around.

When he reached Mr. Madden, The Plague acknowledged the chanting crowd and asked for quiet. Then before Madden could say anything, The Plague started,

"I am here tonight, Mr. Madden, because my friend Chief Hungry Owl is on the card and so is that sorry excuse for a human being, The Masher. I'm sure that other animal, The Mongolian Chicken, is lurking somewhere in the building, and I am making sure that Hungry Owl is not interfered with in any way."

Mr. Madden then asked, "What can we expect tomorrow night, Plague?"

"I'll tell you what to expect." One of the handlers produced a small waste basket and handed it to the Plague who said, "When I get finished with the Mongolian Chicken, all that's left of him will fit in this trash can." He then pulled a dish towel from the waste basket and continued, "And here's a crying towel for all the Chicken's fans." Then he threw the towel into the crowd.

There was cheering and Purple Plague chants, but as all that was happening, The Mongolian Mool, and his two handlers came charging out of the stairway door on the left of the stage. The Mool was shouting, grunting, and growling, and when he reached Madden and The Plague, there was pushing and shoving between the wrestlers, the handlers, and some of the crowd, with Mr. Madden in the middle, trying to get control of the situation.

Order was restored, the wrestlers and their handlers were separated, and the crowd back in its place. Then a flustered Mr. Madden declared, "Gentlemen, please let's not have any more of that." He turned to The Mool and asked, "We have heard from The Plague about expectations for tomorrow night. What is your prediction, Mr. Mool?"

Mool looked at The Plague with a death stare, and then glowered at the crowd saying, "There will be pain, a lot of pain." He glared back at The Plague and continued menacingly slow, "Let these words I speak paint a picture of just what that petulant disease is in for. I have one vision, and that is to seek and destroy the virulence of The Plague."

The Plague pointed his finger at The Mool, and with an evil eye and an evil voice exclaimed, "The Plague is coming for you, brother, and will chop you down to size. There is no escape and no protection." Then he got his finger almost on The Mool's nose and added, "When the Plague surrounds you, havoc ensues."

The Mool slapped The Plague's hand away, and got in his face saying, "Listen little man, you will be lucky if you escape the ring tomorrow with your life. I am the best of the best and the cream always rises to the top. The bear will eat you up and spit you out!"

The Plague was not intimidated, put his finger right on The Mool's nose, and sang in a guttural voice, "Fee, fi, fo, fum, The Mongolian Chicken your time has come."

Mool was enraged, charged at The Plague, and there was chaos. The wrestlers, the handlers, and the fans were all over one another. The wrestlers would be separated, but they would find each other in another part of the gym and continue the battle. Finally, the wrestlers were brought to their feet, and while being held back, were still pawing, and slapping each other, and trying to get at the other one. Clothes were flying everywhere, and as the bell sounded, Mr. Madden shouted, "You don't want to miss tomorrow night folks. The real fireworks will take place right here on our show. This will be the match of the year!"

CHAPTER 16

The next day, the gym was packed with students, quite a few teachers, and even Father Richards was in the crowd. The sound was ready, the handlers went to their assigned places, and Mr. Madden started the show. "Good evening, ladies and gentlemen. We have now reached the feature match, and it is the match we have all been waiting for." There was a round of cheers, the crowd began moving toward the stage, and there were people packed right up against the edge. Suddenly, Sam Vanacort came out from behind the curtain ringing one of the old-time school bells.

Madden continued, "This will be a Revenge Match to be decided by a pin fall or a submission hold with no time limit." After some light applause, Madden announced, "Okay folks, it's time to get down and dirty! LETTTTTTT'S WRESTLEEEEEEE!"

There was loud cheering with "MOOOOOOOOL", and "Purple Plague" chants thrown around. Madden was able to quiet the crowd and started the introductions. "Let me first introduce from the remote and deadly region of the Khangai Mountains in Mongolia, and weighing 250 pounds, the dangerous Mongolian MOOOOL!!

The crowd starts applauding and screaming. They also began MOOOOLING, that was mixed with some BOOOO-ING from The Plague's faithful. Madden looked down at the two handlers at the door, who shrugged not knowing what to do. The delay reduced the noise level slightly, and then the door on the left side of the stage swung open, and the Mool stomped out grunting and growling. He had a black beard, was wearing a black unitard with high top black sneakers, and a long black wig. After ascending the stage and stomping to the center, he struck the classic arms up showing off the muscles pose. The crowd's reaction was enormously loud and stayed that way while he continued stomping around, and at one point approached the edge of the stage scowling and growling, pounding himself on the arms and chest. He then tramped and plodded back to his handlers emitting guttural noises that were almost drowned out by the "MOOOOLS" and the "BOOOOS."

The crowd quieted down when Vanacort started ringing the bell, and Madden began the next introduction. Let's welcome to the ring now, at a wiry 130 pounds from Parts Unknown, The Purpleeeeee Plagueeeeee!"

There was cheering and the Purple Plague chant rang out as all eyes were focused on the right-side doors. Then the sound of blowing wind, a hooting owl, and eerie organ music enveloped the gym. The crowd was silent, the Mool stopped stomping, and Madden looked down at Plague's handlers.

No one knew what to do. Bobby was about to open the door to see what was going on, when the sound affects halted, and the back doors of the gym slammed open. Every head turned and the people on the stage stood in stunned silence.

There was The Purple Plague. He was resplendent in a purple ski mask, a purple t-shirt with the letters PP in a shield, purple boxer shorts, and purple sneakers. But what capped off the outfit was a purple cape, which was wielded like Count Dracula. As his handlers reached their man, the music started, but was completely drowned out as the gym erupted into almost uncontrollable screams of delight and cheers, and of course, there were Purple Plague chants.

The Plague preened his way through the crowd, swishing his cape and pointing at the stage. The Mool returned to jumping up and down and roaring, while running to the edge of the stage and back. Mool supporters started MOOOOOLING to drown out the noise of The Plague fans. The Plague made it onto the stage and walked to the edge. Twice stopping center stage and raising the cape to its full wingspan. He then began stalking The Mool around the stage, who would turn and growl with The Plague taking a few steps back. When the wrestlers were situated in their corners, The Plague slowly removed his cape, the handlers took their seats, the bell sounded, and it was time to wrestle.

Mool came running out of his corner growling and attempted to grab The Plague, who ducked and stuck out his foot tripping up The Mool. After hitting the mat and rolling over, Mool was flat on his back and The Plague jumped on top of him going for the pin. At the two count, Mool rose with his opponent in his arms. There were oohs and ahhs from the crowd as The Plague was sent airborne, but he righted himself in the air and landed on his feet. However, he was off balance, tumbled to the mat, and Mool jumped in the air trying to land all his weight on his fallen foe.

The crowd was clapping and cheering, and then just before impact, The Plague rolled out of the way and Mool hit the mat hard. The cheering turned to gasps, and both wrestlers appeared dazed, but Mool gets to a sitting position first. The Plague slowly rises to one knee, shakes off his dizziness, and attacks Mool from behind, applying a sleeper hold. The move appears to be working, and the referee runs over and lifts the arm of Mool, which falls to his side. The crowd yells, "ONE!" The ref lifts the arm again and it falls once more. The crowd yells, TWO!"

If the arm falls one more time, the match is over. On the third lift, the arm starts to fall, but then stops in midair, and begins to shake. The crowd starts a rhythmic clapping, and Mool's entire body is now shaking, and he gets to his knees, then to his feet. Standing upright, and no longer shaking, he pulls The Plague's arms from around his neck and flips him over his head onto the mat. The crowd is cheering and the sound of MOOOOOOOOL is resonating. Mool then picks up his adversary and puts him in a suffocating bear hug while stomping around the mat. It appeared to be the end for The Plague, and more of the crowd was MOOOOOOOOLING. Then a rival chant was heard, "Purple Plague! Purple Plague! Purple Plague!"

Seeming to gather strength from his fans, The Plague sends both his arms crashing against the side of Mool's head directly on the ears. With his bell rung, and pain flashing through his head, Mool opens his arms, dropping his enemy to the mat. It was a somewhat soft landing, but The Plague grabbed his chest and rolled over in obvious pain. There was more MOOOOLING and cheering, with The Plague fans shouting, "No, no, get up, get up!"

The pain was still showing on The Plague's face as he got to a sitting position. There was not much of a respite because Mool recovered quickly, uttered a guttural sound, and pounced on his rival. Picking up The Plague with both arms, he proceeded to fling his foe through the air to the other side of the mat. Then Mool stomped over, grunting and growling, and attempted to grab The Plague's arms. The crowd was fired up, whistling, and shouting, sensing the end might be near. The Plague was able to elude the grasp this time, but when Mool lost his balance, there was no way for The Plague avoid his falling adversary. While it was not a direct hit, the force of the blow took its toll.

Mool was also feeling the effects of the fall, and was lying on his stomach next to The Plague, who was flat on his back. Lifting his head and seeing the situation, Mool took his massive arm and dropped it across the chest of his opponent. With the crowd cheering and shouting, the ref rushed over, and on one knee hit the mat once, then a second time, and just inches from his hand reaching the mat one last time, thus ending the match, The Plague rolled away with the arm of Mool dropping to the mat. The crowd reacted with cheers and screaming protests at the ref's slow count.

The Plague was now on his hands and knees crawling away. The Mool got to his feet, grabbed his foe around the waist, and threw him in the air. Landing in a heap, The Plague was dazed and struggling to find his legs. The enraged Mool was on him in a flash, grabbing an arm, pulling him to his feet, and in one motion tossed The Plague across the mat. He came to rest flat on his back with his outstretched left hand just inches from the edge of the stage. Mool snarled, walked over to the prone Plague, lifted his foot, and with a hundred eyes focused intently at close range, brought it down heavily on the wrist of his adversary. There was a slight delay in the reaction, and then The Plague howled in pain and brought the injured hand to his chest. There were mouths agape, gasps, cries of "Oh no!," and people hiding their eyes.

Lying on the mat, The Plague watched as Mool was stomping around beating his chest and making all kinds of animal noises. As he kept backing up, the referee stopped him and whispered in his ear. Then the ref looked at The

Plague and held up one then two fingers, which meant that there was not much time left in the period. Mool was now about twenty feet away, and he jumped up and down while roaring loudly. He pointed at his helpless foe, swept his hands in front of his chest, and dragged his finger across his throat. The crowd was going wild, yelling, clapping, MOOOOLING, and there were shouts encouraging The Plague. Then Mool stomped his way toward the prone Plague, ready to land one last crushing blow, and end the match with a pin. When The Mool was just a few feet from his target, The Plague got to his knees, and with all his strength, delivered a one-two punch at the middle of his enemy's chest. There were ooohs and ahhhs from the crowd with chanting for the Purple Plague.

Mool lost his breath and bent over in pain. The Plague rose to his feet, locked his hands together in a big fist, and smashed it down on the neck of The Mool, who went face down on the mat. The Plague quickly rolled him over and jumped on the massive chest, while holding down both arms. The ref was Johnny-on-the spot, and with the crowd counting with him, rapidly hit the mat one, two, three. The Plague jumped to his feet, Vanacort rang the bell forcefully, and the ref raised his hand announcing, "The winner is The PURPLLLLEEE, PLAGUUUUEEE!"

There was pandemonium in the gym as more of the crowd pressed forward to get closer to the stage. There were dueling chants and noise of all kinds, with the fans of The Mool shouting in protest of a quick count. On the stage, Mool was on his feet chasing the ref and his conqueror around the mat. The handlers got involved, and there was much pushing and shoving. The bell ending lunch period sounded, which only cut down the chaos slightly. The gym was finally emptying, but slowly and nosily, with the participants on the stage ending the scuffle. They were now laughing, glad-handing, and congratulating one another, when I said to Russo, "That stomping on my hand was amazing. I was so surprised that it didn't hurt I almost didn't react. And did you see the faces of the people standing right there? They were convinced!"

In the middle of all this excitement, we heard Sam Vanacort say, "Oh, hi Father!"

Everybody looked around to see Father Richards standing in the middle of the stage. We all turned to face him, and the priest said, "That was quite a show, gentlemen. Good Job."

Everyone replied with their own different "Thank you, Father," and he added, "It looks to me like you have some cleaning up to do, and (pointing to Russo and me), you two need to change. So, take your time here, you are all excused from sixth period. Just make sure you make it to seventh period on time."

I made sure everything was under control, and said, "As long as you guys are good here, me and Russo are gonna go change. I really wanna thank you all for pulling this off so great."

After a last round of handshakes, The Mool and The Plague jumped off the stage and started walking across the gym. The Mool asked, "How come you won?"

"Because I beat you fair and square!"

Mool glared at The Plague snarling, and said, "Fair and square! It was a quick count, and if there was more time I woulda had you! No way you can beat me!"

The Plague retorted defiantly, "I'll beat you any time anywhere!"

Mool stopped and put his finger in The Plague's face declaring, "Fine, I want a rematch, pipsqueak!" Stepping forward, The Plague pushed away the finger and exclaimed, "You got it! Let's make the arrangements, animal!"

We stared at each other for a few seconds, and then burst out laughing, pushing one another away and continuing on our way.

When I got to Religion class, there was a round of applause, and Father Hamilton stood up saying, "Okay, okay! Calm down and be quiet." The priest stopped me in front of his desk and with a smile on his face said, "I heard about the match there, Plague, and I guess congratulations are an order."

I bowed my head saying, "Thank you, Father, it was a tough fight, but you know good always conquers evil."

Shouts of "Purple Plague!" rang out, Father motioned for silence, and said to me, "I'm not sure how The Plague got to be a good thing. Now go sit down so we can get this class started."

When I sat down next to Kevin, I attempted to remove a notebook from my book bag. As I did, a book slipped out and dropped heavily on the floor. Kevin was quick, and picked it up before I could get to it. The front cover of the book had flipped open, and he said, "That's not your name here. This isn't your book, is it? Your book was lost.

"First of all, I didn't lose my book, it was stolen. Secondly, this is my book now.

CHAPTER 17

*A*s the first semester was nearing the end, and as Christmas was approaching, my time in JUG remained steady. Mr. Garell, Mr. Starkey, and especially Mr. Jagger were the teachers I enjoyed the most giving me JUG. Once I believed Mr. Jagger unfairly accused me of talking in class and giving me JUG. Standing in Father Richards' office, I assured him that I was innocent this time.

The priest put his hand on my shoulder and stated, "The key words there Loof are, 'THIS TIME.' It was a perfectly natural assumption by Mr. Jagger. You do understand that, right?"

After moving my head back and forth, while turning my palms up, I sighed saying, "Yeah, well I guess so Father. But it's still not fair."

"Only you can change that, Loof." After a short pause he added, "All right, I'll give you a break this time. But try not to show up here so often, okay? Now get out of here!"

My eyes lit up, and with a broad grin exclaimed, "Thank you, thank you Father! I'll do my best!"

As I rushed out the door, I heard Father Richards say, "That's what I'm afraid of.

On the last day of class before finals and Christmas break, I convinced Charlie Russo to find the Santa Claus suit and the elves costumes from the "spider dance." Russo was the perfect Santa, with Kevin and me playing the elves.

At lunch we donned the outfits, and paraded through the halls giving, out candy canes and chocolate. When we got to the cafeteria, Anton Blackman was at the piano and started playing Christmas carols. Blackman and the elves led the signing, and Santa distributed the presents.

When lunch ended, Father Richards had us keep the costumes on and make the rounds of the administrative offices, spreading Christmas cheer. He also told us to report to his office before returning to class. When we arrived, the cleric explained that on Friday, the 23rd, the parish church was having a Christmas party for the neighborhood children. I interrupted asking, "So you want us to play Santa and the elves at the party?"

The priest replied that was the case, and I said, "Well I don't know, Father. You know its short notice, and it's our busy season and all."

They all looked at me with shocked expressions, and not the hint of a smile. I glanced from my fellow students to Father Richards, and exclaimed, "Geeze, guys, what'd ya lookin' at me like that for? It was a joke." Then I said to the priest, "Absolutely Father, just tell us what time to be there."

The Christmas Party was a complete success. Russo was a great Santa, the elves played all kinds of games with the kids, and Anton Blackman was the maestro of maestri on the piano. The pastor of the parish said it was one of the best Christmas parties they ever had. Even Father Nolan was impressed and grateful for our performance and participation. When the afternoon was over, Father Richards caught up with us before we went off to change, "I really want thank you gentlemen for helping us out today. You all did a great job, and I won't forget it."

Speaking for the group I said, "No problem, Father, it

was a lot of fun. But next year, you're gonna have to give us a little more notice, and we'll give you a nice discount."

"Well, you guys are good. Maybe we should pay you." After everybody laughed, he added, "Again, thank you, and I hope all of your families have a blessed and Merry Christmas, and a happy and healthy New Year."

When I joined my friends to change, I gave each of them a liquid filled cup, and they all wanted to know what was in the cups. Then I put my drink down, reached in my bag, pulled out two flasks, and said, "Some Christmas cheer!" I opened one of the flasks and said, "Oops, that one's empty already!" I opened the other flask and began pouring some of its contents into the cups of my friends.

Blackman answered the question the others were all thinking, and said happily, "It's a rum and coke."

I held up my cup and toasted, "To Santa and his helpers, a very Merry Christmas!"

We touched cups and began sipping away. Everyone got a refill on the rum, and then Russo asked me, "Hey, that first flask was empty. Was there rum in it before?"

"Of course, there was!"

Russo asked a little more stridently, "You drank it all?"

I replied in an absurd tone, "Of course not, I shared some of it with the priests."

Kevin said, "Only some of it. What about the...." He looked at me intently and continued, "No Owney! You didn't!"

I raised an eyebrow, and a sly grin slowly appeared on my face. Russo seemed puzzled, Blackman just shook his head, and Kevin slapped a hand on his forehead saying, "You spiked the kids' sodas with rum!"

I shrugged, and declared, "Well not all of 'em. And just a teeny bit."

CHAPTER 18

It was a white Christmas in Rockaway after a blizzard hit on Christmas Eve. After spending Christmas Day with Aunt Anne and the cousins, the Loofs traveled to New Jersey to visit Uncle Jimmy and Aunt Mary. We also visited my mother's cousin Gene and his family. The snow made driving difficult, and we were stuck in Jersey for an extra day. It was not until Thursday, December 29th, before we made it back to Rockaway.

After dinner, my father said that he was exhausted, and went straight to bed. I helped my mother clean up the kitchen and get the dishes put away. Then went to the living room to watch *Batman* and *F Troop*. Before I left the kitchen, my mother said, "Remember Owen I want to watch *I Spy* at eight o'clock."

"Sure mom, no problem."

About fifteen minutes before the end of *F Troop*, my mother called from the kitchen saying, "Owen, Michael's here."

I went into the kitchen and Michael was sitting at the table. "Michael, what's up dude?"

Michael was glancing at my mother and replied, "Not much, I haven't seen you since before Christmas, and I really needed to get out of the house for a little while." Michael again looked to see where my mother was, and asked, "So, how was all your traveling?"

I was now watching him carefully before responding. "It was a little difficult with the snow and all, but it was nice to see all the relatives."

Before we could say anything else, my mother announced, "I'm going to the living room. It's nice to see you Michael, and give your parents my best. We'll see them Saturday at the St. Camillus New Year's Eve Party."

"I will Bridget. I know they're looking forward to it."

When she left the kitchen, I slid forward in my seat, and with my hands on the table, bent closer to Michael, and asked, "Okay, I can tell somethin's up, what's goin' on?"

Michael's face brightened, and he answered excitedly, "So JP and Johnny Portano are at The Circle…"

I broke in asking, "What'd ya mean they're at The Circle?"

"Don't interrupt me and I'll tell you, geeze! Well, they were comin' back from the A&P and when they passed by, they could see that there were only like three people in the place. So, they decided to give it try. They went in, asked for a couple of beers, and got served without being asked for proof. So, Tommy Lawlor, Ed Breen, and Larry McElroy are going over. Come on, let's go!"

I went to the living room, making sure to wait for a commercial, and said to my mother, "Mom, I'm going over to Michael's for a little while."

"Fine Owen. Don't be too late, and be careful."

"Okay mom we will. Do you need anything before I go?"

"Oh yes. Will you please fill this glass with ice and bring me some ginger ale? Thank you, Owen."

After returning with the ice and the soda, I kissed my mother on the cheek saying, "Thanks mom, see you later."

"You're a good boy Owen. Good night, Michael and you both be careful."

When we got to the bar with the others, Mike Woods, whose father was one of the owners, was tending bar. He was hesitant in serving the newcomers, but after some haggling, and since it was a really slow night, he went ahead and served us all, but warned, "We're not gonna make a habit of this, and don't do anything stupid tonight."

For the next three hours, we drank beer and shots of Jack Daniels. We talked about sports and girls. We watched the Rangers beat the Detroit Red Wings 4-2. Football season for the Giants was a disaster with their 1-12-1 record. Then there were NFL and AFL championship games that would be played on Sunday and would determine the teams for the first-ever Super Bowl.

Then it was determined that I was the only one at the table without a girlfriend, since JP was now going out with the pretty blonde, baton-twirling majorette for the St. Camillus band. I took a good bit of teasing, but took it in stride and started singing the Dean Martin song, "Somewhere There's a Someone," and the whole table started laughing, groaning, and throwing things at me.

JP said, "Come on O, you talk to a lot of the girls around here. I've seen you with Michelle O'Brien, Eleanor Angelone, and Mellissa Marks."

I put up my hand, and shook my head, saying, "And they're great girls. They're all pretty, and they're my friends. I don't know."

Michael pointed at me, and then declared, "O, I know you always had a crush on Lorraine Quinn."

I smiled while shrugging my shoulders and said, "Well maybe a little. She's okay lookin'."

My friends again rained down pretzels, potato chips, and coasters on me, and Woods yelled over, "Quiet down over there you guys, and ya know you're gonna have to clean that stuff up."

We also listened to music and played pool. Johnny Portano was the best pool player of the bunch, and after beating all his friends, one of the other three guys at the bar challenged him for beers. Johnny was only sixteen, and this guy was a lot older. It was a pretty close game, and Johnny was winning, when there were some words exchanged. Finally, the guy asked Johnny, "How old are you? Do you have proof?"

Johnny put his pool cue by his side, and answered with his own question, "Do you have proof?"

The guy puts his pool cue on the table, reaches in his pocket, and takes out his wallet. He flips it open to show Johnny a police badge. Johnny puts two fingers on the badge, bends down to get a closer look, and says, "That's good enough."

The guy put the wallet back in his pocket, and smiled asking, "I think I won this game, right kid?"

Johnny hesitated in his response, and looked at the pool table. Michael and I walked over, I stepped between the pool players, and looking at the cop, said, "Oh yeah, you definitely won that game. Come on John shake hands and let's go."

After the handshakes were completed, the cop said to Johnny, "You're a good player, and you have some good friends there, slick. Now you guys are gonna buy me and my friends a beer and head home, right?"

We went to Woods and paid for the winner's beers, while buying a couple of six packs. Then we said goodnight to everyone and headed out the door. When we were all outside, Johnny looked at us defiantly, and said, "I had that guy beat man! Why'd you guys do that?"

Everybody started laughing and threw him into a snow drift.

We trudged through the snow to JP's basement, where the two six packs from The Circle were quickly polished off along with shots of Johnnie Walker Red Label Scotch. Time became very variable, but Michael and I eventually decided to leave, and we left the others in various stages of consciousness. We started around the corner holding each other in as close to an upright position as possible. When we reached my house, we sat down on the porch steps trying to prepare ourselves in case my mother was awake, which I believed would be the case. As we rose to our feet, Michael asked, "Should I come in with you?"

I just shook my head, there was a brief hug, and Michael trudged off unsteadily. I bent down, took some snow, and rubbed it in my face. I took a deep breath, gave my whole body a shake, and marched up the stairs. When I entered the house, I took a quick look into the living room, which was dark, and the TV was off. I sat down and removed my boots, then looked up the stairs, hoping to make it quickly and quietly to my room.

On the second step, the quiet was shattered by my mother's voice calling from the kitchen. A setback for sure, but I felt that all hope was not lost. I thought, "I can do this. All I gotta do is stay calm, make it quick, and don't talk too much."

I walked into the kitchen at what I thought was a very steady pace. Then went right to the counter by the sink for the support it offered. I was not going to initiate any conversation, and only respond to questions. My mother was sitting across the room at the kitchen table. She looked me up and down, and calmly asked, "You do realize what time it is Owen?"

I looked at the clock on the wall, and replied, "Oh wow, it's 2a.m., sorry!"

She was now a little angry, asking, "Sorry, sorry, that's all you have to say?" I just shrugged, and she continued the grilling, "Were you drinking?"

I shook my head and said, "No!"

She then said, "Come over here!"

I pushed off the counter and started toward her chair. The route was rather circuitous, and I stumbled into the refrigerator before landing in front of her. She looked up at me and asked again, "Were you drinking?"

Without hesitation, I again answered, "No!"

She bowed her head, and waved her hand for me to leave the room. On my way out I bumped into the door frame before finding the opening. Walking across the living room and trying to locate the stairs, I was feeling a sense of accomplishment at having escaped without much fanfare. I was unaware that my mother was right behind me. When I was on the third step, I heard her voice, and turned to look down on her. She was only 5'2", and now I added at least four inches to my 5'11" height.

She looked up at me, and asked for a third time, "Were you drinking?"

And like Saint Peter denying Jesus for the third time, I answered, "No!"

I was too inebriated to see it coming, and did not move until my mother's right fist landed square in the kisser. I went down in a heap, like Henry Cooper in the sixth round of his fight with Muhammad Ali. My mother yelled, "That's for drinking and coming home at 2a.m.!"

Even more dazed than I was before, I looked up through blurry vision just in time to feel three kicks to my left side.

Through the pain I heard my mother shout. "And that's for lying!" She then stepped over my body to go up the stairs, and as I was attempting to get to a sitting position, smacked me in the back of the head, which sent me tumbling down the three steps.

When she got to the top of the stairs, my father was waiting, and asked, "Is he all right?"

She replied angrily, "He's just drunk!"

"Should I help him?"

Looking straight in her husband's face, she shouted, "Don't you dare!" And then she dragged him away.

CHAPTER 19

On the first Friday in February, I reported to Father Richards's office for my fifth straight day of JUG. Father Richards looked up from his desk, and said, "Loof you're here again. What did you do now?"

"Father, I think Mr. Jagger just has it in for me."

"Come on Loof, I find that hard to believe. Just tell me what happened."

"Okay, see I was like a minute late for class, and he started yellin' at me, and gave me JUG. So, I started laughin', fell on the floor, rolled around a couple of times, holdin' my stomach, and laughin' harder. Then he came around his desk screamin' at me to get up, he tried to grab me and pull me up. But I rolled over again, he caught nothin' but air, lost his balance, and fell down. It wasn't my fault he fell down. So, I got up and tried to help him, but he just pushed me away, then screamed at me to get to my seat, and gave me another JUG."

Father Richards looked at me dumbfounded asking, "And that's why you think Mr. Jagger has it in for you?"

"Well yeah, I was only a minute late."

"Was that the first time you were late?"

I answered somewhat sheepishly, "Umm no, not really. Maybe I was late for his class a couple of times before."

"So don't you think you can see Mr. Jagger's point?"

I reluctantly conceded, "Yeah, I guess so."

Father Richards shook his head saying, "I don't know what I'm going to do with you Loof. Okay, I'll let you go on the lateness JUG, but the antics you performed must have consequences. You have to do the JUG for that."

"Thanks Father, I'm really sorry and I'll try to do better."

Two weeks later, on a Wednesday, I was in Mr. Jagger's class, and we were studying Hamlet. The "To Be or Not to Be" soliloquy was being discussed. It was said that Hamlet was contemplating suicide to escape the pains and heartaches that the people and events in his life were causing. I raised my hand, and Mr. Jagger acknowledged me. I stood up and said, "I don't think Hamlet was seriously considering committing suicide."

The teacher asked, "Really Loof? Why do you say that?"

"Well sure Hamlet was confused and conflicted. Avenging his father's death, and all the stuff with Claudius and Gertrude was really bothering him. But we've all had some kinda stuff that pushes us to think that our problems can't be fixed. I think he was a strong guy, and in his heart, he knew he'd get over this temporary setback."

There was complete silence in the class. Students were looking at each other not knowing exactly what to make of the situation. Then Mr. Jagger asked, "You really do not know when to stop, do you Loof?"

I stood there with my mouth opened, my hand in front of me palms up and asked, "What? What'd ya mean?"

Mr. Jagger smiled and replied, "You could not be serious with that answer. You are always trying to be funny."

I shot back angrily, "Do you see anyone laughing? I'm not trying to be funny. That's what I think!"

The teacher smiled more broadly and said, "Sure Loof, nice try. Now just sit down."

I did not sit down. I just kept standing stock still, staring at Mr. Jagger. Kevin and Bobby were seated on either side of me, and they both reached out to me. I pulled away from them both, picked up my books, and stormed out of the class.

No one had seen or heard from me since I left the school. A little past seven the next morning, my worried parents heard pounding on the front door, and a voice yelling, "Bridget! Martin! Open the door"

They both rushed through the living room to the front door. When they opened it, there was Michael O'Connor holding me up. I lifted my head slurring, "Hi mom, hi dad, I'm home."

My mother held the door open, while my father and Michael helped me over to the couch. She looked down at me lying on the couch, and asked, "Is he drunk?"

My father answered, "I don't think so. But look how he's shaking. He's really cold."

My mother then asked Michael, "Where did you find him?"

"He was asleep or unconscious on McCarthy's stoop when I got to the bus stop."

"Did he say anything?"

"He was trying to talk, but I really couldn't make out too much except, don't take me home."

They got my heavy clothes off and put two blankets on me. Then they gave me a little oatmeal and warm milk. Slowly but surely, as I warmed up, I became more awake, and relatively coherent.

With my parents and my best friend standing there, I knew exactly what they wanted, and figured there was no sense delaying giving it to them. "Okay, you don't even have to ask the question. Why don't you all sit down, and I will tell you what happened and where I went."

As the audience settled in their seats, my mother asked Michael, "Shouldn't you be going to school?"

"Ahh come on Bridget, I found him. I gotta know what happened."

I chimed in, "Mom really, let him stay. He's like one of the family. It's okay."

When my father also gave his okay, a still reluctant Bridget Loof agreed, and said to me in a decidedly annoyed tone, "Just tell us what happened. It better be the truth and leave nothing out. And you know Michael cannot save you."

I started by recounting the events in English class. After leaving school, I went to the bank and withdrew all but ten dollars from my bank account, which gave me two hundred dollars in my pocket. Then I got back on the train and went into the City.

"My plan was to get on a train or a bus and go somewhere. But after I had some food, I found out that there was WWA wrestling at the Garden."

After the matches were over, I said I went to the movies. I knew they would ask what movie, so I quickly volunteered the information. "I saw "The Spy in the Green Hat." It's like a Man from Uncle movie with all the TV characters, and Jack Palance plays one of the bad guys."

My mother interrupted the story asking, "By this time it must be close to 2a.m. Did you ever stop to consider that we might be worried?"

"I'm not gonna say the thought never crossed my mind, but I was still annoyed at everything, and was still planning to go off somewhere."

My mother sighed deeply and shook her head. I could tell she was really trying to hold her temper. She folded her arms against her chest, and with raise eyebrows said, "I don't know Owen. I just don't know." Then after a short pause she asked, "Okay, then what happened?"

I continued the story by relating that I was a little hungry. It was cold, and there was a bar right there, so I walked through the door and sat down. I saw the look on my mother's face, and before she could say anything I said, "Mom, he wouldn't give me any alcohol, but he made me a nice sandwich with some potato salad, and I had a soda."

She eyed me skeptically, but said nothing, and I continued the story. The bartender asked me what I was doing there, so I told him about the events of the day, what I was feeling, and how I was contemplating remedying the situation. Then I said to the listeners, "Without going into great detail, the guy told me I was being stupid, that my plan was stupid, and in fact, I had no real plan at all. He said I should call you guys and go home."

My father asked, "So why didn't you do that?"

"I was gonna, I really was. But I didn't wanna call from the bar, and decided to wait till I got to the train station.

He asked the next obvious question, "So what happened?"

The answer was delivered forthrightly. "I paid for the meal, and the bartender said it was cold out, so he gave me a hot chocolate to take with me. I thanked him and headed out the door."

I continued by explaining that I had only proceeded a few steps when I heard the door open and close behind me. The bar was on a corner, and when I made the turn up the block, two guys hurried around the turn. I realized they were obviously following me. I stopped to face them, but before I did, I took the lid off the hot chocolate.

I took a deep breath before continuing, "So when I turned around, they both stopped. They were about three feet away, and I asked what they wanted. So, the one guy, who was actually shorter than me, but heavier says, 'What'd think kid? Give us your money!'"

My mother covered her cheeks with both hands and said almost in shock, but also relief, "Thank God, you gave them your money and they didn't hurt you."

With just the hint of a smile and a slight head tilt, I declared, "You're right mom. They didn't hurt me, but I didn't give them my money either."

She was horrified, my father looked puzzled, and Michael asked excitedly, "So how'd ya get outa there O?"

"Well, I says to the guy, I don't think so."

And he says, "Come on kid, ya not gonna fight us. Just give us the money and you don't get hurt."

So, I said to him, "I have another option. If you can catch me, you can have my money. Then I threw the hot chocolate at them and took off running."

My mother shrieked, my father grinned, and Michael applauded saying, "Way to go Big O!

"I could hear them scream, and I had a 50-to-60-yard head start."

Michael glanced at my parents, and said, "With a head start like that, there's no way they were gonna catch Owen Loof."

I slapped hands with my friend and said, "I ran for three blocks, and when I looked around, they were a block away, and had given up the chase."

My mother's reaction was mixed between being happy

I had escaped without getting hurt, and thinking of all the ways the situation could have turned out differently. My father also expressed how pleased he was that I was not injured, and praised me for my quick thinking in eluding the danger. But then he kept up the questioning by asking, "Now wait a minute. You had your money and were out of danger, why didn't you go to the train station and call us then?"

I explained that I was on the way to the station when I heard someone screaming for help. I ran in the direction of the screams, and eventually found the source. There was a woman being dragged along the ground by a man. She was doing the best she could to fight him off, but he hit her, and was trying to get her coat off. So, I started yelling at the guy to stop, but he didn't. He didn't even look up. There was a garbage basket with this metal pole in it and I pulled it out. I started yellin' like a banshee, and charged at the guy. This got his attention, and he jumped off the woman and started running.

When I reached the woman, she was trying to button her coat and get to her feet, and I was able to see her face. First, she was absolutely stunning, and second, she was not much older than I was. She said she was okay, only a little shaky and upset, but did not seem to be hurt.

My mother interjected, "Oh! That poor girl. It's lucky that you were there Owen, and I'm proud of you, but you could have been hurt."

"Well, I had to do something. But when she got herself together, she told me that the guy took her pocketbook and money. She then thanked me for saving her, and told me her name was Rebecca, but I should call her Becky."

I went on to say that Becky was twenty years old and had been in the city with her boyfriend and some other friends.

There was some kind of an argument with the boyfriend, and then she got separated from her other friends. Now she just wanted to get home, but she had no money.

Now it was my father's turn to chip in. "So, of course you offered to pay her way home."

"Well what else was I supposed to do? However, I said we should at least find a cop and make a report. She said she didn't want to get the police involved since she really wasn't hurt. Then I told her that the mugger got her ID and stuff, and she should report it. She got really twitchy about the cops, and when a squad car drove by, she absolutely tried to avoid it."

My parents looked at each other knowingly, and then turned to me. I did not let them say anything before matter-of-factly stating, "Yes, yes, she was a prostitute. When we were on the way to the bus station, we stopped to get some food, and she finally admitted it to me."

With a look of alarm on her face, my mother asked, "Owen, what did you do?"

I reached out to touch my mother's hand answering, "Relax mom, I offered to give her all the money I could as long as I had enough to get on the train. She made me an offer, but I just told her to take the money."

My father then asked, "So you couldn't call, and you got on the train to come home. But why did Michael have to find you passed out in the cold?"

"That was the plan, but I figured I would just sit down for a minute before I walked up the block and I fell asleep." I pointed at Michael and said, "The next thing I knew, this guy was picking me up and carrying me here."

My mother stared at me saying, "I don't know what we're going to do with you Owen! This little stunt was totally unacceptable. You worried us half to death, and there will be consequences." Then she reached over, hugged me, and said, "But thank God you're home safe!"

Michael and my father joined in the brief celebration, and when all the hugging finished, they went into the kitchen so Michael could call his mother. I then asked my mother, "What are we gonna do about school?"

I could see that my mother was thinking, and finally she responded, "I am going to call the school and tell them that after you left school, you got sick on the train. So, you got off the train, and sat on a bench to get yourself together. You fell asleep, a police officer finally got you awake, and after making sure you were all right, he put you back on the train. When you arrived home, there was no one home, and you went right to bed. We didn't discover you until much later." Then she stopped for a second, and continued, "Oh! And you are feeling much better today, but since tomorrow is Friday, as a precaution you will not return to school till Monday."

I smiled, stared lovingly at my mother, and said, "Thanks mom. I got it!"

She looked at me, not so lovingly, and wagged her finger declaring, "Don't thank me, you are not off the hook for this yet." Then she walked into the kitchen.

A short time later Michael came back, sat down, and I asked, "What'd ya mother say?"

"She said to come home whenever I'm ready. And that was quite an adventure you had last night pal."

A sly little smile appeared on my face as I said, "Yeah it sure was, wasn't it?"

Michael's head twitched, his eyebrows raised, and his mouth opened in surprise. Then he peered intently at me saying, "Oh no, come on O. I know that look. Was any of that story true?"

I shot my friend a shocked look, and exclaimed, "I am really hurt. Do you think I would lie to all of you and make up a story like that?"

Without missing a beat Michael replied adamantly, "Three years ago, no way you could do it. But now, yeah, of course you would!"

I placed my hand over my heart and closed my eyes feigning a faint. Michael pulled the pillow from under my head and hit me with it saying, "Stop that you idiot. Did you really make up that whole story?"

There was a delay in my response as I bowed my head. Michael waited patiently for an answer, and it was finally forthcoming. I lifted my head, and saying with a broad smile, "Well, the wrestling matches were really cool in person."

CHAPTER 20

When I returned to school on Monday, of course everybody inquired about what happened after walking out of English class. I asked, "Do you want what I told my parents or my mother's version?"

Bobby responded by saying, "Why not tell us what really happened."

I proceeded to tell them how I went to the bank, had a bite to eat, and attended the wrestling matches. Then after the leaving the arena, I went to a 42nd Street porno movie, had a couple of drinks in a bar, and got picked up by a hooker. She and an accomplice tried to roll me, but I was able to escape. Then I met Becky, who was from Omaha, and was trying to get home. She left Nebraska for the glamour of the big city, found out it was not that glamorous, and just wanted to go home. She was conned out of the money her parents sent her, and had not eaten in two days.

Kevin interrupted and said, "Oh come on Owney, you didn't fall for that sob story."

"Well, if you're asking if I just gave her the money, the answer would be no."

I then continued the story saying that we had something to eat and called her parents, who also wished for their daughter to come home. They said that they would be happy to reimburse any money spent for the trip. We went to the bus station, bought her ticket, and waited for the bus.

Kevin then asked, "So she just got on the bus and left?"

"Well, there were some tender moments before the bus got there, and just before she boarded, she gave me a big hug and kiss. She also said she would never forget me."

My two friends looked at each other, then to me, and back to each other. There was silence as Kevin was scratching his head, and Bobby was just shaking his head. Finally, Bobby asked, "So, she gave you a kiss and you actually saw her physically get on the bus?"

I threw my head back and my hands in the air while protesting, "Geeze, you guys sound like you don't believe a word I'm saying."

The two friends shouted in unison, "That's because we don't!"

I waved a finger at them and said indignantly, "Oh yeah? Well have you ever seen wrestling in person? It's the best. Nothin' like on TV."

We all started laughing as Bobby swatted my finger away, Kevin pushed me out of my seat, and they both playfully slapped me around.

The next week Bishop Loughlin varsity basketball team was again visiting Prep. Michael and his father were coming to the game. I was in the teacher's parking lot when they arrived at the same time as the Loughlin team bus. I showed Michael a box of tissues saying, "I got them ready for ya. You're gonna need them again."

"I got a towel in the car that you're gonna need this time pal."

We were laughing as the Loughlin players passed by greeting Michael. One of the players stopped and said to Michael, "This is a friend of yours?"

"As a matter fact he is. I know him almost my whole life."

The player looked at me and asked, "Weren't you doing the clock the last time we were here?"

"Yeah, I was."

The player said to Michael, "You know our guy believes this one was fooling with the clock and the book at that game."

Before Michael could respond I said, "Why would I do that? It wasn't necessary, you guys are easy."

The player took a step toward me, and I did not back down. Michael stepped between us saying, "Now, now ladies calm down."

A couple of other Loughlin players gathered around, and Michael pulled me in the opposite direction away from the action. As the Loughlin players escorted their teammate away, I yelled, "They didn't need my help then, and they won't need it tonight either!"

Michael shouted at me, "Will you shut up fool!"

I replied in a calm voice, "Yeah, yeah, I'm sorry. I just want to see a good game."

After a little hug, we started back through the parking lot. A green Volkswagen Bug pulled into a space right next to another green Volkswagen Bug. As the man who exited his green Bug approached, Michael said, "Hey Coach!"

"Oh, hi Michael, good to see alumni come back to support the team."

Michael pointed to me saying, "Well, my best friend goes here. I couldn't miss this one."

As his coach hurried off, I asked, "That's your coach's car, huh?"

"Yeah, it is. Look man, I gotta find my dad."

As we walked away, I looked back eyeing the two green Volkswagen Bugs, and my face brightened as if a light bulb turned on above my head.

I was right about not being needed on the clock or the book this time. Prep won the game by eighteen points. Loughlin had no answer for our sensational sophomore Kenny Charles, who led all scorers with 26 points.

He also recorded 12 rebounds and 7 assists. Dan McHale, John Alleva, and Bobby Atanasio all scored in double figures, with Atanasio cleaning the boards for 15 rebounds. It was a total team effort with everybody getting to play and contributing to the victory.

After the game Michael, was a little dejected, but I decided not to rub it in this time, and he went to the parking lot see his former team's bus leave. After saying so long to Bobby, John Alleva, and the other Prep players, I started for the parking lot. As soon as I walked through the door, I noticed a crowd around the Green Bugs.

Michael was standing there, so I joined him and asked, "Is everything okay? What's going on?"

"Well, we're not sure, but Coach's key won't work, and he can't get in his car."

"Really, wow!"

"Yeah, I watched him try all the doors. Nobody can figure it out."

Michael's father went over to see if he could help, but there was no getting the door opened. The father and the coach spoke for a few more minutes, then Mike O'Connor wished the Loughlin coach good luck with solving the problem, and the three of us walked to our car. As we were exiting the parking lot, we noticed that there was a person trying to open the door of the green bug parked next to the Loughlin coach's green bug, and being equally unsuccessful. Michael asked, "Hey O, is that one of your teachers?"

"Yeah, that's Mr. Polerzarri. He teaches bio and is the assistant coach of the JV basketball team."

Michael's father remarked, "You know, those two cars are exactly the same. Maybe they just got them mixed up."

When I arrived in homeroom the next morning, Kevin and Bobby were waiting for me. Bobby grabbed me right away, pushed me down in a seat, and demanded, "Okay how'd ya do it? I know you did it! And who helped?"

I pushed my friend's hand away, replying in a perturbed tone, "Watch your hands there, bud. What are you talkin' about?"

Bobby pointed at me, saying adamantly, "Mr. Polerzarri and Father Richards are on the warpath, and you know why. So don't play with me!"

Sam Vanacort, Mike Hoffman, and a few other guys crowded around to hear the answer. I looked at Kevin who shook his head imperceptibly. Then scanned the rest of the faces, and replied, "Maybe somebody could tell me what the hell you're talkin' about."

"Okay, you wanna play games. As you well know, 'somebody' not only switched the plates on Polerzarri and the Loughlin coach's cars, but also switched the parking spaces."

I looked at my friends incredulously, and said, "Oh come on, the plate switch is easy, but how could they switch the parking spaces?"

Vanacort answered the question, "Well, the cars are not that heavy, and with enough people they could've just lifted them up."

"So, Sam, how many guys you think it woulda taken?"

Vanacort thought for a second, and responded, "I dunno, if they were big enough guys, five or six maybe."

I jumped up, and pointing at Vanacort exclaimed, "See? It was Vanacort. He knows exactly how they did it!"

Everybody started laughing, and Bobby put his hand on my shoulder saying, "Oh, all right. We understand why you don't wanna say anything."

Vanacort and Hoffman also patted me on the back before returning to their seats. Then just before he sat down Bobby looked down at Kevin, and with a pensive look said, "You know, you were pretty quiet throughout this whole discussion."

Kevin just shrugged his shoulders, smiled, and asked, "Was I?"

Two days later, I was passing by Father Richards' office after school, and there were only two students on the JUG line. When he saw me, he stopped talking to the first student, and called out, "Loof wait, don't go anywhere. Go in my office and sit down."

I did as I was told, and as I sat there, I prepared for Father Richards' questioning. People were talking about the car switch, but there was not even a whiff of who was responsible.

Finally, Father Richards entered, and I asked, "Slow day at JUG, huh Father?"

"It's always a slow day when you are not here Loof, and you have not been here for a while. Oh, and by the way I am glad to see that you are feeling better after last week, but you can't just leave the school without telling anyone. You have to come and see me first, all right?"

I told the priest I would remember that, and started to rise from my seat, when Father Richards said, "Sit down Loof that's not all." I returned to my seat, and he continued, "I was wondering if you and your group of entertainers could help us out again. You see, we are going to be having a St. Patrick's celebration for the children, and since you guys did such a fine job at the Christmas Party, the parish priest asked if we could get you back."

I took a deep breath of relief, and answered, "You know I have no problem doing it Father, but I'll talk to the other guys and let you know tomorrow, or at least by Monday. Oh, when is it Father?"

"Thank you, Loof. Its Saturday March 11th."

I stood up and said, "Okay, that's good Father. I'll let you know." Then I reached across his desk to shake hands, and turned to leave. I had only taken a few steps, when Father Richards stopped me by saying, "Oh, one more thing Loof, that was quite a prank, switching the cars."

Before I could turn around and say anything, the priest put up his hand and said, "Don't say anything. I just know it was your idea, but it obviously took a few other people to pull it off. Of course, there is no proof and nobody is talking. But I have to tell you Loof, and do not tell anyone I said this, that was a good one. Even Mr. Polerzarri, who was very annoyed that night, laughed about it, and gave you guys a lot of credit."

I smiled saying, "Thank you Father. If I find out who did it, I'll let them know."

Father Richards laughed, "You are a piece of work Loof. Now get out of here, and watch yourself."

The kids had a great time at the St. Patrick's party, as did the entertainers. The drama department supplied the leprechaun costumes for Kevin, Anton, and me. But they only got a green suit for Bobby because there was no leprechaun suit big enough for him. I said it was just as well for there are no giant leprechauns.

When Anton, who was black and from Jamaica, saw the suit, he asked, "Well how can I wear the suit?

I answered, "Oh, we'll just tell them you're one of the Black Irish!"

The Prep boys had a great time with the kids, keeping order and playing games. There was also singing and dancing, along with teaching the kids about St. Patrick. At the end of the night, when we were backstage changing, Kevin asked, "Hey Owney, ya got the flask with ya?"

When I pulled the flask out of my pocket, Bobby threw his hands in the air and said, "Oh no! You didn't spike the kids' drinks again, did you?"

"Well, I really had no intention of doing so, but two kids came up to me and asked if I had any of the good soda like at Christmas."

CHAPTER 21

The second week in April, I arrived in homeroom obviously annoyed. Bobby said to Kevin, "Uh oh, somebody's got a bug up their ass."

Kevin asked, "Okay Owney, what's wrong now?"

I snarled out an answer. "Some son of a bitch stole my history book again. This is the third time."

Bobby patted his friend on the back saying, "Relax man, maybe you should buy one this time."

I pushed the friendly hand away, and answered derisively, "Oh yeah, that's a great idea. So they can steal a brand-new book. Fine! They wanna keep playin', but I better not catch 'em!"

When I got to History, I had only calmed down a little, and then Mr. Quinn asked everyone to take out their books. I was the only student without a book on his desk. Mr. Quinn approached and asked, "No book again, Loof?"

"Yeah Mister, somebody took it."

"You have used that excuse one too many times. Nobody gets their book stolen so many times without being irresponsible. I'll give you two days to get a new book, and then I'll take a point off your grade every day you don't have one."

I replied in a not so pleasant tone, "Fine, whatever. I'll have a book, don't worry."

"Watch your tone, Loof! You want JUG or points off your grade now?"

I sat there in silence, and when Mr. Quinn turned around, I flipped him the bird, which caused a little laughter. The teacher turned around quickly, and I was bent over getting my notebook.

The next period was Mr. Garell's French class, and Kevin told Bobby what had happened in History. He said to me, "You're gonna have to buy a book, ya know."

"Will you shut up about buying a book? I'm not going home asking for money to buy a book. We're moving into a new house in a couple of weeks, and it's costin' more than they thought. I'm not askin' them for money. Arggg! This is such bullshit. I'll get a book. Leave it alone."

"Okay, okay, don't bite my head off. You'll get a book!"

The bell sounded, and Mr. Garell entered holding an apple in his hand that he placed on his desk. I sat through the class very sullen and slumped in my seat. The teacher actually asked me to sit up straight at one point. Then fifteen minutes into the class, there was a problem with the slide projector that was being used to transmit images that represented French phrases. Mr. Garell left the classroom to find a remedy for the situation. As soon as he was out the door, I jumped out of my seat, ran to the teacher's desk, picked up the apple, and took a big bite. I then placed the apple down in such a way that the bite mark was not visible.

Mr. Garell returned about five minutes later and announced that the class would have to move to another room. We all rose from our seats, Mr. Garell went to his desk, and picked up the apple. There was still some moisture on the bite mark when he touched it, and dropped the apple in disgust. He yelled, "Who did this. I do not find it the least bit funny!"

Everybody stopped in their tracks, and he continued furiously, "Hurry up and get next door. This is not over!"

When everyone was seated in the new classroom, Mr. Garell was still visibly upset and said, "No one is leaving this room until someone owns up to this misdeed."

The class sat in silence for five minutes. Then ten minutes went by, and there was still silence. I then silently polled the class for guidance on how to proceed.

The vote was almost split down the middle. There were thumbs up for turning myself in, and there were thumbs down for remaining silent. I waited a few more minutes, then raised my hand, stood up, and confessed. Mr. Garell gave me a lecture and JUG, and I apologized.

The last ten minutes of the lesson were uneventful, but the teacher made a point of saying that my stunt had cost the class valuable instruction time. When the bell sounded ending class, a few people passed by to have a laugh with me over the incident. I stood up to leave and said, "Oh crap!"

Kevin heard and asked, "What's a matter?"

"I really can't do JUG today!"

"So, ask him if you can do it tomorrow."

"Yeah, yeah, I'll ask. You guys go, I'll catch up with you later."

Kevin and Bobby left, and I walked to Mr. Garell, who was still at his desk, and said contritely, "Listen Mister, I am really sorry about the apple thing. I don't know what I was thinkin'."

"What you think, Loof, is that everything is a joke. You are going to find out one day that life is not all jokes. And the time you are wasting now will have consequences in the future."

"Yeah, I guess you're right Mister. But I was wonderin' if I could do the JUG tomorrow?"

"No, you will do it today!"

"But Mister, ya see my parents are buying a house, and they have an appointment with a lawyer or something, and there's a delivery coming, and they need me to be there."

"You should have thought about that before pulling the stunt you did!"

I pleaded, "Oh come on Mister, I really gotta be home today. Gimme three days, gimme five days, I just can't do it today."

Mr. Garell shouted, "I don't care what you have to do! You must be taught a lesson. Your actions have consequences, and you will do the JUG today."

I started continuing to plead my case, but before I could say anything, Mr. Garell put up his hand yelling, "End of story, think the next time, Loof!" Then the teacher picked up his briefcase and left the room leaving me standing there stewing.

I stood for a few seconds boiling, finally pounding my fist on the desk, and stomping out of the room. When I got to the cafeteria, I threw my books down on the table so hard the whole table shook nearly spilling some of the drinks. Bobby sighed, and asked quietly, "Okay what happened now?"

I responded curtly, "I don't wanna talk about it! Leave me alone!" Bobby tried to respond, but I said more loudly, "I said! I don't wanna talk about it!"

Bobby was perturbed and raised his voice. "Well fine, don't talk about it then!"

I took a deep breath, and bellowed, "AHHHHH! The fuck is makin' me do the JUG today even after what I told him I had to do! This is all bullshit! They keep stealin' my book, and now this guy won't give me a break. It was just a joke. God dammit!" Before my friend could utter a word, I got up in a huff, picked up my books, and walked away saying, "Shit, shit, shit!"

When I got to English, Kevin and Bobby both asked if I was feeling better, and wanted to know where I went. I stated, "I'll feel a lot better when I take care of Garell after school."

Bobby then asked, "What are you talkin' about?"

"I'll tell ya what I'm talkin' about. I knocked on the teacher's lounge door and that schmuck opened it. Then I told him I knew where his car was parked, and I was gonna be waitin' for him after school, and we'll settle this like men."

"Your tellin' us that you threatened to beat up a teacher?"

"Yeah, I did! And don't try to stop me!"

Bobby said, "You nut job, you'll get expelled."

I just sat there without saying a word. Kevin attempted adding to the conversation, but I put up my hand and said, "Enough talk!"

I was quiet through English and religion, but I did participate in all the activities Coach Sullivan put us through in gym. As I was changing my clothes, Coach Sullivan informed me that I was being summoned to Father Richards's office. On my way out of the locker room I said to Kevin and Bobby, "We who are about to die salute you! I'll see you guys tomorrow."

Bobby asked, "You sure about that?"

I smiled saying, "Yeah, yeah, don't worry. I'll be here!"

There was a line at Father Richards' office that as far as I could tell, consisted of mostly freshman. At the front of the line, the priest was screaming at a little freshman, who looked terrified. On any other day I might have found this amusing, but there was nothing to feel amused about today.

When I looked down the line again, Father Richards was so mad at this kid, his face was red, and the veins were popping out of his neck.

Then in the middle of the tirade, he raised his head, and spied me at the end of the line. In the middle of a rage-filled sentence, the redness drained from his face, the neck veins returned to normal size, and he very calmly called out, "Um, Owen, would you come into my office right now please?"

I walked down the line of underclassmen, who looked at me like I was a star on the red carpet. On arriving at the head of the line, Father Richards put his hand on my shoulder and said evenly, "Owen just sit down, and I will be with you when I'm finished here."

It was not as long as I thought it would be before Father Richards came through the door. I rose quickly from my seat, threw my hands up in the air, while shaking my head, and declared, "I know, I know Father! Before you say anything, I know I shouldn't have done it. It was stupid. But you know I really wasn't gonna do anything. I was just mad, and then I calmed down."

"That's all well and good Owen, but you can't be going to the teachers' lounge threatening teachers. What were you so angry about?"

I related the entire story, from biting the apple to the reason I could not do JUG today. When I was finished, the priest fixed his gaze at me, and asked quietly, "Did you ever think of coming to me, and asking if you could do the JUG tomorrow?"

I looked at the priest dumbfounded and speechless. Then I finally answered, "Uhh, well, no I didn't."

As soon as the last words were out of my mouth, Father Richards gave me a slap upside the head, and said, "I overestimated you, Loof. I thought you were smarter than that. You'll do the JUG for the apple tomorrow. Now get out of here before I change my mind. Oh, and before you leave school go apologize to Mr. Garell."

I replied excitedly as I rushed out the door, "Don't worry! I will Father! Thank you, Father! See you tomorrow, Father!"

The next day when I reported for JUG, Father Richards again asked me to wait in the office until he was finished with everyone else. The wait was a little longer this time, which gave me time to prepare answers for any possible questions. However, like a good counter puncher, I was certainly going to let the priest throw the first punch.

Father Richards entered, and without saying a word, he went to his desk, took out a metal cash box, and placed it on the desk. I sat there wondering what the heck was happening. Finally, the priest asked, "Are you ready for JUG today, Owen?"

"Sure, I guess so Father."

"Good, so here's what you are going to do for your JUG. I have pictures from the St. Patrick's party ready to be picked up, and I need a couple of rolls of film. I want you take care of this for me. Here is money for everything, including train fare. Oh, and here is the address and directions."

I eyed the priest skeptically, and said, "This is not a joke. This is really my JUG."

Father Richards replied slightly perturbed, "Yes, this is really your JUG. Now take the money, and get going so you can get back."

I collected everything I needed for the excursion, and said, "Gotcha Father. See ya in a little while."

It took a little more than an hour for me to complete the mission, and after looking at the pictures with Father

Richards, I went to my locker. Then I walked past the gym where Bobby and some of the varsity basketball players were shooting around. When Bobby saw me, he walked over and asked, "So how was JUG instead of gettin' expelled?"

I explained what Father Richards asked me to do, and added, "Best JUG ever. I'll have to get JUG more often!"

On Friday of the same week, I had already been without my history book for two days. When I entered homeroom that morning, Kevin, and Bobby could see in my face that I had something to tell them. Kevin said, "You look like the cat that ate the canary, so tell us already."

I sat down, reached in my bag, and plunked a history book on the desk. Slightly shaking his head, Bobby groaned, "Oh no, you stole another history book."

"Yes children, I certainly did. However, this is no ordinary history book."

Kevin asked, rather impatiently, "What are you talking about? Will you get to the point?"

I put up a waving hand in front of my testy friend, and answered, "Relax my good man relax." I opened the front cover of the book, pointed to the box containing the owner's names, and asked, "You see the second name on the list?"

Bobby slapped Kevin on the arm, and in an animated tone shrieked, "Holy shit, he stole back his own book!"

I closed the book, picked it up, and hugged it close to my chest saying, "Yes kiddies, and the third time's always the charm. I knew I'd get you back eventually." Then I kissed the book adding, "And nobody's gonna take you away again."

CHAPTER 22

On the Saturday after Memorial Day, there were waves, and I went surfing with Michael and Johnny Portano. Their girlfriends were all out together at the movies watching *Barefoot in the Park*, starring Robert Redford and Jane Fonda. The three of us met at JP's around nine o'clock. After a couple of beers I said, "Okay what are we gonna do now?" There were gestures of indecision and blank stares, so I added, "Well, this might be a gamble, being Saturday night and all, but we know Mike Woods is behind the bar, so let's try The Circle for just one or two?"

Michael answered, "More of a crowd means more people that could know us."

"I just said that it was a gamble. But if we stay in the back and keep a low profile, Mike can bring us two pitchers, we drink up, and get out. Besides, anybody got a better idea?"

After a short discussion, the plan was a go, and I said to Michael, "I already called my parents and told them I was staying here for a while. So, go call your mom and tell her you're with me."

Michael left to make his call, and when he returned, I asked, "So what'd she say?"

"She said okay, and that I better not be drinkin'"

I laughed and said, "My mother said the same thing. So come on, let's go get some beers!"

When we got to the bar, it was moderately crowded and there were definitely a few people who might recognize us. Michael and JP were reluctant to carry out the mission, but I convinced them that since we walked all the way over, it was worth a try. So, in we went and waved at Woods as we walked to a dimly lit table in the back of the bar. Most of the crowd was gathered around the TVs toward the front of the bar watching the Yankee/Red Sox game that was in extra innings. Woods came right over to our table and said, "Guys, come on, it's Saturday night. You can't be in here now."

I replied, "Yeah we know that Mike. It's been discussed. Look, just bring us two pitchers, and we'll sit here quiet, drink up, and leave. Nobody will even know we're here."

He agreed, but was really not pleased, and with a well-placed finger, said, "Okay fine! Just shut up and drink your beer." He left in a huff, returning a few minutes later with the beer and some glasses. However, before he went back behind the bar he said, "You guys owe me big time!"

We sat there making guy talk about sports and girls, with summer plans being added to the mix. Portano said he was going to Maine with his family for most of the summer, and JP stated that he was getting a job as soon as school ended.

After Michael explained that his college was probably going to set up an internship, and his father was trying to get him a job, he looked at me and asked, "Hey wait a minute, didn't you tell me your school was havin' a junior prom?"

"Well yeah, as a matter of fact they are."

He inquired tactfully, "So, you haven't told me who ya takin'?"

"I didn't tell you, 'cause I'm not takin' anybody, 'cause I'm not going."

My three compatriots greeted the news with a mix of surprise and mock sympathy, and Michael expressed the majority opinion asking, "What? Owen Loof, the main man of Brooklyn Prep, not going to the prom. It can't be."

Slightly annoyed, I answered, "Oh stop, you sound just like the guys at school. They're all sayin', 'Owney, ya gotta be there.' 'It won't be the same.' 'We'll fix you up.' I don't wanna go with just anybody, and I have no one to go with, so I'm not goin'. No big deal!"

Michael asked, "Well, did you actually ask anyone?"

I became a little more annoyed, replying, "No I didn't! And who was I gonna ask anyway? So just drop it okay!"

There was a chorus of, "AWWW, poor widdle Loofy, can't get a date for the prom!"

I stood up and said, "You know what? Fuck you guys!" Then I angrily wheeled away from the table. Just at that moment, one of the baseball watching patrons was passing by to use the restroom. He was my height, but was a lot heavier, and about ten years older. He also had a little more alcohol under his belt. When I crashed into the guy, it ordinarily might not have been a big deal. However, because the guy was taken completely by surprise, multiplied by the effect of his alcohol consumption, he lost his balance and landed on the floor. At the sound of the crash, every eye in the bar was focused on me standing over the guy.

I was frozen in word and deed for a few seconds, and after returning the stares of the assemblage, extended a hand, and said, "Geeze, I'm really sorry."

The guy on the floor was not happy, or in the mood for an apology. He slapped my hand away and said, "What's the matter with you? You stupid fuck!"

I was trying to explain what happened, and convey my expressions of regret, but the guy got to his feet, and began yelling something unintelligible, along with an expletive or two. I tried my best to strike a conciliatory tone, but the guy seemed determined to exact some sort of satisfaction for the wrong inflicted on him.

After a few more shouts, and expletive laden name-calling, I felt he was about to escalate the situation to some sort of physical action. My feeling was proven correct, as the guy attempted to land a well telegraphed, sloppily thrown punch. Not only was I prepared, but it was also a blow a blind man could see coming, and I was able to step sideways and evade it easily.

As the guy glided passed, I helped increase his forward motion with a little shove, which sent the puncher into an empty table that tipped over, sending them both crashing to the floor. While most of the bar just watched, two guys were rushing over, and it was obvious they were not peacemakers. My back was turned to these two, and Michael, who along with JP was checking out the guy on the floor, called out, "O, behind ya!"

I turned, ducked out of the way as a fist whizzed by, and pushed the guy away. Woods, and the other bartender, jumped over the bar, grabbed the other guy, and pulled him away. Between the two bartenders and cooler heads, order was restored with handshakes, apologies, and cleaning up. Once everything calmed down, and we were reseated finishing up the last pitcher of beer, a tall guy in his early twenties approached the table. He greeted each one of us by name, and when no one else was able to utter a reply, I said, "Hey Andy, how's it going?"

Andy Judge was a 96th Street neighbor, whose mother

Essie and my mother were as close as sisters. Judge answered, "Well everything was going really good, and it was a quiet night, until you guys started throwing people around."

I protested, "Geeze, I bumped into the guy by accident, and he's the one who started throwing punches. I never threw a punch!"

"That really doesn't matter now does it. What does matter is, what are you guys doing in here in the first place?"

I answered the question honestly, and without hesitation, "Well, we're havin' a beer, just like you."

Judge cocked his head, and raised a finger saying, "Whoa, there's a big difference! None of you guys are eighteen!"

With a slight tilt of my head, and a wave of my hand, I brushed off the comment by stating, "A minor detail my good man, a minor detail." Then I stood up, draped an arm around Judge's shoulder, and asked, "You're not gonna give us up to the authorities, are you?"

A surprised Judge shook his head, and replied adamantly, "Of course not Owen, why would I call the police. That would only get Mike in trouble."

I gave Judge a soft tap on the chest and said, "No, no! I know you wouldn't call the cops! But would you tell an even higher authority?"

Judge laughed, replying, "Oh, I got ya! Don't worry Owen, I won't turn you or your friends in to your mothers." Everybody breathed a sigh of relief, and after we all thanked Judge, I added, "We'll pay you back for this Andy, starting with a drink on me, and you'll never catch us in here again till we're legal!"

Judge shot back, "That's a lie, and you know it, Owen."

With a sly smile, and an upraised finger, I stated, "I said you'll never catch us!"

Everybody laughed, and Judge said, "We'll see Owen, we'll see! Just don't start any trouble you bully!"

Judge went back to his friends, and as we drained the last drops from our glasses, Mike Woods came over to the table. He exploded, "What the fuck is wrong with you guys? I'm sure glad you just sat quiet and drank your beer! You're gonna hafta stay outa here for a while!"

I reached over, and patted him on the arm saying, "Well you how we always keep a low profile."

CHAPTER 23

With summer on the horizon, I knew I had to make it through the final weeks of school, especially the finals, before I could even think about making plans. During those weeks, I was almost invisible. It seemed like I always had my nose in a book. I was taking notes, asking sensible questions, and staying out of JUG.

Finally, Bobby and Kevin confronted me, with Bobby asking, "Owney are you okay? What's going on? You've been really quiet lately."

"Yeah, see we'll be movin' into the new house in a couple a weeks, and things have been crazy. My parents are really stressed about the money, and I guess I don't wanna give them any more worries."

The third Friday in June was the last day of regular classes, which would begin on Monday with trigonometry that was our first class of the day. The bell sounded, and after about a minute, Kevin and Bobby burst through the door with clown masks covering their faces, and brandishing cap guns. Kevin screamed, "Okay, everybody on the floor, and if you all do what you're told, nobody gets hurt!"

Mr. Benny attempted to intervene and protest, but Bobby pointed the gun at him, and shouted, "Put your hands up, and don't make another move or I'll plug ya!"

Before the teacher could say anything else, Sam Vanacort got up from the floor, and lamented, "There's only one person who can save us!"

Then the window opposite the teacher's desk opened, and I jumped into the room dressed in a Superman suit. Kevin started shooting at the caped crusader, and cried out, "Oh no, it's Superman!"

Bobby was also firing his gun, I raced over, grabbed their guns, and punched each bad guy to the floor. Billy Ward rushed to Superman's side, and while fawning over him with dreamy eyes cooed, "Oh, my hero! Thank you, Superman!"

Superman replied, "Protecting the innocent is my job in the never-ending battle for truth, justice, and the American way!" Then after waving to the class, Superman helped the villains to their feet, and escorted them out of the room. There was laughter, and a round of applause, with even Mr. Benny giving his approval.

When Bobby got to second period for Mr. Quinn's history class, the teacher asked him, "Loof isn't with you? I know he's in school, where is he?"

Bobby just shrugged his shoulders and took his seat in silence. Mr. Quinn inquired suspiciously, "Come on, come on, don't give me the silent thing. Something's up, right?"

The words were not out of the teacher's mouth, when I confidently walked in dressed in pink stripped bell bottoms, a paisley shirt, love beads around my neck, and sandals on my feet. In addition, I was wearing John Lennon-esque circle-shaped sunglasses, a long black wig with a bandana, with a fake joint, and an "End the War" sign. As I walked around the room, some of the guys followed, producing loose-leaf signs with antiwar slogans, and some of the class went to the front of the room and sat down.

They all followed my chants, "Hell no! We won't go!", and "Draft Beer, not me." Mr. Quinn quickly stopped the

"One, Two, Three, Four…" chant before the vulgarity popped out. The teacher also wanted to make sure that it was not a real joint I had in my hand. The "protest" went on for a while, and finally Mr. Quinn restored order, and sent me to change clothes.

I took a little time returning to class, and when the period ended, I went to Mr. Quinn and said, "Mister, I need a little favor."

"That depends on the favor Owen."

"It's nothin' big like givin' me the answers to the final or anything. Could you just grab Mr. Garell, and delay 'im for a few minutes?"

Mr. Quinn looked at me suspiciously, asking, "Oh Owen, what are you going to do?"

"Come on Mister, ya know I can't tell ya. But I promise it's nothin' bad. Ya know I wouldn't do that to Mr. Garell after what happened. I just wanna make it up to him."

Mr. Quinn eyed me up and down, then finally said, "I trust you about as far as I can throw you. Fine, but you better be careful. Oh, and good luck on the final."

"Thanks Mister, see ya next week!"

When the bell sounded, Mr. Garell had not yet arrived, and when he did the whole class was standing outside. The classroom door was closed and locked. He found the door key, and when it was opened, everyone could see the teacher's desk was ringed with apples, and in the middle of the display were three cream pies.

Mr. Garell laughed lightly, saying, "Very funny, Loof, very funny."

I stopped in front of the desk, and said, "What Mister, what? I don't know how that stuff got there. You could see the door was locked.

Everybody took their seats except for Kevin and Bobby, who were standing on either side of me at the teacher's desk. Mr. Garell pointed at the apples and asked, "I get the apples, but why the pies?"

I picked up one of the pies, and responded, "I don't know anything about anything Mister, but I think this pie smells funny." I turned to Bobby, and asked, "What'd you think?"

Everybody knew what was coming, and they were not disappointed when Bobby bent forward toward the pie, and I mashed it in his face. The guys laughed, Mr. Garell gasped, and Bobby picked up one of the other pies, and let it fly toward me. I ducked, and the pie hit Kevin square in the face. Pointing at Kevin, I was doubled over with laughter. Mr. Garell picked up the last pie, walked around his desk, and tapped me on the shoulder. When I turned around, the teacher mashed the pie in my face.

There was cheering and laughing all around. I shook hands with my teacher, and asked, "How'd ya know?"

"One of the other teachers told me what you were doing with those crazy, noisy answers, so I watched some episodes of *The Soupy Sales Show*, and I learned about the pie thing. Now you guys go get cleaned up, and get back here quick." The three pie filled faces left the room to a standing ovation.

After lunch, it was time for Mr. Jagger's English class. When the bell sounded, Bobby, Kevin, and I were not in the room. Mr. Jagger was well aware of what had been going on throughout the day. He threw up his hands, bowed his head, and sat down saying, "Okay, let's get it over with."

Pat Santisi stood up, and announced, "*Hamlet the Sequel*, Act 1, Scene 1: On the street with Laertes, Francisco, and Horatio."

Kevin and I enter dressed in Shakespearean costumes. I am walking in front of him, and he calls to me, "Hey Laertes, how's it going? I haven't seen you since your sister passed."

"Ah, Francisco, it is good to see you. You know, it has been very hard getting over my sister's death, and I did not forget who caused it. I searched all over Europe, in all the capitals and small towns, and I finally found him."

Francisco interrupted, "Oh yeah, Hamlet."

Laertes eyes widen in rage, he clenches his fists, and grits his teeth. Then he turns his shoulder, and lifts his leg, while saying, "Slowly I turned, step by step, inch by inch…" Then he rushes to Francisco and starts punching and slapping him, pulling at his clothes, and shaking him vigorously. Suddenly Laertes stops the assault, and says, "Oh, Francisco, I am so sorry. It's just that every time I hear that name…"

At that point Bobby enters the room in costume, and asks, "Hey Laertes, Francisco, what's going on?"

Francisco answers, "Hey Horatio. Everything's cool, but Laertes is still having a hard time with his sister's death."

Laertes interjects, "And it was all because of your friend!"

Horatio starts to answer, but is stopped by Francisco. "Whatever you do, for your own good, don't mention his name, okay."

Horatio says, "Oh, you mean Hamlet!"

Francisco screams, and Laertes begins, "Slowly I turned…" But instead of going after Horatio, he beats up on Francisco, knocking him to the floor.

At this point, Mr. Jagger stands up, starts applauding, and is joined by the entire class. Then he says, "The Three Stooges do Shakespeare. Unbelievably silly, but inventively well done. Now sit down!"

THE BEST DRESSED MAN IN ROCKAWAY

As the period was drawing to a close, Mike Hoffman raised his hand and asked, "Um, Mister, I'm a little confused about the kings. You know Claudius and Polonius. What play were they in again?"

Mr. Jagger shook his head answering, "Okay Hoffman, Polonius was not a king. Claudius was the king, and they were both in Hamlet." He stopped, realizing the word he had uttered, and exclaimed loudly, "Oh no!"

Bobby, Kevin, and I stood up and began in unison, "Slowly I turned…." We rushed toward Mr. Jagger, the bell sounded, and the teacher picked up his belongings, and ran from the room laughing, with the three costumed players in hot pursuit.

Sixth period was Mr. Starkey's Latin class. When the bell sounded, Kevin, Bobby, and I walked in quietly past Mr. Starkey's desk, said hello, and sat down in the last three seats of the last row. Mr. Starkey had of course been told about what had gone on in the other classes. He smiled happily, and started the review for the final exam. Halfway through class, Bobby raised his hand and asked Mr. Starkey to write some vocabulary on the board. When the teacher turned his back, I left my seat and opened the window. I climbed out on the ledge, and closed the window.

The teacher finished writing, and turned around to explain what he had written on the board. In the middle of the explanation, he noticed the empty seat, and asked, "Okay, where's Loof? Where did he go?"

No one in the class moved, or said a word. Mr. Starkey walked around the room, and even went to the window, opened it, and checked the ledge. The teacher walked back to the front of the room obviously flustered and angry. "I am going to get Father Richards, and Loof will not get away with this. Russo come up here while I'm gone."

As he turned to leave, Bobby opened and closed the window, which made a sound that caused Mr. Starkey to run to the window again. This time, the whole class got up, and crowded around the teacher.

When Mr. Starkey was satisfied that he could not see anything, he started walking back toward his desk. Everyone returned to their seats, me included. Mr. Starkey stopped at his desk to speak with Russo. I raised my hand, and asked, "Excuse me Mister, before you go wherever you're going, how many questions did you say were going to be on the test?"

Mr. Starkey screamed, "What are you doing Loof? You are in big trouble young man!"

"What? I just asked a question."

"Don't give me that. Where did you go and how did you do it?"

"I didn't go anywhere!"

Bobby volunteered, "He's right Mister. I saw him sittin' right there." There were nods and murmurs of agreement all around.

With that, the bell sounded, and a red-faced Mr. Starkey pounded his fist on the desk while sitting down. The students began filing out, and they all said so long to their teacher. Kevin, Bobby, and I were the last to exit, and wished Mr. Starkey the best. The teacher looked up at me and said, "I don't know how you did it, Loof! But I'll find out!"

At the end of the day, I was walking past Father Richards's office. As the priest was coming through the door, we almost collided. Father Richards said, "Be careful there Loof!"

"Oops, sorry Father."

"You had a little fun today, Owen. You're lucky it's the last day of classes, or you really would be in trouble. Now get out of here before I change my mind, and go start studying for the finals."

We shook hands, and I smiled saying, "I think Mr. Garell had the best time. Thanks Father have a good weekend."

CHAPTER 24

*M*onday and the trigonometry final arrived in the blink of an eye. When I got to school, I could not find Kevin and Bobby right away, but I ran into a couple of other guys from my math class. Billy Ward, Jack Fredreck, and Johnny Killbride were waiting in the gym before the classroom for the test was opened. I asked them excitedly, "You guys see Kevin or Bobby?"

The response I received was three shaking heads, with Fredreck asking, "Somethin' up Owney? Come on tell us."

"Okay, okay. Look, just come with me, and when we find the other two, I'll tell ya all!"

We left the gym, and began our search. Finally finding our quarry on a bench outside the cafeteria. I inquired adamantly, "What are you guys doin' out here? This was literally the last place I looked."

Bobby answered, "Whoa there Sherlock, what the hell is your problem?"

I blew out an annoyed breath, waved my hand, and replied, "Whatever, look there's not much time. I have come into possession of some valuable information."

Now it was Bobby's turn to be annoyed, and he said, "You just said there's not much time, so get to the point will ya!"

I put up my hand, and apologetically responded, "You're right, you're right. Okay, here's the deal." Then I opened my notebook, removing a sheet of paper, and holding it out, continued, "What I have here are the answers to Mr. Benny's trig test."

Everybody's interest was piqued, and Kevin asked, "Are you sure, and where did you get them?"

"One hundred percent sure these are the answers, and I can't tell you where I got them."

Kevin said, "You could, but you're just not gonna."

"I don't care how you say it, do you want the answers or not?"

They all took out paper to write on, and began copying down the answers. There was silence as everyone was carefully examining their paper, and Killbride noted, "So according to this there are twenty multiple-choice questions, and two problems."

Fredreck interjected, "And the multiple-choice answers go, A,D,B,D,A,D,B,D right down the line. There are no C answers?"

Everybody was looking at one another skeptically, and I threw up my hands saying, "If that's what it says, that's what it is. Look, I'm givin' you the info. It's your choice to do what you want with it."

Bobby raised his hand with a question, "You said it was the answers to Benny's test. I have Breen, how do they help me?"

I patted my friend on the shoulder saying, "I don't know if they're using the same test, but see what happens." Then I looked around at my classmates and said, "I know there's not much time left, but let's try to get these to as many guys as we can. And we'll meet back here afterward, okay?"

True to their word, we all assembled outside the cafeteria after the test. Kevin spoke up first, "Well, it was twenty multiple-choice and two problems, which by the way, were pretty easy."

I laughed and said, "Yeah I know, they were so easy even I could do them!"

Fredreck added, "I'm still not sure about that A,B,D,B thing though."

I replied, "Tell ya the truth, I wasn't either. So, I sat next to Alwill and Avitabile, who everybody knows are the best math people, and they had a couple of Cs, so I put in one."

Bobby was sitting there frowning. I looked at him and said, "I guess it wasn't the same test, huh? But you did pretty good all year, you probably didn't even need the answers."

"You're right it wasn't the same test, and it was pretty hard. I wish I had the answers though, and if you get a higher mark, I'm gonna be pissed!"

Two weeks later, I found a bunch of the guys on the beach with a case of beer. Michael gave me a beer and asked, "You're pretty quiet there pal, what's goin' on?"

"Well, there's the good news, and the complicated news."

"Just tell me the story."

"I got a 96 on the trigonometry final."

"Wait, you got a 96 on a math test?"

I told him the whole story about the test, and ended by saying, "It really is a good thing I changed an answer, because if I didn't, I woulda got a hundred. Then you know there woulda been an investigation."

"That's for sure, but what's the rest of the story?"

"So, remember last year when I failed geometry and English, and I told my mother I would do better this year." Michael nodded in agreement, and I added, "I really did do better this year. I failed three subjects: Latin, religion, and English."

"Oh crap, are they gonna kick you out?"

"They could have, but no. Since I didn't pass any quiz or test in Latin the whole year, they're treatin' it like I was never in the class. I really don't need the credit to graduate. Then my religion teacher is the new headmaster, and he's takin' care of that, which means, officially, I only failed English."

"That's great! Hooray for Brooklyn Prep and Owen Loof. But I know that look, what'd ya thinkin'?"

"I don't know. The deal just sounds too easy. I'd like to know what my mother really did to get them to take me back."

"Well, you're back! That what counts.

"You're so right! Senior year here I come!"

Senior Year

CHAPTER 25

When I exited Michael's car on Woodfield Avenue, he also got out, and walked around to me. While shaking hands, he said, "Well, barring unforeseen circumstances, this will be your last year at this place. But, as we all know with you, unforeseen circumstances are the norm."

I laughed and replied, "Come on, man, gimme a break here! Ya know fuckin' up that test in the eighth grade and not gettin' into Loughlin, then my mother not lettin' me go to Brooklyn Tech, might've been the best things that could've happened. I couldn't imagine the last four plus years anywhere else but right here, and it all starts with Tom Collins. He's still been with me these last three years, and I can't wait for this year."

Michael gave me a hug saying, "I got ya dude! You're right. It's senior year! It's your year!"

In a solemn tone I replied, "Wait, I don't know. Maybe a low profile would be better this year."

Michael looked at me askance, laughed quietly, and remarked, "Low profile? Right. Where have I heard that before? Good luck with that." He shook his head, smiling, and gave me a playful punch on the arm. Then he turned, got back in the car, and drove away.

I watched the car leave, then turned, looking through the fence across the field at the stately Brooklyn Prep building. I took a deep breath, smiled broadly, and started up

Carroll Street. As I approached the entrance to the gym lobby, I made sure to slip in unnoticed, and spoke to no one.

As usual, the day began with an orientation assembly with introductions, speeches, and homeroom assignments. Father Hamilton was introduced as the new headmaster, and there were several new teachers. After all of that, Father Hamilton announced that there would be a slight change to the day's schedule. Students would not be dismissed to their homerooms until after the Student Government had finished a special presentation. Then the priest invited the Student Government officers to the stage.

The president of the Student Council, Charlie Russo, began his speech, and then he got to the key part: "This will be a great year for Prep both on the field and in the classroom. The Blue Eagle is the embodiment of what our school is all about, and he will lead us to greatness all year. The Eagle will infuse within all of us here today, the spirit that we need to act as one body, and support each other through any obstacle we need to overcome. So, let us rise as one, and feel the power of the Blue Eagle."

The school song blared over loudspeakers, and the back doors swung open to reveal a large egged shaped object being wheeled in by Kevin and Bobby. There was singing as the egg rolled down the middle isle between the juniors and seniors. The egg then stopped in front of a portable stairway that led up to the stage.

With Kevin and Bobby on either side, the egg was pulled open, and I jumped out in front of the egg dressed in a blue and white jump-suit. My head was covered with a bright blue eagle's head, and strapped on my back, a pair of large flowing blue and white wings. The Blue Eagle spread his wings to their full glory, and after a few seconds of whooping and hollering, ran along the front row of seats. He stopped dramatically in front of the egg flapping his wings, and then ran up the portable steps. While standing there spreading and flapping his wings, Kevin and Bobby attached a wire to the back of the wings. Once hooked up, The Blue Eagle was lifted in the air, and pushed to swing back and forth over the first few rows of the crowd.

After a few swings, The Eagle was lowered back to the stage, and unhooked. Then he ran down the stairs, up the freshman side of the gym, down the sophomore side, and up the middle isle between the juniors and seniors. All the while, The Eagle spread and flapped his wings, howling and shouting to raucous applause. On his arrival at the rear of the gym, the Blue Eagle stopped, jumped up and down, flapping his wings vigorously while whooping noisily, and ran out the door.

The Blue Eagle flew out onto Carroll Street, where he encountered two cops who went hysterical when they saw the bird flapping past them. Continuing up the block, there were a group of first graders, who The Eagle entertained by letting them chase him around. The Eagle finally made his way to the locker room, where he met Kevin and Bobby. Those two he expected, but he did not expect to see Father Hamilton and Father Richards.

Before even taking off the eagle head, I greeted the two priests with a hello and a flap of the wings. Father Hamilton started the conversation in a tone that indicated displeasure. "First of all, Loof, take off the eagle head." When I complied with the request, the priest continued, "Are you three crazy? I realize that may be a rhetorical question, but you never cleared that harness swinging with anybody. All you said you were going to do was pop out of the egg and run around."

I asked, "So Father, would you have given us permission to hook up the harness?"

"Of course not!"

My response surprised everyone. "That's why we didn't ask."

The headmaster was really not pleased with my statement, and said angrily, "Not the right thing to say, Loof! Watch yourself here! That was a dangerous stunt, and could have gone wrong in so many ways, and the school would have been responsible."

I said sheepishly, "I do see your point Father, but wouldn't it have been worse if you said no, and we did it anyway. Look nobody got hurt, it went great, and everybody loved it."

"You are certainly correct that it would have been worse, like expelled worse." Then he pointed his finger at me saying, "You were lucky this time, and you should probably get some time with Father Richards…"

I put up my hands, and with a slight tilt of my head, interrupted, "I hear ya Father, and if you want me do some JUG it's okay, whatever you want. And I promise we'll clear everything with you or Father Richards in the future."

Father Hamilton shook his head, and looked first to me, and then to Father Richards saying, "Yes you will Loof, yes you will. There better not be a repeat of something like this. He's all yours Father."

After Father Hamilton was gone, Father Richards told us our homeroom would be 4E, and the teacher would be Father McCartney. He also gave us a copy of our complete schedules. Glancing at Kevin and Bobby the priest said, "You two can report to your next class, but I need to speak with you, Loof."

We all looked at each other. Then Kevin and Bobby shook hands with me and said goodbye to Father Richards. Then I asked, "What's up Father? So how many days?"

Father Richards began, "For the stunt you pulled, you are nuts and should not have done it, but you're right everybody loved it. So don't worry, but I do need a favor."

I looked at the priest in puzzlement, and inquired, "Sure Father, what'd ya need?"

"Well, I have some pictures at the camera store that need to be picked up, and I can't get there today or tomorrow,"

"Oh yeah, for sure Father, but I can't do it today. How about tomorrow?"

"That's fine Owen, thank you."

I sidled up to the priest, and put my arm on his shoulder saying, "I don't mind at all doin' this for ya Father, but I want ya to put down that I got JUG when I do it."

Now it was the priest's turn to look puzzled, as he asked, "You don't want to do it just it for me, you want the JUG?"

I threw up my hands, looked at the priest, and said, "Come on Father, I got a reputation to uphold!"

When I looked over my schedule, Bobby and Kevin were with me in chemistry, French, and pool/gym. It was also noted that pool would be in the first semester and first period. We did not make it to homeroom after the assembly, so it was not until the second day of school that we met the rest of 4E. It was hands down the ultimate eclectic group of guys you could find.

There were guys with really good grades, near the top of the senior class. There were guys with grades that were at the very bottom of the senior class, and everywhere in between. There were good athletes from every sport, and all the arts were represented from writing to, photography and painting, to performing. There were no real troublemakers, but everyone knew how to make a joke, and take a joke. The class had Walter McClean, a seventeen-year-old bartender who worked three jobs; and Giacomo Avigliano, the son of an Italian diplomat who arrived at school every day in a limo with bodyguards. Everybody said the E in 4E stood for "Experiment", for if the building was still standing at the end of the year, and no teachers had quit the profession, the school could survive anything.

When we arrived at homeroom, Kevin and Bobby went through the door first, and I followed close behind carrying a cardboard box. It was early, and less than half the class was there, but John Alleva and Jack Fredreck started a "BLUE EAGLE" chant that was picked up by the rest of the early birds. I put the box down on the desk beside Fredreck, then waved and took a bow. Nick Sama and Jim Eagan wandered over, and Fredreck asked, "What's in the box Owney?"

"Take a look and see." The three students opened the flap and looked inside.

Eagan exclaimed, "Water balloons!"

I said, "Yeah, and if you look, our windows overlook the entrance from the field that most of the freshmen use. So come on let's go before McCartney gets here!"

Fredreck picked up the box, and the others followed him over to the windows. With the window opened, we saw several freshman targets. In a few seconds, the bombs began to fall with a few of them finding their mark. Kids were looking up trying to determine from where the missiles were being dropped. Anton, the piano player warned, "McCartney's almost here!"

There was only one balloon left, and I let it go. I was closing the window as it dropped. However, just before the window was completely closed, I noticed Mr. Jagger had come out of the building, and was talking to some of the freshmen. I kept the window opened just a crack, and as I peeked through the tiny opening, watched the balloon hit the teacher in the back of the leg. Mr. Jagger looked up but could see nothing.

Jumping into my seat, I said to Fredreck, "Oh shit, the last one hit Jagger in the leg."

My friend reacted with surprise and alarm, but before anything else could be said Father McCartney appeared, and asked, "What about Mr. Jagger?"

I looked at my new homeroom teacher, and answered, "Oh, morning Father! I was just tellin' Jack how much I enjoyed Mr. Jagger's English class last year."

The priest looked back at me skeptically, and said, "Oh yeah, I'm sure that's what you were saying, Laertes."

The bell sounded, and Father McCartney went about making some announcements, and addressing chemistry topics, since most of the homeroom were also in his science class. In the middle of this discussion, Mr. Jagger and Father Richards entered the classroom. Mr. Jagger pointed at me and said, "See Father! It had to have come from this room. Loof is here."

Father McCartney asked what the problem was. Father Richards did not take his eyes off me, and explained what had happened with the water balloons. When asked if he had seen anything, Father McCartney said that he had not seen anyone near the windows, and they were all closed when he entered the room.

Mr. Jagger started up to the window, and I gave Fredreck a soft elbow nudge and whispered, "I forgot to get rid of the box."

When the teacher got to the window, however, the box was not there. He did open the window, and protested to the priests at the front of the room. "Look! you can see the wet pavement from here!"

Unbeknownst to me, there had been one more balloon left in the box, but it had been removed by John Alleva. The box was now folded up, and hidden from view. The balloon had been passed around the room, and was in the possession of Giacomo Avigliano, the Italian diplomat's son.

Questions were asked, and no one reported seeing anything. Father Richards concluded that there was no proof the people responsible for the balloon attack were from this room. Still not satisfied, Mr. Jagger said, "Father, you and I both know it had to be Loof."

Father McCartney stated, "Mr. Jagger, maybe he did it, and maybe he didn't, but nobody saw him. You cannot punish him without proof."

Mr. Jagger waved his finger, pointed around the room, and said, "They know who did, and they're all protecting him. Punish the whole class!"

Father Richards put his hand on Mr. Jagger's shoulder, and grabbed his arm, easing him toward the door saying, "You have a class now Mr. Jagger. I'll take care of this." As Mr. Jagger walked out the door, he looked at me staring daggers.

Father Richards said to Father McCartney, "Sorry about all this. I will look into the situation further." Then he looked at me and said, "I'll talk to you later, Loof."

As Father Richards walked out the door, the bell sounded, everyone got up, and started to leave the room. Anton came over and handed me the folded-up cardboard box. Then Giacomo neared, and gave me the water balloon.

I smiled in surprise and said, "Hey Mo, thanks man, that's great. But ya know you coulda given me up?"

With a heavy Italian accent, but in perfect English, the new student replied, "I'm not crazy, and I'm not stupid. I could see what was going on, and I've heard people talking about you. So doing something good for you seemed like a smart move. And besides that, my grandfather always said, 'Mai tradire gli amici, e tenere sempre la bocca tappata'"

I grinned broadly, and asked, "Okay, and that means?"

"Never betray friends, and always keep your mouth shut!"

I threw my head back and laughed, saying, "A man after me own heart! Way'd go dude! Come on we gotta go to the pool, and boy do we have a surprise for you."

We turned to leave with me holding the balloon in my hand. I bumped right into Charlie Russo, who was now standing with Father McCartney. The balloon broke, and sent water mostly on me, but also on the priest, Russo, and the floor. Everybody looked at each other, the floor, and then to me. The look on Father McCartney's face told the whole story, but before he could say anything I shouted, "Oh no, get me to the hospital quick. My water just broke." I then grabbed Giacomo, and the two of us ran out of the room as fast as we could.

That afternoon, when I reported to Father Richards's office so I could pick up the receipts and money needed for the camera store, the priest said, "I talked to Father McCartney you know."

I replied nonchalantly, "It's so nice to hear that the priests get along so well. I'm sure you always have a lot to talk about."

With a warning tone the priest stated, "Be careful Owen, you know exactly what we talked about today." I shrugged, and said nothing, so Father added, "Owen please, he told me about the water balloon."

"Oh yeah, that. I saw it rolling on the floor and picked it up. Then Russo was standing there and bumped right into me. I have no idea how it got there."

Father Richards looked at me intensely, and asked, "So you did not throw the water balloons, you did not see anyone throw water balloons, and the water balloon that broke in your hands was not yours?"

I raised my left hand, and stated emphatically, "That is absolutely correct Father!"

The priest shook his head, and with a slight hint of a grin remarked, "It might be better if you raised the other hand." I quickly switched hands, and Father Richards continued, "Okay, Mr. Jagger is going to find out about the balloon, but it doesn't prove you threw any. So, you have two days JUG for possession of the water balloon, which you will serve the next time I need you to run the errand for me. Now get out of here before I change my mind."

CHAPTER 26

Father McCartney did the best he could to keep an eye on me, and anyone who was my lab partner, or those sitting near me. However, with this lab made up of mostly 4E students, a lot more pairs of eyes were necessary. When coupled with the fact that first period pool class afforded the opportunity slip out of the class early, the combination was fateful.

For instance, one time, the ingredients for making smoke bombs were procured, and the devices were produced. With cover from Bobby, Giacomo, and McClean, Kevin and I were able to leave the pool area undetected, and made our way to the fourth floor, where all the classrooms were for seniors. There were stairwells at either end of the hall, and Kevin was stationed at one end, and I was at the other end. Timing was going especially important in this escapade.

We synchronized our watches with the school clock, and at T-minus ten seconds started rolling the devices down the hall, and the hallway was completely filled with smoke at the moment the classroom doors were opened. Our pool mates had created a diversion that delayed dismissal of the class until we had returned.

The next week in homeroom, Father McCartney was late, and Bobby, John Alleva, and I discovered that the chem lab door was unlocked. We were not looking for anything in particular, when I opened a cabinet and pulled out some tape, remarking, "Hey, maybe we can use this scotch tape for something."

Bobby and Alleva came over to look at what I was holding, and Bobby said, "You idiot, that's not scotch tape. It's magnesium tape. They use it in some experiments to generate heat. Once lit it produces a flame."

Alleva saw the look on my face, and he said to Bobby, "Oh no, I don't like the look on that face."

I started to unroll the tape from the one I was holding, and then did the same from the other roll. Bobby asked, "Why don't you just take the whole roll?"

"Right, only an idiot wouldn't take the whole roll." I finished the unrolling, combining it all into one roll, and added, "You see, this way when anybody looks in the cabinet, it still looks like there's two rolls there."

A few days later, Bobby and I used the same game plan as the smoke bombs. We lined as much of the hallway as possible with the magnesium strips, and lit them up as the classroom doors opened. One of the teachers pulled the fire alarm, and we just barely made it back to the pool as everyone was evacuating.

During the investigation, Father McCartney reported that no magnesium strips were missing from the lab. Several students vouched for my presence, and even Mr. Gorman was convinced that everyone from the pool class had never left the pool.

It took a little over a week for the case to be closed, albeit unsolved. The next time I reported to Father Richards's office for JUG, the priest asked, "I can't find the slip with your name. I know it was from Mr. Watts. What did you do?"

"So, we were talking about vocations, and somebody said that maybe priests should be allowed to marry as a way to get more guys to become priests. There was more discussion back and forth, and all I said was that my father told me priests should be married."

"Wait, that's all you said?"

"Well, no. I told him my father said that it was a good idea, because that way they would know what hell was really like."

Father Richards bowed his head, and rubbed his rubbed his temple, saying, "Owen, was that really necessary, and that's when he gave you JUG?"

"No Father, it was a little while later. He asked us if we could think of something positive about being a priest. So, I raised my hand this time, ya know I didn't wanna just yell out an answer."

Father Richards interrupted with a question. "And he called on you? Well, he should have known that was a mistake. What did you say then?"

"Give 'im a break, Father, it's early in the semester, and he's a new teacher. But anyway, I said that it's a fact that priests have a very low divorce rate."

"So, he correctly gave you JUG for disrupting the class. Wait, is this the only thing you've done in his class?"

"I refuse to answer on the grounds it may incriminate me!"

"That's all I need to know. Will you please take it easy on Mr. Watts, we would really like to keep him. Now get out there and start walking." I waved, and as I reached the door Father Richards called to me, "That was a little dangerous with the magnesium strips Owen."

"I'll, um, uh yeah, you're right Father, that could of started a fire or somethin'. I see the floor up there is a little burnt. I'll keep my ears open for ya."

The priest smiled and said, "Almost had you there Loof." I gave the priest a wink and a wave while rushing away.

That week at school, I mostly succeeded in keeping a lid on my antics so as not to bring too much attention to myself because the fourth-floor hallway needed some repair, and the administration was concerned someone could have been injured. The only exception was Mr. Watts's Religion class.

On Monday, Mr. Watts asked, "What can we do before we can expect forgiveness for our sins?"

I yelled out, "Sin, we have to sin!"

An angry Mr. Watts shouted, "Shut up Loof, shut up!

On Tuesday, there was a discussion about people who wanted to convert to Catholicism. Mike Hoffman asked, "So Mister, can anyone of any religion become a Catholic?"

Mr. Watts replied, "Yes absolutely. The church accepts all denominations."

I shouted out, "That is so true. The church will accept 10s, 20s, 50s, and really enjoy accepting 100s"

Trying to stay in control, the teacher walked around his desk, but suddenly stopped. With a scowl, and through clenched teeth, he growled "I'm warning you Loof. I'm warning you. You can't disrupt my class like this."

On Wednesday, the discussion revolved around some differences between Protestant beliefs. Johnny Killbride asked, "What is the problem that the Baptists have with sex?"

Mr. Watts was only standing a few feet from me when I answered, "They believe it will lead to dancing!"

The teacher glared at me, and his face was red with rage. He started toward me saying, "That's the last straw Loof. I warned you."

I did not wait for the teacher to get near me, but jumped from my seat, and started toward the front of the room with Mr. Watts right behind me shouting, "Stop! Get back here Loof!"

I stopped right behind the teacher's desk in front of the blackboard. As the teacher neared, I put my hands in front of me, palms up, started laughing, and said, "Mister, come on relax."

Mr. Watts stopped, and yelled, "Are you laughing at me Loof? You think this is funny?"

Through my laughter, I answered, "Yeah, it is kinda funny, and you look hilarious right now."

The teacher was now beyond enraged, and balled his right hand into a fist. I saw what was coming, and when the telegraphed punch was thrown, moved deftly to my left. The fist whizzed past my head, and landed square on the blackboard hard. The whole class heard the crack as the punch hit home, and there was a collective groan as Mr. Watts grabbed his hand shrieking in pain. The bell sounded, and as everyone else started for the door, I went to the teacher's side, and asked, "Can I do anything to help?"

Mr. Watts sat down at his desk in great pain, and answered angrily, "Get out of here Loof! Just go!"

Two days later, Mr. Watts arrived at school with a cast on his right hand, and as I passed Father Richards's office on the way to homeroom, the priest stopped me in the hall. He asked, "Did you see Mr. Watts today, Owen?"

"I did Father, looks like he hurt his hand."

"He did Owen. He says he tripped in the teachers' lounge, and broke his wrist."

"Wow, that's a bummer Father."

"But I'm hearing rumors that something happened in religion class the other day. Can you shed any light on that for me Owen?"

"Gee Father, I don't remember anything happening."

"So, nothing happened between you and Mr. Watts that might have caused him to hurt himself?"

I shook my head saying, "Not that I can remember Father. He said how he hurt his hand, maybe we should believe him. He is a religion teacher, right?"

The Priest put his hands on his hips and looked at me intensely saying, "Get to class you! Go!"

CHAPTER 27

The football season started well enough, but after a nice win against another Jesuit school, Xavier High School, there were two lopsided losses to Herricks and Monsignor Farrell. Then there was a third straight setback by the score of 20-13 to Fordham Prep. With key players like Tim Delaney, Nick Sama, and Richie Walters sidelined, the Eagles just did not have the running game or defense to handle Herricks, nor the size and strength to cope with Farrell. What the team had all season, though, was heart and spirit. They never quit on the field, and with the Blue Eagle leading the way, spirits were always high. The Eagle did his job both on the sidelines during the games, and even more importantly at the rallies in school before the games.

Whether the Eagle was flying around the gym, performing with the female cheerleaders while wearing one of their outfits, or interviewing players and coaches, people were always fired up for the team. Attendance at the games was at an all-time high, which contributed to the team's never-say die attitude. However, all the rallies and team preparation were pointing to the most important game of the season. Thanksgiving Day would be the fiftieth confrontation with archrival, St. Johns Prep. It really did not matter if the team was winless going into the St. Johns game, a win in that game made the season a success.

On the day before Thanksgiving, I had to leave my last period class early so that I could change into the Eagle costume for the pep rally. Last period was Father Flaubert's French class, and I raised my hand to ask if I could be excused. The priest acknowledged me by saying, "Ah, Monsieur Loof. Vous avez une question?"

"Father I gotta go to…."

The priest put up his hand, and interrupted, "Ah, Monsieur Loof, en Francias, s'il vous plait!"

I threw my hands up in protest saying, "Oh come on, Father, really?"

With his arms outstretched, palms up, and with a nod of his head, Father Flaubert replied, "Oui Monsieur, oui!"

I stood there thinking, and said haltingly, "Euh, puis-je, euh etre excuse, euh, parce que…"

Then I paused trying to find the right words, and Jack Fredreck pulled me down, and whispered, "Tell 'im, J'ai une fille chaude attendant le sexe."

I repeated the phrase well enough to get the point across. The half of the class that was advanced enough in the language went hysterical and, while Father Flaubert's face went slightly red, he smiled, and said, "Eh bien, eh bien, je veux certainement pas faire obstacle a l'mour. Allez, monsieur, allez!"

I hurried down to the locker room, and became the Blue Eagle. I then flew upstairs, and took my position on the stage behind the curtain. When the gym was filled, the school song was played, and then the curtain opened. The Eagle jumped off the stage, making several passes around the gym as the girls on stage led the crowd in the usual rousing cheers. Father Hamilton appeared on the stage, and started a string of speeches. The coaches received a loud round of applause for their words of inspiration. Then some of the players like Charlie Russo, Tim Delaney, and Rich Walters really got the gym rocking with their predictions for the game.

There was a surprise guest, who was well known to almost everyone in the gym. It was John Dougherty who was one of the best athletes ever to attend Prep. After graduating, he was a two-sport star at Harvard. From there he played minor league baseball in the Boston Red Sox organization, before switching to football, and was now a defensive back with the New York Jets. He reminded the players and students that he had played in three of these Thanksgiving classics, winning two of them. But he remembers each one as the most important of his sports memories, and emphasized that would always be the case.

Then, as he was nearing the end of his speech, his tempo was increasing, along with the loudness and excitement of his voice. The last words of the speech are always remembered by everyone who was present that day: "Go out there tomorrow and knock their jocks off!" Then he jumped off the stage and waded into the fired-up crowd.

As all that was going on, Alex Avitabile grabbed me and said, "Quick take off the costume and change into this trench coat and fedora."

"Whoa, wait! What's going on?"

"Look just be quick. We're gonna line up the team behind you on the stage. You are the St. John's coach, and all you gotta do is introduce your team. Let us know when you're ready. Just hurry up!"

I ran into the wings, where Kevin and Bobby were waiting to help me in the transformation. I was not happy, and said to my friends, "They never told me I had to do this. I have no idea what I'm supposed do!"

Suddenly, we heard the introduction for the St. John's coach, and the chorus of boos and cat calls that ensued. Bobby handed me a clipboard and a pen saying, "You're on pal! Knock 'em dead!"

I sauntered to the middle of the stage, and took my position in front of the football team. I bowed to the team, then turned and waved to the crowd, soaking up all the negativity being thrown my way.

I began the address by saying, "I want to thank Father Hamilton and your coaches for letting my team participate in this event." I went on to expound on the great tradition of the game, and what it represented to both outstanding learning institutions. Then I stated, "My hope is for a good, clean, hard-fought game that will unfortunately break the hearts of the Brooklyn Prep faithful because my team is primed for victory." The noisy boos from the crowd were deafening, and Russo, along with Delaney, took a few menacing steps forward only to be restrained.

Holding up my hands to quiet the crowd, and after glancing over my shoulder at the subdued players, I announced, "Let me now introduce my team, the St. John's Prep Redmen, who will undoubtedly win the game tomorrow." The boos got even louder, and the entire football team was clearly agitated.

"First is our record-setting wide receiver, at 6 foot 5, and one hundred and fifteen pounds, Chuck Wagon!" Some little freshman ran across the floor in front of the stage.

"Next is our outstanding left tackle, at 5 foot 2 and five hundred and twenty-five pounds, Jim Beam!"

There were nine more players to introduce, and the next five went smoothly with the likes of Bud Wiser, Johnny Walker, and Al Kaholic. The last four got progressively more difficult, and I really started reaching. For my eighth and ninth players I used the names Cal Seeum and Willie Maykit. When I got to number ten, I was thinking of a name at the same time announcing, "Our star running back at 4 foot eleven two hundred and sixty pounds, the human bowling ball…" I paused to think and blurted out, "Ben Derhover!"

I got a signal from the wings that I had to hurry, so without hesitation I started, "And last but not least, our captain and starting quarterback at 7 feet tall, and six hundred pounds…" My mind was a blank. I could not think of anything, and then a name popped up. I thought, no, I can't use that, but it was all I had, and the kid was running to his spot. So, I yelled out as loud as I could, "DICK HERTZ!"

There was laughter, applause, raised fists, and chants of "Knock Their Jocks Off! Knock Their Jocks Off!" I looked over to the wings, and Father Richards was standing there, holding, and shaking his head. Russo, Delaney, and Walters picked me up, and ran off the stage into the noisy rowdy crowd.

The bell sounded, ending the rally and the school day. The gym was emptying out, but with the excitement lingering, I had to practically fight my way back to the stage to retrieve the Eagle costume. When I got there, Bobby and Kevin had the costume all packed up, and ready for me to take back to the locker room. John Doughery was standing with Father Richards, and while I wanted to meet the famous Prep alum, I was really trying to avoid the priest. However, Father Richards saw me, and called all three of us over. I said, "I know Father, sorry, it wasn't planned, I mean it. I had nothin' left, and it just popped out. See ya for JUG on Monday."

The priest replied with a smile, "Unless you do something else, there's no JUG on Monday. I'd like you all to meet Mr. Doughery."

Everybody shook hands, and we talked for a few minutes. We were a little in awe of the star athlete, but he really made us feel comfortable, especially mentioning our shared connection of attending Brooklyn Prep. The conversation ended with Doughery singling me out for congratulations. "That was a great performance kid, and I don't know whose line they'll remember more. And I sure wish we had a Blue Eagle like you when I was playing here. See you at the game tomorrow!"

When I left the stage with Bobby and Kevin, I spied Jack Fredreck about to exit the gym and called out to him, "Jack, hey Jack! Wait up, man!"

Fredreck turned around, and asked, "Yeah Owney, what's up?"

"What did you tell me to say to Father Flaubert, and what did he say?"

My friend laughed, answering, "You told him you had a hot girl waiting for sex. And he said he didn't want to stand in the way of love."

CHAPTER 28

I arrived at school the next day too late to take the team bus to the game. So, I donned the Eagle costume, and made the forty-minute trip to the field on public transportation. The bus driver let me on the bus for free, and only one or two people took notice. It was as if a blue eagle riding the bus was not the least bit unusual.

The Blue Eagle reached the field in plenty of time, and was front and center as the two teams were introduced. This was important because the game was being televised on WPIX-TV. The two teams lined up for the opening kickoff, and finally the whistle blew unleashing the pent-up emotion that had been building in the players, the fans, and the Blue Eagle.

The Eagle kept the adrenalin pumping by exhorting the players on the bench and the fans in the stands. He rarely sat down or took a break. This was a major factor in the titanic defensive struggle that took shape between the two powerful archrivals. The ball was exchanged from side to side until there was one minute and fifty-six seconds left in the first half, when Charlie Russo, behind the "big butt" offensive line, pushed the ball over the goal line for a touchdown. The defenses continued to dominate in the second half, and the game ended with Brooklyn Prep victorious by a score of 6-0.

At the final whistle, the BP side of the field exploded in joy, and fans swarmed out of the stands to join the celebration with the players. The Blue Eagle was right in the middle of the revelry, and the TV reporter corralled him for a comment about the game. The Eagle proudly declared, "Winning the 50th edition of this classic is even more special than any other defeat of our rival. No one here today will ever forget it, and all our Alumni, all our students, and especially the seniors, are rejoicing in today's victory. It was a truly memorable milestone for the school."

The bus ride back to the school was a raucous affair, and the celebration continued in the gym with all the families. The team party would have to be delayed because there were Thanksgiving dinners to attend. After almost two hours, most of the players and their families had departed, leaving ten or twelve guys who were on their own traveling home. I was standing with Kevin Kane, Kevin O'Rourke, Sam Vanacort, and Louie Stathis, and the conversation turned to taking public transportation generally, and today in particular.

There were different opinions on how dangerous the routes each of us had to take to reach our destinations safely. I announced, "Stop it all a ya! The neighborhoods I gotta go through are worse than any of you guys. But I'm prepared today. My friend gave me this." I reached in my pocket, and pulled out a large hunting knife encased in rawhide sheath.

Stathis grabbed the covered knife, and removed the blade from its sleeve. Everybody was oohing and ahhing, and Stathis called out to the others, who all gathered around. The knife was passed from one to another, as they all wanted to hold the cold steel. I am not sure how it happened, or who threw the knife first, but the blade was suddenly flying through the air, landing in the wooden men's bathroom door that had only recently been installed. A great time was being had by all, as everyone was taking turns throwing the knife, with some guys making multiple flings.

At first, I was nervous about the whole thing, but decided it was no big deal, and just wanted to have a go at the door. I took the knife from Mike Hoffman, and took aim sizing up the target. To the right of the bathroom door, there was a pair of large metal doors that led to a stairwell. In between the bathroom door, and the metal doors, there was a two-inch sliver of marble. I was ready, and drew my hand back. Then I brought it forward in one swift motion, sending the knife hurling toward its mark.

It looked and felt good as the knife left my hand, but as it neared the door, everybody could tell something was a little off. We were all using our bodies, trying to move the blade closer to its intended destination. But alas, the knife missed the wooden bathroom door, and it also missed the large metal doors. It did, however, hit the two-inch sliver of marble.

Only I could make a shot like that, but there was no time for celebration or teasing laughter. The knife hit the marble, and bounced to the right, landing right in front of the stairwell doors. Just as it hit the floor, a black-robed scholastic opened the door. Guys were scattering in all directions, but I ran directly to the knife on the floor. I couldn't leave it there because it was not my knife. O'Rourke and Kane had not run away, and after I retrieved the knife, joined them in attempting to back away slowly.

None of us had ever seen the teacher, and we found out later that he was not yet teaching, but observing as part of his training. Just as we reached the door, the scholastic caught up, and told us to stop. Instead of running out the door, we obeyed, and I said, "Hey Mister, Happy Thanksgiving! You have a great day now!"

"Not so fast you three. Stay right there." Then he pointed to Kevin Kane, and asked," What's your name?" The scholastic wrote it down, and the process was repeated with Kevin O'Rourke.

Then the scholastic turned to me, and said, while already writing, "I know you, Loof!"

CHAPTER 29

On Monday, I met Bobby in home room, and told him what had happened after the game. Then I asked, "Have you seen Kane yet?" Bobby replied in the negative, and by the time we got to the pool I said, "Wonderful, Kane's not gonna show up today."

When I arrived at religion second period, I discovered that Kevin O'Rourke was not in school either. Bobby asked, "What's the big deal?"

"Well, it would be good if we talked before going to Richards, so we could get our stories straight. We certainly don't want to tell three different lies. I guess I'll figure somethin' out."

Bobby gave me a pat on the back saying, "If anybody can do it, you can!"

Sure enough, during chemistry class the note came from Father Richards. Most of the class knew what was going on, and offered their silent support. I got the impression that even Father McCartney knew the story when he said, "Good luck Owen, you know what to do."

I stopped just outside Father Richards's office, put my hands on my hips, closed my eyes, and tilted my head back. I stayed in that position for a few seconds, then opened my eyes, shook out my whole body, and with a big smile on my face, entered the lion's den saying, "Mornin' Father, hope you had a great Thanksgiving!"

"Thank you, Owen, and I hope you and your family had a blessed Thanksgiving. But let's get down to business."

"Sure, Father! What can I help you with? Am I going the camera store today?"

"Owen don't make this difficult. You know you are here because of the knife incident."

I gave the priest a surprised look, and asked, "Knife incident, what knife incident?"

Father Richards pointed a clearly perturbed finger at me, and said, "Look, do not try to play it this way. Mr. Smythe saw the knife, and the damage to the bathroom door speaks for itself."

I threw up my hands saying, "Okay, you got me Father. It was my knife, and I'm the only one who threw it in the door. I can't believe I missed so badly on that last throw."

"So, it was just you, Kane, and O'Rourke there?"

I looked puzzled again and said, "Who? I didn't see anybody else."

Father Richards shook his head saying, "Owen, Owen, I have their names!"

"Oh yeah, right Father, Kane and O'Rourke. No, ya see Father they were there just walkin' out, and stopped to say so long. I think that's why I missed that last throw so bad. They distracted me"

"All right, enough of this Owen. Go back to class, and I will let you know what the punishment will be."

"Okay Father, thanks and keep me posted." Then I rushed out of the office before the priest could say anything else.

The next day, Kane and O'Rourke returned to school, and the three of us were summoned to Father Richards's office. We were informed that the punishment for the indiscretion would be ten days JUG, plus payment for the repair of the door. When the priest finished handing down the sentence, I protested, "Father I don't think that's fair to these two guys. They were just passing through at the wrong time, and neither one threw the knife."

"Don't argue with me about this Owen. That is my decision, and it's final. So, stop your lawyering, and get out of here. You are all to report to Mrs. Joplin at the front desk tomorrow to start your JUG."

I stood there staring at Father Richards, the other two each hooked an arm, and practically dragged their mouthpiece toward the door. As we reached the office door, I muttered rather loudly, "It's just not fair!"

The next day I was leaving last period with Kevin and Bobby, and I said, "I can't figure out why we gotta go to the front desk for JUG."

Kevin just shrugged saying, "I guess we'll find out in a few minutes."

Bobby put his arm on my shoulder, and said, "He told everybody how good you were in trying to get them out of it."

"Well, I wasn't good enough, but I had to try."

Bobby added, "'Cause that's who you are Owney. That's who you are! Anyway, I gotta get to practice. They must have somethin' special for you guys. See you tomorrow."

Kevin O'Rourke was waiting at the front desk with Mrs. Joplin when I arrived with Kane. She came around the desk and said, "Good, you're all here, so come with me, and I will show you what you will be doing."

She led us down the hall, and stopped at an office door. When the door was opened, the room had a desk and three chairs. On the desk were boxes filled with envelopes and letters. She explained that there were two different letters that had to be enclosed in each envelope, and an address label was to be affixed to each envelope. One of the letters was the school newsletter detailing events that would be taking place during the second semester. The other was the School President's holiday message and prayer. Before leaving, Mrs. Joplin said, "You people can set up any system you want to get the job done, as long as it's done correctly. I will be in to check on you periodically. I don't know what you boys did to get ten days JUG, but thank you for helping out."

After the woman closed the door behind her, we divided up the responsibilities, and through trial and error, quickly worked out a way to make the job easier. Then for an hour a day for the next ten days, we stuck to the system, and did the job. On the tenth day of JUG, the clock was ticking toward the end of our required time. I stopped what I was doing, which disrupted the well-oiled envelope stuffing machine, and Kane asked, "What are you doin'? Why ya stoppin'?"

"Well look around, we're not gonna finish all this today. We probably need one more day to finish the job."

"O'Rourke asked, "So, what'd we do?"

I smiled broadly, and gave my friends a wink, replying, "Come on guys, what'd ya think we're gonna do?"

As we passed the receptionist, we called out in unison, "See you tomorrow Mrs. Joplin!" She rose from her chair, and watched us walk down the hall looking very confused.

The next day we reported to Father Richards's office for JUG. When we walked in together, the priest looked up from his desk puzzled, and said questioningly, "Wait, your ten days was up yesterday. What are you doing here?" Then he shuffled through the JUG slips on his desk, and found two that answered his inquiry to some degree. He asked, "Loof and Kane fighting in English class?"

O'Rourke was standing between us, I glanced over at Kane, and said adamantly, "Yeah, well he started it Father!"

Kane raised his voice, and said, "You're crazy! You hit me first!"

We began pawing at each other over O'Rourke, and Father Richards shouted, "Stop it both of you! Stop it right now!"

The fighters stopped trying to have at each other, exchanged dirty looks, and when we were all facing Father Richards, Kane said, "He's a nut job Father! You can see he started it!"

The priest yelled, "I don't care who started it! It's finished now!" In the confusion, he dropped the JUG slips. He tried to find the other slip, and finally gave up saying to O'Rourke, "And what are you here for?"

"I fell asleep twice in math, Father."

Father Richards gave him a quizzical look asking, "Twice O'Rourke?"

"So ya see Father, the first time I was snoring kinda loud, and Mr. Lennon woke me up. But the second time, I fell completely outa my seat. That's when he gave me the JUG."

An angry Father Richards said, "Okay, you all deserve it! Go to RM. 103, Mr. Quinn has JUG duty today."

I said matter-of-factly, "Um, no Father. We're gonna go to Mrs. Joplin again."

"She did not say anything to me about needing people today."

In a reassuring manner I told the priest, "Trust me Father, she needs us today."

Farther Richards looked askance at us, picked up his phone, and dialed Mrs. Joplin. After a brief conversation he said, "Okay, I'll send them right over."

THE BEST DRESSED MAN IN ROCKAWAY

We were already walking toward the door, and before the priest could say anything, I remarked, "See Father? I told ya she needed us."

"Yes, she does, now hurry up and get over there." We all waved, and said thank you before heading out the door. We were halfway down the hall when we heard Father Richards's voice from inside his office, "Wait you idiots! I know what you did! Get back here!" The idiots took off running and the priest had to go back to his desk to answer a ringing phone.

When we arrived at the reception desk, like the proper gentlemen we were, we greeted Mrs. Joplin warmly. She looked at her three workers intently, and asked, "I thought you boys were finished with your JUG yesterday?"

I answered, "Well, you really do need us today, and it just so happened we all got JUG again." All three of us gave the receptionist a wink and broad smiles, and started toward our office. I turned my head saying, "The Lord works in mysterious ways, Mrs. Joplin, mysterious ways."

CHAPTER 30

The following Monday was the last day of classes before finals, and the Christmas break. Pool class was first period, and the week before, Bobby had an idea to get Santa hats and Christmas-themed G-strings. Then, while guys kept Mr. Gorman busy, some of us would get costumed up, run out one pool door, and down the hall to the other door. Between Kevin, Bobby, and me, we had scrounged up enough money to outfit twelve guys, and that morning everything was ready to go.

The plan went into effect, and with Mr. Gorman suitably distracted, the twelve scantily clad elves made their exit, and were off running and skipping their way down the hall. Everything was going well, and the air was filled with Christmas cheer as the entrance door at the other end of the hall opened, and the elves disappeared inside. Kevin, Giacomo, and I were the last three in line with the Italian student lagging well behind the two of us.

Kevin went in, and when I followed closely, Bobby slammed the door shut, and locked it. I looked at my friend with surprise, and asked, "What'd ya doin' man?"

"Remember, we said the last one in line we lock out."

"No, I don't remember that!"

"Well, that's the deal. I feel bad for the guy, but that's the breaks."

Then we heard Giacomo pounding on the door saying,

"A couple of people saw us, and there's a teacher coming. Let me in, please!"

I opened the door, and pulled Giacomo inside quickly. Then I said, "Hurry up and get to the locker room with the rest of the guys."

"But what are you going to do!

"Don't worry, just go!"

Giacomo was barely out of sight when the door opened, and Mr. Wood the school registrar appeared, and asked loudly, "What's with that get up, and was that you out there?"

"Now what would I be doin' out in the hall Mr. Wood?"

"Look, not only did I see you, but Mrs. Warwick saw you too. Father Richards' going to hear about this."

At that moment, I heard Mr. Gorman's voice behind me shouting, "Loof, what are you doing!" Then he said to Mr. Wood, "I'll take care of this one Hank!"

"Father Richards still should know, Sam."

"Oh, he will! Now go change Loof, and wait in my office!"

About an hour after dismissal that afternoon, I was passing Father Richards' office, and the priest was coming down the stairs directly opposite his office, and we bumped into each other. After we exchanged an excuse me, the cleric said, "Since I have you here Owen, come into my office for a minute please."

When we walked into the office, Father Richards went behind his desk, and I slumped down in the chair that was always right in front of the desk. Before he sat down, the priest said, "Make yourself at home. But then again you're here enough for it to be partly your office."

"Sorry Father, I'm just kinda tired, and I just wanna get home and start studying for the finals."

"I really wish I could believe that Owen. But I have some questions about this morning's escapade."

"Okay Father, shoot. But not literally of course, and you know I'll tell you the truth."

"Now that I absolutely know I can't believe, but I'll ask the questions anyway. Now you say you were the only one out in the hallway half naked?"

"That's right Father."

"Owen, Mr. Wood and Mrs. Warwick both say they saw more than one person."

"Well, I don't know how that could be because I was the only one out there, and it was all my idea."

"So, you are going to stick with contradicting the two adults?"

I looked right at the priest saying, "I don't know what they thought they saw, but I'm tellin' you the truth, I was the only one out there."

The clergyman shook his head, and looked at me saying, "All right Owen, if that's how you want it go. Mr. Gorman has informed me that you are going to be helping him over the Christmas break clean up around the pool and the gym, and I agree that is punishment enough. But you know you do not have to do it alone?"

I rose from my seat abruptly, and throwing up my hands said, "Stop it Father, will ya! Yes, I do, okay! If that's all, I'm goin'. All right?"

"Yes Owen, you can go."

I reached across the desk, shook hands with Father Richards, and after saying thank you, I added, "See ya tomorra' Father." Before I turned to leave the priest said, "You are a piece of work Owen Loof!"

CHAPTER 31

The first homeroom after the break, I walked in, and sat down in a huff with Bobby, John Alleva, and Jack Fredreck. Bobby said to Alleva, "Is it that time of the month already?"

Alleva looked at me asking, "Okay Owney, what's goin' on?"

"Did you guys get your grades?"

After they all nodded their affirmative responses, Fredreck said to me, "So you must've got yours, and that's what wrong. How many did ya fail?"

"I didn't fail anything."

My friends gave me funny looks, and Bobby asked, "So what's the problem?"

"Well, if you look closely, there's a rank in class number buried in the corner. Guess what my number is?"

Bobby glanced at the other two guys, and then back to me answering, "I dunno 180!"

I laughed heartily, and said, "You're really funny, ya know. No, I was 217 out of 218 which is so annoying."

Alleva leaned closer to me inquiring, "Annoying? I don't get it. What's annoying about it?"

This time it was Bobby's turn to laugh, and he said, "Wait for it, wait for it! Go 'head Owney you tell 'em."

"Somebody beat me out for being last in the class. And it's all because I'm doin' so good in history." My three friends started laughing, and playfully slapping me around, then I said indignantly, "It's not funny. A lot of famous generals finished last in their class at West Point, it's almost an honor, and they get money too. I'm gonna find out who's 218 though, he's gotta be in this class."

The bell sounded, and everybody began drifting out the door, but Bobby and Kevin were waiting for me to catch up with them. When I did, I stopped suddenly, put up my hands and exclaimed, "Oh wait, I just remembered! We gotta have a meeting. I got an idea to run by you guys after school."

Bobby said, "Ya know I got practice, right?"

"Yeah, yeah, I know, but it won't take long, I promise. I need help with it." The three friends quickly arranged the place to meet, then walked down the hall on their way to the gym with Giacomo right behind.

Fifteen minutes after last period, I entered the cafeteria, and my assistants were waiting, including Giacomo. When I reached the table, I asked, "Hey Mo, what's up? Isn't the car waiting?"

"I told them I had something to do, and they're waiting. I heard you needed help with something, so I'm here."

"Okay cool, I can use all the help I can get."

Bobby said, "Come on, I don't have much time. What's this big idea?"

"I know, I know, well I was at my uncle Red's bar…"

Kevin broke in saying, "Uh oh, there's gonna be money involved here."

"That's right my good man, and it involves the NFL/AFL Championship game that some people are calling the Super Bowl." I went on to explain that my uncle made this big chart that was divided into one hundred little squares, and each box was numbered. Then people would buy one of the boxes. As I was talking, I pulled out a facsimile to use as an example.

Bobby asked, "How much does a box cost, and what do you get for buying a box?"

"I'm gettin' t'dat, if you'll shut up." I continued by showing them that the name of one team is written on the top of the chart, and the other team is written on the side of the chart.

I could see they were getting impatient, and I said excitedly, "Now for the important part. You take the numbers, 0 thru 9, pick them randomly, and you place them on top of the boxes across the top of the chart. Then you repeat the process for the boxes down the side."

When I finished writing in the numbers, I waited while my team analyzed the paper in front of them. Giacomo responded first by saying, "I think I got it. Each numbered box corresponds to a number on top and a number on the side."

"Ding, ding, ding, give that man a cigar! So, Bobby, if you have box 27, what two numbers would that give you?"

After examining the chart, Bobby answered, "3 for the Packers, and 0 for the Raiders." I congratulated my friend, and then let Giacomo and Kevin go through the exercise. When that was finished, Giacomo asked, "So what do those numbers represent?"

"They represent the score at a certain point in the game. Look, let's say at the end of the first quarter the Packers are winning 3-0. Bobby wins money. Before you ask, in a two-digit number, it's the second number that counts. So, if the score is 33-10 Packers Bobby wins. Got it?"

After the three students indicated they fully understood the concept, I went on to explain that each box would cost ten dollars meaning the chart would be worth one thousand dollars. We would take two hundred off the top, and distribute the remaining eight hundred as follows: first quarter and third quarter/$100, halftime/$200, and final Score/$400.

The next day, I had the chart all ready, and set up for business in the gym at lunch. In the first twenty minutes thirty-five boxes were sold, and enough people had expressed interest that the brain trust was confident that they would have no trouble quickly selling out. Just before the period ended, and as the workers were closing up for the day, they were engrossed in counting the money and discussing the possibility of a second chart. Then they heard the imposing voice of Father Richards. "Okay, what's going on here?" Before any of the students could say anything, the bell sounded the end of lunch, and the priest said, "Loof, you gather up all this paraphernalia, and come with me to my office. You other three go to class."

As I walked with Father Richards, I asked, "Hey Father, how come I'm the only one goin' to the office?"

"Because I know whatever is going on, it was all your idea."

When I met with my three compatriots later, they peppered me with questions. "All right, calm down I'll tell ya everything." Then I proceeded to lay out the plan that I created with Farther Richards.

"Okay it's gonna be a fundraiser for the school. We're gonna make five charts, one from each of us, and the one for the school, which we have almost half sold already. So, when it's all over, that's a thousand dollars for the school."

Kevin asked, "Anything for us?"

"I'm still in negotiation on that point. So, you guys know what to do and how it works. Go home, get your charts together, and start sellin' boxes."

By the following Thursday which was three days before the game we actually had six completely filled and paid for charts. Bedside the one I had put in The Circle, I also placed one in Flynn's. The next day Giacomo surprised us by bringing in the money for another chart. I asked, "What's this? Why didn't you tell us you were doing another one?"

"Because I didn't know, you see my father was talking to my grandfather, and when this whole thing came up in the conversation, my grandfather made a phone call. Then last night, these two guys showed up at my house with a completely filled-out chart, and the money."

"Wow, that's cool! That's great, right guys? We'll have to thank your grandpa!"

Bobby and Kevin looked at me and Giacomo, then to each other, and paused before replying with shrugs and raised eyebrows, "Yeah sure. Great.

Father Richards was happy with the fact that there would be an extra $400 for the school because of the two extra charts. In fact, he was so pleased that when we gathered in his office before leaving for the weekend to hand in Giacomo's money, he said, "Thank you all for doing such a good job. You know Owen, the fourteen hundred dollars we made this time is more than you made with Father Knox and the Kentucky Derby."

"You are very welcome Farther, anything we can do to help the school."

"You know what Owen? Twelve hundred would be a nice amount also." The priest then handed each of us a fifty-dollar bill.

We all thanked our benefactor, then there were handshakes, and best wishes for the weekend. When we were out of the office, I held up my fifty saying, "The Circle on Sunday! First two rounds are on me."

On Monday, the morning after the game, which ended with the Green Bay Packers defending their championship in a 33-14 victory that was a surprise to no one, I bounded into the room and looked around quickly, asking out loud, "Anybody see McClean?"

There was shaking heads or just silence, and then Jim Egan who was standing with Kevin and Bobby asked, "What'd he do now?"

"No, he didn't do anything. Somethin' good happened." Then I walked over and got the school's box chart, and said, "He had the 3 for the Packers and the 4 for the Raiders. He won the $400!"

Kevin piped up, "Yeah damn it, if not for that touchdown pass to Miller with nine minutes to go, I woulda won the money. I had 7 for the Raiders."

I tapped him on the arm, and said, "Woulda, shoulda, coulda. Famous last words of the gambler, but that's the thrill. I'm just glad he won, and I can't wait to tell 'em."

When homeroom ended, Walter McClean was still not in attendance. He was only in two other classes with me, and when he was not in Mr. O'Donnell's Speech class sixth period, it was clear that he had not been in school all day. After last period, I met Kevin and Bobby, and said, "I'm gonna go over to Father Richards's office to check the JUG list to make sure someone from 4E is there."

Bobby asked me, "What'd doin' that for?"

"You tell 'im, Kev."

"Ya see Bobby, we got a streak going. So far this year someone from 4E has been in JUG every day, and we wanna see if we can keep it goin' all the way to the end of the year."

I pumped my fist, and said loudly, "We got this guys! We can do it!"

I was standing outside Father Richards's office checking the names, when Walter McClean walked out the door. He was rubbing his eyes, and looked like he just got out of bed. McClean did not see me, and started up the stairway right outside the office. I hurried over, and called after him, "Walt, hey Walt! Wait up!"

McClean stopped, and looked down the stairs asking, "Owney, how ya doin'"

I caught up with him, and as we continued up the steps, asked, "Hey man, where ya been all day?"

"Oh man, it was a long weekend. I had to tend bar both Saturday and Sunday night. You know Saturday night is my regular night, and I was only supposed to work Sunday afternoon, but the regular guy didn't come in, and I had to stay. I didn't close up till four this morning, and I came right here."

"But nobody saw you all day. What'd ya doin' comin' outa Richards' now?"

"If ya gimme a chance I'll tell ya. So, I come into school, and Richards sees me. He tells me I look terrible and wanted to know what happened. When I tell 'im the story, he brings me in the office and tells me to go to sleep. And I just woke up."

"Wow, that's a cool thing to do. So, did you watch the game?"

"It was on, but it was really busy. I didn't get to see much. I do know the Packers won."

"Yeah, they won 33-14."

McClean stood in silence for a few seconds, and then blurted out, "Oh shit! those are my numbers! I won, didn't I? How much was it again?"

"Four hundred dollars, man!"

"Yes, yes, yes! Oh man that's great! Thanks, Owney, I really need that money!"

"And I'm glad you won!"

The rest of the week was mostly uneventful. I was banned from the Chemistry lab for causing a small explosion and fire. Then in French class Father Flaubert showed a slide with a mother, a father, and two children. When the next slide was shown, the children were not in the picture. Father Flaubert asked, "Ou sont les enfants?" (Where are the children?)

Jack Fredreck was sitting behind me, tapped me on the shoulder, and whispered an answer. I quickly raised my hand, and probably without thinking, the priest acknowledged me. I stood and announced, "Ils sont morts."

Most of the class started laughing, and I had no idea why, because I did not know what I had said.

Father Flaubert raised both his hands to try and stop the laughter, and said, "Attendez, attendez, c'est un peu morbide, mais c'est une bonne reponse. Ils pourraient etre morts!

When I sat down, I turned to Fredreck and asked, "Wha'd I say?"

"You told him the kids were dead!"

Even though the priest had said the children being dead was a correct answer, although a little morbid, he did not call on me to give a response for the rest of the year.

A few days later, Father McCartney entered homeroom to find me sitting alone in the classroom. He asked, "Okay, where is everybody?"

I shrugged, and replied, "I don't know Father, haven't seen anybody."

The priest smiled, nodded his head, and sat down at his desk. He kept watching me while checking his watch.

Finally, he stood up and said, "Owen, what's going on, you want me to mark everyone absent?"

"Father, I dunno what to tell ya. If that's what you gotta do, I guess."

Obviously a little flustered, Father McCartney went to the door of the chemistry Lab, and found it was locked. He glanced over his shoulder at me, and used his key to open the door. Then, he went into the lab and looked around the place thoroughly. When he was satisfied that there was no one hiding, he walked back through the lab. As he got to the door, the priest was able to see into the classroom, and all the 4E students were in their seats, except for me. Father McCartney entered the room shaking his head and smiling, then asked, "Now Owen's missing?"

Everybody looked, around, and Kevin answered, "Gee Father, we haven't seen Owney."

Father McCartney went up to the window, and opened it to check for me. Then he exited the classroom, and walked around the hall checking the two stairwells. When he came back, there was no one else in the room but me, and I said, "I guess you're gonna have to mark them absent Father."

"You know, you guys are going to drive me out of the priesthood!"

When the bell sounded ending the period, I rose from my seat, helped the priest gather up his belongings, and with my hand on the teacher's shoulder said, "Come on Father, I'll walk you out."

As we reached the door, Father McCartney said, "Wait, the lab door!"

"Don't worry Father I'll get it." Just before closing the door, I gave the okay sign to the guys in the lab.

CHAPTER 32

On the last Monday in January, Father McCartney announced that he would not be in homeroom the next day due to a doctor's appointment, and that Mr. Jagger would be covering for him. He would however be back in school by third period for Chemistry. During the day, I was able to talk to every member of 4E, and outline a plan for the morning. I gave everyone the option of participating, and asked if they choose not to, would they please wait five minutes before entering the classroom. Of the twenty-seven classmates, two said they were not going to be in school, and three opted out of the plan. It was also made clear to the twenty-two people still in that it was required to be present twenty minutes before the bell, and if running late, they should also adhere to the waiting period.

The next morning, Mr. Jagger arrived at the Chemistry room five minutes before the start of class. He was surprised to find there were no students waiting, and the door was closed and locked. He was able to get a glimpse inside room by looking through the small window in the door. From what he could see, there was no one in the room. Then, as planned, Sam Vanacort approached and asked if Father McCartney would be out for the entire day. The conversation lasted less than a minute, and when Mr. Jagger opened the door and entered the room, he saw twenty 4E students sitting in their seats wearing nothing but their underwear.

We all rose from our seats, and in one voice exclaimed, "Good Morning Mr. Jagger."

The teacher was not amused, and hollered, "This is not funny! Sit down you idiots! Father Richards is going to hear about this." At that moment, Jim Egan entered the room, and Mr. Jagger shouted at him, "Eagan, I want you to go and tell Father Richards, I need him up here right away!" Eagan hesitated, looked over at me, and with a wave of my hand, I indicated it was all right.

It took a little less than ten minutes for Eagan to return with Father Richards, and when the priest saw what he was there for, he just hung his head, shaking it with his hand on his forehead. A still upset Mr. Jagger howled, "Do you believe this Father!"

The cleric looked at the teacher, then to the twenty underwear clad students, and remarked, "To be honest Mr. Jagger, nothing surprises me with this bunch, but even they might have gone too far this time."

Mr. Jagger then started pointing at me saying to Father Richards, "You know this was Loof. It was all his idea!"

"I don't think we can blame this all on Loof." Then turning his attention to the students, the priest announced, "This is the first time since I've overseen discipline at any school that I have given JUG to an entire class. You will all report here for JUG this afternoon. And make sure you have your clothes on. Now get dressed!"

As Mr. Jagger walked Father Richards to the door, Jim Eagan sat down in his regular seat next to me and Jack Fredreck, obviously annoyed. I patted him on the shoulder saying, "It's okay man, you had to go get Richards. You had no choice."

"I know that Owney. That's not it."

"Then what?"

"If damn train wasn't late, I woulda been here. I really wanted to be here. Now you guys all got JUG, and I feel left out."

That afternoon, all the participants in the underwear caper were seated in the chem room, fully clothed, waiting for Father Richards. Everyone looked up when Jim Eagan entered the room. Before he sat down, I asked, "What'd ya doin' here? You don't have JUG."

"Yes, I do, I didn't turn in a Physics paper that was due today, and Father Watson had said if anybody didn't turn it in, they would get JUG."

Giacomo interjected, "Wait a minute, I was having a problem finishing one of the experiments, you took out your finished paper, and helped me out. I saw your paper."

Before Eagan could say anything, I gave him a playful slap on the arm and asked, "You got JUG on purpose just to be here with us, didn't you?"

Eagan replied in a strong tone, "Well maybe!"

February was coming to an end, and Father McCartney was again going to miss homeroom. This time, Mr. Watts was going to be covering for him. On that morning, I arrived earlier than usual, but more than half the class was in attendance. I showed them I had two twenty packs of firecrackers. I then proceeded to go to the window, open it up, throw some of the projectiles out the window, and watch them explode in the air. Almost the entire class was at the windows for the show, watching the students down below entering the school, and scrambling around at the sound of the explosions. More than one person joined in throwing the firecrackers, until they were being tossed from all the windows of the room.

I knew that Mr. Watts would be getting to the class soon, so I stopped the fun, and said, "Okay, okay. Look, there's only a couple left. I got an idea." I laid out the plan, and with help, began preparations.

When Mr. Watts arrived, twenty four of the twenty-seven students assigned to the class were in their seats quietly reading. The teacher looked around cautiously, and said, "Good morning gentlemen!"

Twenty three of the twenty-four heads lifted, and answered, "Good morning, Mister."

Mr. Watts looked over at the only person who did not respond, and asked, "Loof, you can't say good morning?"

I did not answer right away, but after a few seconds, I jerked my head up saying, "Oh, sorry, Mister, I'm studying for your religion test. Good morning, Mister."

With that, the bell sounded, and all eyes were on the classroom television for the announcements and news from B.P.E.T.V. station. The morning telecast always ended with the anchor person leading the school in the Pledge of Allegiance. Everything was going just as normal as any other morning, and the words of the Pledge could be heard throughout the school. Then in the 4E homeroom, when they finished the last line, "With liberty and justice for all," six firecrackers were thrown in the air, and a loud round of applause was mixed in with the sound of the explosions. Then everyone sat down, opened up a book, and started reading as if nothing had happened.

Mr. Watts was livid, and started shouting, "Who is responsible for that? I am warning you all! I want the names of the people who did this, and I want them now!"

There was complete silence, and no one even raised their head. Mr. Watts then said, "Oh, so that's how you're going to play this. Loof, I know you must be one of the people who threw a firecracker. So, stand up in front of the room."

I stood up, and asked, "Did you actually see me throw a firecracker, or did you see anybody else throw one?"

"Well, no I did not. My back was turned, and I was looking at the TV. But I know you did it! Didn't you all see him?" The question was answered with blank stares and silence.

At that moment, Father Richards entered the room, and was brought up to speed on what had happened. He told me to sit down, and then asked, "Look, we know that firecrackers were thrown from the windows in this class, and we know what happened later. All I want is the names of the people who threw the firecrackers." There were only blank stares and silence. Five minutes went by, then ten minutes went by, and still blank stares and silence.

A frustrated Father Richards finally announced, "Okay, have it your way! You are all to report here after school, and we'll get to the bottom of this. You're already late for first period. Get going!"

When I, and some of the other 4E guys got to gym, Mr. Sullivan was aware of the situation and put us right to work in the class. During a break in the exercises, Jim Egan asked what had happened. After he was given the whole story he said, "That damn train made me miss it all again! Shitin' railroad!"

At three o'clock, the twenty-four 4E students were in their seats when Father Richards and Mr. Watts entered. He did not beat around the bush. "You know what I want, and you know what you have to do to end this. We will be here as long as it takes. There is to be no talking, no reading, no writing, and no sleeping."

After half an hour, Father Richards rose from his seat, and said to Mr. Watts, "I am going into the next room, and

I want you send in each of these idiots one at a time. And I want Loof last."

And so it went, the twenty-four students went in for questioning, and each returned without the priest, and shaking their head. When Father Richards finally came back into the room, he said, "You have now all been threatened with suspension, but I am going to give you one more chance to give me the names I need."

I turned my head, and scanned the room, receiving a mix of thumbs up and thumbs down. Finally, I stood up and announced, "I was the only one who threw a firecracker, Father."

Before the priest could say anything, Kevin stood up and said, "I was the only one who threw a firecracker, Father." Then one by one, the other twenty-two 4E members stood up and made the same confession.

Father Richards was stunned, and at a complete loss for words. He did try to stammer out a few words, then looked at Mr. Watts, and finally said, "I don't believe this. Fine, I'm done with this! You're all suspended from school tomorrow. Now get out of here!"

The students exited quietly single file, and remained that way until we were outside. Then the celebration began. There were hugs, handshakes, back slapping, and I tossed the last firecracker in the air. Then I asked, "Did anybody get threatened with less than five days?"

There were various answers, but no one said less than three. The celebrating began anew, and somebody yelled, "Party tomorrow! We meet in the city at noon!" There were cries of agreement and the plans were made."

In the weeks after the class suspension, 4E and I toned it down a little, but still managed to keep the class JUG streak going. In homeroom on the Friday before St. Patrick's Day, I was making like Notre Dame football coach Knute Rockne before a big game. Holding a chart, I said, "Okay you guys, we're doing great, but remember this is a team effort. We win as a team, and we lose as a team, but everybody has to contribute to reach our goal. Kane and Fredreck have been doing a great job."

Jim Egan called out, "What about you coach?"

"Well, I am leading the team…" I was then interrupted by a round of applause. I raised my arms and waved my hands to quiet the crowd, and continued, "But like I said, it's not about one person. We're all in this together. So, Rovegno and you other baseball players, I know the seasons startin'. I've got that noted."

There was a brief pause while I looked over the chart, and then said, "You know there's a couple of you guys who have not contributed at all. We're gonna need you to step up here. Now, Alleva and Atanasio, basketball season is almost over so I expect you both to pick up some slack too."

Alleva nodded, and said, "Got ya coach!"

Bobby smiled, and said, "I'll try my best sir!"

With a grim-face, and gritted teeth, I exclaimed, "There's no tryin'! There's only doin'!"

"You're seniors now, and you'll never forget this. Now let's get in there together and fight, fight, fight! St. Ignatius Loyola…" And the whole class joined in, "Pray for us!" Then I was showered with an assortment of paper, socks, and a jock or two.

CHAPTER 33

The last Monday in March I reported for JUG, and Father Richards asked, "Owen, really, Mr. O'Donnell?"

"Well, ya' see Father, Mr. Watts is just too easy, and I figured out that Mr. O'Donnell was the only teacher who has never given me JUG. Since it's comin' to the end of my career, I thought the time was right."

The cleric just shook his head saying, "I don't know, I just don't know. You will probably be fine someday, and I wouldn't be surprised if you wind up selling ice to the Eskimos. Anyway, here's the money. Get back as soon as you can."

After returning to school, and leaving Father Richards's office, I stopped by the gym to see if anything was happening. There were a couple of pick-up basketball games being played, and some other guys just hanging out. Jim Eagan and Jack Frederck were sitting in the bleachers waiting to get in a game, and Bobby was out on the court. I sat down with my fellow 4E'ers, and told them about the day's JUG. When Eagan protested mildly, "Man, how come I never get JUG like that?"

I replied, "Rank has its privileges, my man! But I'll put in a good word for ya!"

When Bobby's game ended, Eagan and Fredreck ran out to warm up for their game as Bobby came over and took a seat. I asked, "Lookin' good out there, dude. Any word on what college wants you?"

"Not exactly yet, but there's a couple of things in the works," After wiping his sweaty face, he asked, "Hey wait, what about you? You shoulda got your SAT's back by now?"

"Yeah, yeah, I got 'em. So, before you ask, I got 450 on the Math and 450 on the English."

"Well, that's okay."

"Oh yeah, just great. Harvard here I come."

"Stop it will ya'. Seriously, what'd ya think ya' gonna do?"

"I dunno, my mother's been makin' noise about a couple of Jesuit colleges. St. Louis University and Xavier in Cincinnati. It seems she's already made some phone calls."

"Well, that's good."

"I dunno about the whole goin' away to college thing, and then there's the cost. Yeah, of course they say don't worry about the money, but my father's working two jobs now. Sometimes I don't see him awake for weeks. How much more can he do?"

"But ya' gotta go somewhere?"

"Yeah, maybe the Navy. I could see the world." After we both laughed, I added, "Oh, wait, you'll really get a kick out of this. Remember I told ya' my mother sent me to that counseling center psychologist? Well, we got his report. She didn't want me to see it, but I found the hiding place."

"So, it probably says you're crazy. Everybody knows that."

Pulling some papers out of my bag, I said, "Well, I don't know about crazy, but I'll read you exactly what he wrote."

I believe this failure was due to a lack of an essential condition in learning, namely, maturation. Owen simply does not have the psychological readiness for learning.

"So, I'm not crazy! I'm just immature, and not ready to learn anything. So, take that!"

"Well, excuuuuse meeeee!"

We were both laughing, and I put up my hands, and said, "Wait, wait! There's more!" I leafed through some pages to find what I was looking for, and said, "Here!"

An intensive examination of his personal activities enabled us to identify a number of reasons why Owen did not do as well as he could in his academic endeavors. To begin with, he has little, or no conception of what study involves. Added to this, is the fact he lacked interest in academics. In other words, not only did he not know how to study, but he did not want to do it either.

Bobby laughed heartily while shaking his head saying, "And this guy got paid for that. Again, who doesn't know that?"

With a smile I responded, "Yeah, yeah, but besides resentin' all that stuff, this is what really annoyed me."

It is conceivable that a student will achieve academically without some organizational approach if he has a strong desire to do so. This implies being properly motivated or wanting to achieve a specific goal.

"Isn't that bullshit? You know how motivated I am to achieve a specific goal!"

"Of course! Everybody knows how really hard you are trying to finish with the worst grades in the class!"

I stood up, and took a bow saying, "Thank you, and thank to all the little people who helped me along the way to this great honor."

While I was still standing, Bobby asked, "By the way, have you figured out who your competition is?"

"No, I haven't, but I got it narrowed to some good suspects. I'll have to steal some answers for them."

CHAPTER 34

On Tuesday April 2nd, I hobbled into homeroom with a cane, and a cast on my right ankle. Father McCartney looked at me, and asked, "Owen, what did you do now?"

I sat down in the nearest seat, and with most of the class gathered around, I began, "Well, I woke up yesterday morning, and really didn't feel too good. And no, I was not hung over! I stayed in bed most of the day, and when my mother got home from work, I figured I'd go downstairs. I slipped on the stairs, missed the last three steps, landed feet first, and broke my ankle."

Father McCartney asked, "And you came right into school this morning?"

"Well, ya know Father, I didn't wanna miss any work. Senior year's important!"

John Alleva stepped in front of me, grabbed my arm, and said, "Okay you, whoever you are, what'd ya do with the real Owney Loof?"

Bobby put his hand on my forehead saying, "He's got a fever, Father. Somethin's wrong!"

I remarked stiffly, "Okay, okay, have your fun. It's fine!"

Everybody laughed, returned to their seats, and Kevin said to me, "Ya know, everybody was waitin' for ya yesterday. They wanted to see what you would do."

"Yesterday? What was so special about yesterday?"

"Come on Owney, it was April Fools' Day. It was your day!"

I put a hand on my friend's shoulder asking, "Kevin, really, do you think I could have said or done anything that woulda gotten over on anybody in the school?"

"Ahhh, you're probably right, but did you see the paper?"

"What paper?"

"The school paper. The Blue Jug."

"Oh no, I didn't. Was there somethin' in there I shoulda seen?"

"Yeah, they did a whole April Fools edition, with all kinds of funny shit, and instead of doin' the spotlight on one of the nerds or a jock, they did it on you."

With a surprised smile, I asked, "Is that right, really?"

"Ya really didn't see it? Here, look."

Spotlight on:

OWEN

One glance at Owen Loof is hardly enough to plumb the depths that lie here latent. He is, of course, typical of the average, run-of-the-mill Brooklyn Prep intellectual. He is looked upon as a shining blight, the acne (as in Fernanda Waldemiller) of the student body.

To those of us here at the Prep, Owen is invaluable for a variety of reasons: 1) He is a living example of righteousness, 2) He worked his way up from a Weblow Cub Scout to one of the biggest B. S. A.'s in the world. 2) (Remember?). He is the cause of the CLT course in junior year (Mr. Devlin gave up). 4) He filters the pool free of charge (but not of soot) every Friday afternoon; and last but far from least (that is for the treasurer), he is four years behind in tuition.

The blue eagle.

Owen has always been a leader in the Prep. From the first day of his high school career, when he fell down those blood-stained marble steps leading to the frosh corridor, there have been changes. He first was a member of the Dance Committee, acting as its public relations man. (The tickets were printed "Big Beer Bash with Hash".) Next, by revamping, reorganizing, and regurgitating, he fashioned a new BP magazine, which was appropriately named *Mad*. He inspired the idea of Communion under two species when he took a swig of his "Twister" (the wine of wierdoes) at the altar. He was the hero of the sophomores when he brought his portable fan into the lavatory.

Owen also shares a few distinctions for some outstanding achievements. Scholastically, he holds two records of merit. He is now a Road's Scholar and for this distinct honor Fr. Rector has declared another official holiday. He is in addition one of the few students in the entire nation or the world (what's left of it) on the six year plan (high school level). What's more, B.P.E.T.V., that award winning station televising from the plushy flushies—has offered Owen a contract for his own seven minute series Monday through Friday mornings.

Rumor has it that Owen may be the recipient of Prep's valedictory award. (A word to the wise, not to mention any names, Charles Russo).

And so, to sum up this small but sincere little article we have the words of Fr. John D. Alexander, S.J.: "Would that all were as he".

After scanning through the article, I laughed, and said, "That's really good. I'm glad they did it."

Kevin raised his hands saying, "Hey wait a minute, the picture! You had to know about the article because they dressed you up for the picture."

"No, I swear. I didn't know. They never told me what the picture was for. I thought it was for the yearbook or somethin'"

Kevin pursed his lips and squinted his eyes in a questioning manner, saying, "Yeahhh sure....., okay."

I shrugged and said, "Believe whatever you want. I'm just tellin' ya what happened."

The rest of the day I moved unsteadily around the school with the cast and the cane, retelling the story of what happened to anyone who asked. The next morning, I shuffled into homeroom, taking my seat with a little difficulty. Father McCartney asked, "How's it feeling today, Owen?"

"Not too bad Father, and somebody even gave me a seat on the train. So, that was cool."

As that was happening, a few of the guys were coming over to get the latest news. In the middle of the discussion, Jack Fredreck looked at me, and asked, "Umm, Owney, didn't you say yesterday that you broke your right ankle?"

"Yeah, that's right. I fell down the stairs and broke my right ankle."

"Well, then how come today, the cast is on your left ankle?"

I looked down, and replied, "Oh yeah it is." Then I unfastened the cast in two pieces, taking it off my left leg, and fastening it onto my right leg. I grinned at Fredreck and said, "Thanks a lot Jack!"

My classmates lifted me from my seat and jostled in the air as the fake cast was removed. They dropped me on the floor, taking turns playfully beating me with the cast pieces.

Finally, they threw the cast pieces on me, along with my books, my coat, and the contents of the classroom's waste basket. Father McCartney actually supplied the waste basket, and as I lay there, I looked up and declared, "April Fools'!"

Two nights later, which was one night after Martin Luther King Jr. was shot and killed in Memphis, Tennessee by James Earl Ray, sparking unrest in cities across the country. I was on the A train traveling between Howard Beach and Broad Channel. It was not really that late, but I was the only person in the train car. I had been reading, but was now dozing on and off. Suddenly, I was startled by voices, and looking up, there were three Black kids, about my age or a little younger, standing over me.

The tallest kid demanded, "Okay white boy, give us your money, and we won't fuck you up!"

I yawned and shrugged, saying, "You guys picked one poor white boy. I got one dollar on me, and if you want it, you can have it."

One of the other kids demanded, "Let's just fuck 'em up anyway!"

I shrugged, and replied, "Well, you were probably gonna do that anyway. So, are you ready?" I jumped out of my seat, bulldozed through them, as if going for the goal line, and jumped up on the seats across the aisle.

The tall kid pulled out a knife saying, "You're one crazy white boy, and you are definitely gettin' hurt now. It's three against one."

Then out of nowhere, another voice was bellowed, "No it's not! It's three against three!"

The three attackers turned to see who the voice belonged to, and I recognized my teammates from the Hammels-St. Francis basketball game, Curtis Brooks, and Ray Alford. I said, "Curtis, Ray, what's happenin'? Good to see ya!"

The tall kid with the knife asked, "Who the fuck are you, and what'd you care about this white boy?"

Alford answered, "We are the guys that are saving your sorry butts from this crazy ass white boy that you don't wanna fuck with, and he's a friend of ours. So, I would advise you three to put the blade away and take a walk!"

One of the other kids said to the knife wielder, "Wait, the white boy is right! That's Ray Alford. He organizes basketball games in the project park, and he went to school with my brother."

Alford said, "That's right, I've seen the three of you playin' out there, and I was with your brother last night."

The kid with the knife pointed at me, asking, "You really know this guy?"

"Yeah, we do, and besides being crazy, he's a good player, and a good guy."

The kid looked at me, and said, "Get down off the seats you crazy white boy. If you know Ray, then everythin's cool."

I jumped down, and shared hugs with Ray and Curtis, while shaking hands with my former attackers. There was not a lot of time, as the train was approaching Broad Channel where I had to change for the shuttle to Rockaway Park, but the other guys were remaining on the A to Far Rockaway. We briefly caught up on old times and new times, and talked about playing a few games together.

When the train finally arrived at the Broad Channel station, there were goodbyes with more hugs and handshakes. Then, just as the doors opened, the kid who had the knife asked me, "Were you really ready to fight us?"

I stepped out on the platform, smiled, and answered, "I dunno, but I'm sure glad I didn't hafta find out." Everybody laughed and the doors closed.

CHAPTER 35

*O*n the Wednesday after Easter, Kevin, Bobby, and I walked into homeroom to find Alex Avitabile and Charlie Russo waiting for us. I took one look at them and said, "I was gonna say good mornin', but you guys look too serious. What's up?"

Russo scanned the room, then said to Avitabile, "Well most of them are here, and really as long Owney's here, I think we can go ahead."

I waved my hand, saying, "By all means, now that I'm here, please go ahead and say what you gotta say."

Russo announced, "Okay, fine. You know there hasn't been a senior boat ride since the piano was thrown off the boat a couple of years ago."

There was laughter, and I exclaimed, "Yeah, that was Atanasio's brother's class! Wish I had been there for that one!"

Putting up his hands to quiet everyone, Russo continued, "Whatever, the point is me and Alex have been working really hard to try and get the boat ride this year." There was cheering and applause, and Russo waited for the noise to abate before adding, "We have a tentative date, and Father Hamilton and Father Richards have all but agreed to let it happen. The decision has to be made by Friday, and they wanted us to talk to you people before they gave the final go ahead."

I asked Russo, "So what do we have to do with the decision?"

"Well, they are concerned about letting this class go." Then pointing at me, Kevin, and Bobby, he said, "Especially you three."

I looked at Kevin and Bobby, and asked, "Do you think we should be insulted?" Then I said to Russo, "Why would our names even come up like that?"

"Come on Owney, they know you just like everybody else does. There's no telling what you'll do to try and top the piano throwing."

From the top row of seats, John Alleva shouted, "Yeah that's why we want him to go!"

There was more laughter and applause, which Russo put a stop to by saying, "Wait, wait! Like I said, it's not just Owney you know. They talked about banning the whole class." There were boos and cat calls, and Russo continued over the din, "Okay, okay, calm down! We were able to talk them out of that, but they want to warn you that there will be dire consequences if you do anything really stupid. And I would just like to remind you, that you could be messing it up for next year, and future years."

I rose from my seat, and said, "Alex, Charlie, you can go back to Richards and Hamilton, and tell them that I promise to be on my best behavior." The rest of the class stood up, and with whistles, shouts, and clapping, added their agreement. Then I pointed my outstretched arms toward Russo saying, "There you have it! We know what we have to do."

The next week, Kevin, Bobby, Giacomo, Jack Fredreck, and I were all in JUG, along with a few underclassmen. Since the weather was pleasant, our JUG was being spent walking the courtyard. After about ten minutes of walking, Kevin, Jack, and I sat down. One of the freshmen asked, "Why are you guys doing that? What if Father Richards comes back?"

I answered, "Watch and learn, he won't do anything the first time."

There was a discussion concerning the boat ride, and I related the piano story to the freshmen.

They wanted to hear more, but suddenly Father Richards opened the door, and yelled, "Okay you three, you'll be back here tomorrow! Now start walking!"

The three slackers got up, and joined the line of march. There was a round of laughter, and the freshman, who had spoken before, asked me, "I thought you said he wouldn't do anything?"

"If you remember correctly, I also said to watch and learn. So, did you learn anything?"

The kid answered, "Yeah, I learned not to believe you!"

"Good! Always remember, trust no one! People will lie to you! Check everything and everybody out before you decide what to do.

Giacomo put his hand on the kid's shoulder saying, "Besides, even the best of us is not infallible."

I added, "That's right, even the Pope is only infallible on religious stuff."

There was scattered laughter, and I announced, "Come on guys, let's show them how to really walk JUG." Then I started to hum a little tune and perform a Rockette-like leg kick. I was quickly joined by Giacomo, Jack, the rest of the seniors, and two freshmen.

The line of dancers was leg kicking their way around the courtyard, when the door opened and Father Richards shouted, "What is going on here? What's wrong with you people? JUG is not a joke! All you Rockettes will be back here tomorrow, and Loof, Kane, and Fredreck, you will be here for the next three days!" The priest turned to reenter the building, but did an about face, and said calmly, "Oh, Owen, I want to speak with you before you leave."

When I got to Father Richards's office, I was told to have a seat, and the priest got right to the point. "You have probably heard that we okayed the boat ride to Rye Beach Amusement Park on May 11th."

"Yeah Father, I got some of the details. There's two other schools going, and one is a Catholic girls' school. We also know that one of the schools is a public school, but nobody knows where the girls' school is from."

"Well, the final details were only worked out yesterday. Owen, you live in Rockaway, correct?"

"Sure Father, all my life."

"So, you know the girls' high school there, Stella Maris?"

"Absolutely Father, most of the girls from my grammar school go there." I paused for a second, and before Father Richards could say anything, added, "Wait a minute Father, are you tellin' me Stella Maris is goin' on the boat ride with us? Shouldn't it be St. Brendan's?

"Yes, Owen it should be St. Brendan's, but the nuns are reluctant to let them go with your class. They still remember the spiders. So, Stella Maris will be with us this year. And now listen, you especially, but all of 4E, were very close to not being allowed on this trip. Now hear this well, and heed it! I want you to know, and be sure to remind the other reprobates in your class, that there will be the direst of consequences if there is any kind of misbehavior. I hope you understand what I am saying Owen, and you better get that message across to the rest of your class."

"Well, um, okay Father… I got the message, but it's not like I can tell everybody what to do."

Owen Loof

"But Owen, you can set the tone. And I'm thinking, it may be a good thing you are familiar with the girls from Stella Maris."

"Look Father, I'll pass along the information, but you may be overestimating my influence. There's a lot of guys in this class who are smarter than me and can come up with their own funny stuff."

"Come on now Owen, this is me you're talking to. Nobody does it better than you. Just be careful on the boat ride this year for the sake of the underclassmen. Besides, I would hate to lose you now."

I stood up, reached across the desk to shake hands with the cleric, and said, "Thanks Father, I'll just have a good time, and keep as low a profile as possible."

CHAPTER 36

*O*n the Friday night before the boat ride, half of 4E came to Rockaway for pre-ride festivities. Michael and JP joined the group, and everybody met at The Circle. Michael and I were surprised that neither Mike Woods, nor Joe, the other regular bartender, were behind the bar. When the Prep guys ordered their drinks, the bartender asked for proof. Each one down the line produced the necessary document, and received whatever alcohol they desired. Michael and I were the last waiting to be served, and I asked, "Hey man, how's it goin'? You're new here?"

With a thick Irish brogue, the barkeep answered, "That's right, I'm a cousin of the Woods brothers, new in the country, and my cousins are trying to help me get settled."

I reached out my hand, and while handshakes were being exchanged, I introduced myself, Michael, and JP, and the bartender said, "My name is Liam, and I'm from Westport in County Mayo."

My face brightened as I exclaimed, "Wow, you don't say! My grandmother is from Ballycastle." Then pointing to Michael, I added, "And my friend here also has deep roots in the old country."

Liam responded, "Ah yes, Ballycastle, know it well. And what will you gentlemen be havin'?"

I said, "Three Harps Liam, my good man."

He got the bottles of Harp, and when he placed them

in front of the three patrons, he asked, "And may I be seein' your proof, please?"

I laughed, and said, "Liam, Liam, please. We've been drinkin' in here for years, even before we were legal."

"Well, I don't know about that lad, but the rules are the rules, and my cousin told me to check proof."

Obviously miffed, I glanced over at Michael and JP for support, but they were in the process of going through their wallets, and Michael said, "Come O, the guy's only doin' his job."

I pulled the wallet from my pocket, and while searching the contents, I was still complaining. "I don't think I've ever been asked for proof anywhere in Rockaway!"

Michael and JP were already taking the first taste of their beer when I blurted out loudly, "Shit, shit, shit, I don't believe this!"

Michael asked, "What are you yellin' about?"

"My card's not in here!"

"What're talkin' about?"

Kevin, Bobby, and couple of the other guys gathered around as I answered, "My proof's not in my fuckin' wallet, and I don't know where it is." Then I looked at Liam, and pleaded my case, "Liam, your cousin Mike is a friend of mine, and the brothers know my family. Just call them."

"Well, I would if I could, but one of the reasons I'm working, is that they're all at a wedding for the other side of the family."

"So, you're really not gonna serve me?"

"Look lad, it's not that I don't believe you. It's just that me cousins said that the authorities have been checkin' up on them, and told me to be strict with the rules. And in my situation, I can't afford to get in trouble."

I smiled and said, "It's fine Liam. I gotcha, don't worry about it. Gimme a coke, okay." I took the soda, walked over to a table, and sat down. Michael and JP grabbed a couple of seats with some of the others following. Jack Fredreck had a shot of rum in his hand and poured it into my soda.

Bobby asked, "So what's the plan O?" Michael and JP laughed heartily. Bobby looked over at them, smiled, and added, "Yeah, yeah, I know, we'll use his Rockaway name tonight."

After I stopped laughing, I replied, "Well, we're not gonna sit here with you guys feeding me drinks. There's another place a couple a blocks away. Let's go."

The troop made their way to Gilroy's, and I could not get served there either. As we were leaving, I protested, "I do not believe this! If I was in Brooklyn, or somewhere else maybe I could see it, but in Rockaway? I'm eighteen, and except for Michael, none of you are!" Everybody laughed, and I looked at Michael saying, "Come on, there's one place I know this can't happen!"

Michael raised his fist in the air, and shouted, "Flynn's!"

The Rockaway boys were correct, and in Flynn's everyone got their drinks. It also worked out well for another reason. A half an hour after we arrived, a group of girls from Stella Maris showed up, including Michael's girlfriend, Maryanne, and the party really began in earnest. The alcohol flowed, the music played, and the Prep boys and the Stella girls had a great time together.

At one point, I was standing with Maryanne and some of her friends, when John Alleva and Jack Fredreck joined the conversation. After the introductions, I asked Maryanne, "So where's Veronica, out with Mr. College?"

"Yes, she is Owen. Why would you ask?"

I did not answer right away, and then just asked, "And will she be gracing us peasants with her presence tomorrow?"

"You don't have to be that way, Owen. You two could try to get along."

Before I could answer, one of the girls grabbed my arm saying, "Come on O, dance with me!"

I winked at the group, and as my dance partner and I headed for the dancefloor, I heard Fredreck ask Maryanne, "Veronica? Veronica? Wait, didn't she have something to do with O and the junior prom?"

"Yes, she certainly did, but there is a lot more to their story than last year. They spin around like an amusement park ride, and then find one another before spinning again."

"And she's gonna be there tomorrow? Verrrly interesting!"

About midnight, all the girls were gone except for Maryanne and two of her friends. Michael was still there, as well as Kevin, Bobby, and Giacomo, who were all staying at my house for the night. I walked over to join the group at their table. When I was settled in my seat, Bobby asked, "Everything's ready for tomorrow, right?"

"Don't worry, man. I have people puttin' on the finishing touches, and it's all set!"

Then Alleva and Fredreck, along with the remaining 4E crew, came over to say so long, and I said, "Okay guys, sorry about the bar hoppin' problem. But you know, I think this place worked out better."

After some laughter, murmuring, and nods of assent, I continued, "Okay look, I just want to stress that nobody bring booze tomorrow. I've already talked with Russo, and the word is out. Remember, they're gonna be lookin' at us especially."

Fredreck asked, "But you do have a plan, right O?"

"Listen, the less you know the better. All I'm sayin' is nobody has to bring anything tomorrow!"

There were smiles and handshakes as the 4E guys headed out the door, and when they were all gone, I looked at my three remaining classmates saying, "Okay you guys, we got a little work to do."

We all stood up, and Michael said, "I'll meet you guys there in a little while. I'm gonna take Maryanne home."

The Prep boys started for the door, and after a hug with Maryanne, I turned to leave. When I heard her ask her boyfriend, "So what's going on?"

Michael wrapped his arms around his girlfriend, kissed her lovingly on the cheek, and answered, "I'll let O tell you tomorrow."

The next morning, Michael dropped off my three classmates and me at a spot a block and a half from the dock, and more than an hour before sailing time. We emptied out the trunk, which contained eight boxes, a folding table, and two chairs. When the boxes were all on the table, and I was sitting behind it along with Bobby, Michael said to me, "Watch the car for me, I'm gonna go find Maryanne."

I gave my friend a thumbs up, and then said to Kevin and Giacomo, "Okay, you guys go over to the boat and direct the 4E guys, and whoever you think we can trust, over here."

After fifteen minutes, the first of the 4E people arrived at the same time Michael returned with Maryanne, Veronica, and a couple of their girlfriends. The Prep students formed a line, and Michael along with the girls walked behind the table, and stood behind me. Each person in the line was given two bottles, and a choice of three pieces of fruit.

Maryanne finally asked, "Okay, what's in the bottles?"

I turned my head, saying, "Michael, sit here and help Bobby so I can fill in the girls. We switched positions, and I explained, "The bottles are filled with a special recipe boat ride Bash, and the oranges have been injected with vodka and the apples with rum."

Veronica asked, "What's the special recipe?"

"Well, you know when we make our Bash, we usually use any kind of juice we can find and all kinds of liquor." The Rockaway girls all nodded, and I continued, "But for this one, we wanted to make sure of the taste, so we only used orange juice, vodka and gin."

Maryanne looked around at the boxes on the table, and pointed to one under the table asking, "How many bottles did you make, and what's the one there?"

"We got a hundred bottles, eighty to give out, and twenty in the box under the table for us. Plus, Giacomo somehow got a connection with one of the deck hands, and there's some more boxes on the boat already."

"Where did you guys get all the money for that much stuff?"

I pulled Maryanne and Veronica aside, whispering to them, "Don't say anything, but Giacomo financed the whole project."

The rest of the distribution went smoothly, and when it was time to go over to board the boat, there were eight bottles left. I told the girls to take them, and I added two bottles from my private stash. Then I said, "Here, take some of the fruit too, but be careful who you share it with, and don't tell them what it is. See ya on the boat!"

Maryanne gave Michael a hug and a kiss before rushing off with the other girls. We took the empty boxes, the table, and the chairs, and loaded them back into the trunk.

When the job was complete, Michael shook hands with the three other Prep guys, who started toward the boat. I hugged Michael and he said, "Okay dude, I'll be here later to drive you all home. So, have a good time, and try not to get in too much trouble."

"Thanks man! What kind of trouble could I possibly get into?"

Michael laughed heartily, waved his hands in the air as he entered his car, and I ran to catch up with my fellow passengers. As we neared the boat, Father Richards, Father McCartney, and Mr. Jagger were standing by the gangplank with three other teachers. The four of us hung back to check what was happening as the Prep students walked past the teachers, and onto the boat. From what we could see, it was noted that students were only being randomly searched. I said, "Okay, just follow me."

The four of us fell in line, and when we reached the checkpoint, Mr. Jagger remarked, "Okay here's Loof. Show us what's in your bag Owen!"

I opened my bag, and the first thing seen was three bottles. Before any of the teachers could say anything, I removed one of the bottles, held it up so all the teachers could see it, and said, "Orange juice Father, orange juice."

Mr. Jagger looked at Father Richards, and said, "You know Father, we've seen a lot of orange juice today."

I opened the cap, handed the bottle to Mr. Jagger, and said, "Here you go Mister, you can have that one." Then I gave the other two bottles to Father Richards and Father McCartney.

After Mr. Jagger had taken a couple of sips, he said to Father Richards, "It does taste like orange juice. But do we really know what's in it?"

Father McCartney countered, "I don't think even Owen Loof would take a chance, and give his teachers spiked juice."

My deadpanned reply was, "That would just be crazy Father, thank you. I'll see ya on the boat!"

CHAPTER 37

On the ride to the Amusement Park, I divided my time between Maryanne, Veronica, and the Stella girls, drinking with the 4E guys, and singing with the band. After one number, Maryanne approached me and said, "You know the only other time I've seen you do that was at the Avigliano party. You never do anything like that in Rockaway."

"I dunno it's just different in Rockaway. You all know who I am there, it's home."

Just then the music started, and I was practically dragged out on the dance floor by three girls. When the music stopped, three other girls joined the group, and I stayed there talking and joking with all of them. After a few minutes, I excused myself to the restroom, and departed by kissing the hand of each girl. As I left the dance floor, I passed Bobby and John Alleva standing by the railing. Alleva said, "You look like you're havin' a good time out there with all those girls, Owney."

"Ah, well they're not really lookin' at me, they only see the performer."

Bobby put his hand on my shoulder asking, "Whatever you say, but do ya think ya could save us some of your leftovers?"

Once at the park, I was again trying to split myself in many pieces to be with all my friends. I was walking with

Giacomo, Kevin, and a couple of other Prep guys, and as we passed the line for the roller coaster, I stopped to say hello to a group of Stella girls. They would be the next group to go on the ride. Then four guys came along, and cut the line right in front of them. Two young park employees were monitoring the ride, and said to the four line crashers, "There is a line, and you must go to the end of the line."

The girls were all protesting, indicating their agreement with the employees, when one of the guys while pushing one of the girls, said, "We're goin' on the ride next!" One of the other guys asked the employees threateningly, "You gonna make us go to the end of the line?"

I was standing in front of the Prep entourage, and asked nicely, "Why do you hafta act like idiots? It's a nice day, just get on the line like everybody else."

The line cutters stepped off the line to confront their opposition, and at that moment, the ride employees opened the gate and started letting people on the ride. While there were no punches thrown, or real physical activity, there was a long exchange of expletive-filled shouts, and a little jostling. Then one of the ride employees yelled that security was on the way, and the line crashers took off running. There was a round of applause from the other people in the line, and Father Richards arrived on the scene with Father McCartney at the same time as the security detail.

We were quickly surrounded, and one of the guards announced, "Okay you guys, don't give us any trouble. Just come with us, and we will escort you from the park."

Father Richards approached the lead guard asking, "These boys are from my school, what's the problem?"

"They have been cutting the line on rides, and starting fights!" Some of the people on the line called out in protest,

"No, no, it's not them!" Then one of the ride employees came forward, telling the guard what really happened. The guard apologized, and walked away with the rest of his men.

Father Richards reached out to shake hands with all of his students and said, "Good job gentlemen, but try to be careful and enjoy the rest of the day. Especially you Owen!"

As the two priests walked away, the girls exited the rollercoaster, and ran over smothering me with hugs and kisses. I said, "Hey, wait a minute, I wasn't alone here. Make sure you thank the other guys too!"

After eating lunch with Maryanne and Veronica, I stayed with them, and a few of the other girls, going on rides and playing games. I even won a big stuffed dog at a ring toss game that I gave to Veronica. Then later, I found Bobby and John Alleva at a basketball shooting game, where they had already won three prizes apiece, and the employee running the game was about to ban them from playing.

Jack Fredreck was at the shooting gallery right next door, and was also cleaning out the prizes. There were two guys at the other end of the counter shooting, who were not winning anything. They got progressively angrier, and started yelling at the worker, accusing him of cheating. Fredreck was asking for another reload, and when the worker turned his back to accommodate the request, the two complainers jumped over the counter, grabbed a few of the stuffed animals, jumped back over the counter, and started running.

Without a second thought, I took off in pursuit of the thieves, with Bobby close behind. As the chase continued, I spied Charlie Russo, Tim Delaney, and Pat Santisi walking toward our prey. I yelled, "Hey Charlie, stop those two guys with the stuffed animals!"

The thieves realized the obstacle in front of them, but did not stop running, thinking they would be able to make their way through. The three Prep football players grabbed the thieves like opposing runners at the line of scrimmage, and the larcenists gave up quickly, surrendered their ill-gotten goods, and were sent on their way.

We brought the pilfered articles back to the shooting gallery, and as I was standing in the middle of a circle surrounded by the Prep students, a security detail appeared on the scene. The lead guard had also been at the roller coaster, and when he saw me said, "You again! Maybe we should have thrown you out before. Thanks for catching him, guys!"

Russo answered, "No problem sheriff, take him away!" Everybody started laughing as the guard started toward me, and I held out my hands to be handcuffed. The guard looked around at the laughing group somewhat confused. The shooting gallery employee cleared up the situation by disclosing the real story to the guard, who laughed and said, "Okay, well I want to thank you boys again." Then he looked at me asking, "Does trouble always follow you around?"

Before I could answer, there was a voice heard from behind. Father Richards answered, "More than you would know, sir. More than you would know!"

At the end of the day, the boat was almost ready to start sailing home, and I heard Father McCartney talking to an employee at the top of the gangplank. "Two of my colleagues are not back yet, I'll have to look for them."

I went to the priest asking, "Father Richards and Mr. Jagger aren't here? Where'd ya see them last?"

"They said they were going to take a walk on the boardwalk."

So, Kevin and Bobby joined Father McCartney and me in the search for the lost teachers. Soon enough, we found the priest and the scholastic asleep on one of the boardwalk benches. When the two men were awakened, they were both groggy-eyed and somewhat confused for a few seconds. Father Richards asked, "What time is it? How long have I been here?"

Father McCartney answered, "The boat's just about ready to go. You two left a while ago, but that's not important now, we really have to get to the boat."

Father Richards and Mr. Jagger nodded, and were helped to their feet. They were both a little unsteady, needed assistance walking, and Father Richards remarked, "I don't know what could have caused this to happen."

I said, "It was pretty hot today, and maybe you didn't get enough fluids."

Father Richards replied, "I don't think that's it. The boys kept sharing their orange juice, and we both had some of the fruit."

"So, you were both tired from workin' so hard, and were so relaxed here that you fell asleep. You needed it!"

"Maybe so Owen, maybe so."

We all made it back to the boat before the gangplank was removed, and the two chaperones were settled in comfortably for the ride. As I walked away to join the festivities of the return trip, Father McCartney pulled me aside asking, "Owen, what was in that juice?"

"I dunno Father, juice I guess."

"Don't B.S. me Owen, Richards and Jagger really look like they've had a few drinks, and I was watching some of the students getting on the boat. There were definitely signs some imbibing had been done."

"Geeze Father, is it possible some guys were able to get some kind of alcohol passed you three? Sure it is. But I didn't see anything, and I got my juice from a deli in Rockaway. I don't know about anyone else."

The priest just shook his head asking, "And of course you would tell me if you did know anything?

I gave Father McCartney a determined look, and replied, "Of course Father!"

Still shaking his head, the frustrated cleric said, "Get out of here Owen! Just go!"

Everybody was having a good time on the sail home. The band was great, I sang and danced, and there were a couple of instances of guys being hung over the side of the boat. After one set, the band was taking a break, and I noticed that some guys from the public school were giving the band members a hard time. Suddenly, it got physical, with a guitar and a saxophone being ripped from the musicians' hands and thrown overboard. Three of the musicians were then pushed to the floor, and I ran over, inserting myself between the fallen musicians and their attackers. One of them shouted, "Okay, this guy's the next one goin' over!"

As the attackers moved toward me, they noticed that they were now surrounded by fifteen students from 4E. Since they were outnumbered at this time, the public-school students decided that discretion was the better part of valor, and backed off. Then members of the crew arrived on the scene with Father McCartney and a couple of public-school chaperones.

All the combatants retreated to neutral corners, and order was restored. Father McCartney looked at me and said, "So, you really didn't cause that ruckus by trying to recreate the great piano fiasco."

"No way Father, the band is really cool, and I didn't wanna see any more instruments go overboard 'cause then there would be no music."

"There is always a method to your madness isn't there Owen? You know young man, you are a little nuts. But you have a good heart, and you are loyal to your friends. You're going to be all right!"

There was still music as the boat did have a piano, the band still had drums, and another guitarist. Also, the band member who lost his guitar to the sea had a spare. At one point, I had just finished a song when I saw Charlie Russo standing right in front of the stage, and I made a request of the band. As the band began the first notes, I called to Russo, jumped into his arms, and began singing the song, "Daddy's Little Girl."

As I sang the lyrics, Russo carried me around the dance floor to much laughter and applause. Finally, Russo plopped his cargo down as the band played on, and the crowd joined in the singing. Maryanne and Veronica, along with a group of Stella girls, were now standing right in front of me, and Veronica threw herself into my arms. As we began dancing and singing, I could tell that she was a little wobbly on her feet, and her speech was slurry. Then Maryanne tapped me on the shoulder, and whispered, "There's a couple of nuns coming, get her outta here!"

I quickly and deftly danced my partner and myself off the floor, and out of sight. A giggly Veronica was more than happy to keep hold of me and follow along. I found an isolated spot that had a bench, and sat down with the tipsy Veronica, who was cuddling up and kissing me on the cheek. Then with heavy eyes, and a goofy little smile, she said, "Oh Owen, you found a place for us to be alone together." Then she then began nuzzling my neck, while nibbling on my ear.

I did not exactly resist forcefully, or pull away, but after a deep sigh, I said, "Look Veronica, you've had a little too much to drink. I just wanna get you off the boat without you gettin' in trouble."

"Just kiss me, Owen. It's just me and you right now."

"And your boyfriend?"

"Don't worry about him either. I want you to kiss me." Then she moved quickly forward and put her lips on mine. I did not really return the kiss, but made no concerted effort to stop it either. Veronica ended the kiss, laid her head on my chest, and was quickly off to dreamland.

As I sat there watching the pretty girl sleeping in my arms, many thoughts were racing through my head, but I was snapped out of my daydream when a crewman appeared. I asked, "Is there any other way outta here?" After the instructions were given and I thanked the man, I was surprised to see Father McCartney who said, "What's going on here Owen?"

"Oh, nothin' Father. This is Veronica, and we went to grammar school together. She got a little seasick and fell asleep."

"Seasick, Owen?"

"Yeah, but don't worry we have a ride home. I'll get her to the car."

The priest shook his head, and smiled saying, "A fitting end to your day Owen."

"You know, I'm always just trying to keep a low profile, Father."

Father McCartney laughed out loud and said, "Owen, you wouldn't know a low profile even if it hit you in the head. Get you and your friend home safe."

CHAPTER 38

The last weeks of high school went by quickly, and for me I was keeping somewhat under the radar. On the last class day of high school, I walked into homeroom, and John Alleva said, "It's about time you got here! Atanasio, you gotta talk to 'im!"

"Well, good morning to you John. And yeah Atanasio, you gotta talk to me."

Bobby stood up saying, "Wait a minute, I'm not doin' this by myself. Listen Owney, everybody wants to know why you've been so quiet the last few weeks, and they're lookin' for test answers!"

Jack Fredreck piped up, "And we all remember last year!"

There was murmuring all around, and fingers pointing at me. I raised my hands, and said, "Look, I've just had a lot on my mind, and this year is not like last year. Also, I'm not cheatin' because I gotta finish last in the class on my own, and I gotta make it to graduation."

I was interrupted by the entrance of Father Hamilton and Father Richards. Everyone was surprised and sat down, except for me. The two priests were staring at me, so I said, "Father, I didn't do it, and nobody here did. But maybe we can…"

Father Hamilton broke in, and said with a wave of his hand, "Sit down and be quiet Owen, nobody's in trouble, yet."

As I was sitting down, I asked, "Okay, thanks Father, so if we're not in trouble, what's goin' on?"

Father Richards cleared his throat, and began, "So first, this homeroom has accomplished something that has never been done in the long history of the school." He paused as the we passed glances from one to the other, and then continued, "What you people have done is nothing to be proud of, and I certainly hope it never happens again. You see at least one person from this homeroom has been in JUG every day this year, and no homeroom has ever amassed as many total JUG days.

There was some subdued rejoicing, and I said, "So, what you're saying Father is we're famous."

"I think infamous would be a better term to use. Also, Mr. Loof, no one student has ever received more JUG during their four years in the school."

Now there was real applause and cheering, and I took my bows thoroughly enjoying the adulation. Even the two priests were smiling, and Father Hamilton added, "I don't know how you did this, and are still here today."

"What can I say Father? It's a skill. They said it couldn't be done. Owen Loof graduates from Brooklyn Prep!"

While still smiling, Father Hamilton retorted, "Not so fast young man, you still have to get through today, and finals. I remember last year."

"Don't worry Father, I got this!"

There was more applause, and I walked over to the clerics, first shaking hands with Father Richards. As I was doing the same with Father Hamilton the priest said, "You are quite a guy Owen Loof, and how could you not be? You have exceptional parents, especially your mother."

I thanked the headmaster, and as the priest turned to leave, he looked back at me and asked, "Owen, you still got that knife?"

As soon as the two priests left the room the bell sounded, and cheering was heard throughout the school. Every 4E student stopped by to say so long to Father McCartney, and I was of course the last in line. After shaking hands with the priest, I said, "Thanks for everything Father, and I really do apologize for any grief I caused."

The teacher put a hand on my shoulder saying, "I almost hate to say this, but you were a pleasure. There was never anything malicious nor destructive in the things you did. Well, the magnesium strips notwithstanding, but you were having a good time, and so was everyone else. And just between me and you, you made a lot of the teachers laugh too."

"Remember *Signing in the Rain* Father? "Make em laugh, make em laugh, all the world loves a clown." As long as people were laughing was all I cared about."

The priest gave me a pat on the back, then with a smile on his face, and a shake of his head said, "Go on you nut! Get outa here! And don't ever change."

The rest of the day I was busy giving gifts to all of my teachers. I especially made sure to give something to Mr. Jagger, Mr. Watts, Mr. Delasalvo, and Mr. Garell. I had pennies that said, Brooklyn Prep 68' that I gave to all my classmates. My comrades in 4E also received a class picture that was taken by Father McCartney in the chemistry room.

Then halfway through Mr. O'Donnell's speech class, I realized that I had not checked to see if anyone from 4E had received JUG. When the bell sounded ending the period, the entire class bounded from their seats, and the seniors in the class exchanged handshakes and hugs. We all waited for our turn to say goodbye to Mr. O'Donnell. When everyone was gone, I approached the teacher, and after saying our goodbyes and complimenting one another, I asked, "Mister, I wonder if you could do me a favor?"

"Certainly, old bean! What can I do for you?"

"Without asking any questions, I need you to give me JUG."

"This is the strangest request I've ever received. Why?"

"Mister, no questions. Just write the slip, say I disrupted the class, and I'll see you at graduation."

Confused, the teacher shrugged, acceded to my request, and as he handed me the JUG slip, said, "You are as unpredictable as you are amusing, young Loof. I do not wish you luck, I wish you be true to yourself as you are now, and your future is assured. And from Shakespeare I offer you this, "Love all, trust a few, and do wrong to none."

No other words were necessary, and we sealed our farewell with a final handshake. As I exited the classroom, the realization that my time at Brooklyn Prep was coming to an end really hit me. Two periods later, I left my last high school class with a 99.9% feeling of happiness and satisfaction. Then there was that tenth of a percent feeling of doubt and dread.

I reached Father Richards's office, knocked on the open door, and walked inside. The priest looked up from his desk, saw who it was, and asked, "Owen what happened? Why are you here?"

I handed over the JUG slip, and the priest read it, then said, "Owen, I can't believe you disrupted Mr. O'Donnell's class, besides there's no one else here."

"Father, Mr. O'Donnell signed that slip. Are you questioning your own faculty? He gave me JUG, I gotta do it."

"You're going to go out there, and walk JUG all by yourself?"

"Yes, I am Father. It's the principle of the thing!"

Father Richards smiled broadly saying, "You really are nuts, but in a good way. You want to walk JUG by yourself, go ahead, walk it."

I went out to the courtyard and began walking. I was only out there for a few minutes when the door opened, Father Richards appeared, and announced, "You have company Owen."

Then Kevin walked through the door, handed the Prefect of Discipline a JUG slip, and joined his classmate. Bobby was next, and then John Alleva, Jack Fredreck, and Giacomo repeated the process. However, that was not the end. It was not long before each and every member of 4E was out there with me. An incredulous Father Richards stood there watching, and after a little more than fifteen minutes he stopped the parade, saluted the group, and said, "You people never cease to amaze me. I don't think I'll forget this day, or this class." Then with a big smile he added, "You're a weird bunch of squirrels, but you are all outstandingly loyal, and that will always hold you in good stead. Go do Brooklyn Prep proud. Now get outta here you nuts!"

There were shouts of joy, and 4E did as they were told, ran past Father Richards, and shook his hand. For me, the priest had a playful slap across the back of the head.

CHAPTER 39

At nine p. m. on the Friday after the last day of classes, Kevin, Bobby, and I shuffled into The Circle. Kevin and Bobby went over and seated themselves at a table with Michael, Maryanne, and Veronica. Almost thirty-five minutes later, I finally made my appearance, and along with Mike Woods, I had drinks for everyone. Bobby asked, "Where the heck were ya?"

Before I could answer, Michael replied for me, "Well, I can see one group of older guys from the neighborhood that had to say hello. Then there's a couple of girls who wanted to talk, and finally there's at least six people that asked him about his mother."

I added, pointing toward the bar, "Ya see those two couples over there? I have no idea who they are, but they sure know my parents"

Bobby said, "Oh well, the price of fame I guess!"

When I was firmly planted in my seat, Michael scanned the three males at the table saying, "So, the Prep boys are officially done with high school."

Kevin said, "Well, we still need our diplomas, but the last test was today."

Michael looked at me, and asked, "If this was test week, and you got out early, where were you? I haven't heard from you since last weekend."

After furtive glances in the direction of Kevin and Bobby,

I replied, "Well, ya know I just had some things I had to do."

Michael tilted his head toward Maryanne and Veronica, and said, "Somethin's up, but we're not supposed to ask any questions. So how did the finals go?"

I answered, "I think I did just bad enough."

Veronica leaned forward, and asked somewhat incredulously, "You didn't want to do well on your final exams?"

Bobby laughed, and replied, "Ya see Veronica, the nutcase here is in a competition with another guy to finish last in the class. So, he wants to pass everything, but do bad enough to win.

An astonished Veronica exclaimed, "Owen, really!"

"Guilty as charged, and by the way, I'm pretty sure I accomplished it. Of course, I won't be sure till I see it in black and white, but I'm confident."

It was a fun night of music, laughs, and drinking. At one point, I went to the bar for another round, Michael joined me, and he said, "So, your big day is next Saturday. How many people thought you would never make it?"

"Me included, but it really looks like it's gonna happen."

"Yes, it does, but it's too bad you won't be able to make Maryanne and Veronica's graduation party."

"Yeah, that's a real bummer, but I had no input on either date. I do wish I could be there though." Then I looked at my best friend in the world, and asked, "But that's not what you came over here to talk about, is it?"

"You know me as well as I know you, and that's right. And that's how I know that you and your Prep friends over there have some plan in the works. So okay, you can't talk about it tonight, but I know you'll tell me when you're ready."

Mike Woods put our drinks on the bar, I winked, and said, "People are waitin' for these. Let's get them over there."

At eleven p.m. on my graduation day, Michael exited Maryanne's house, and when he reached his car, I was sitting on the hood. When I saw my friend approaching, I jumped down and said, "Hey man, what's happenin'? I've been waitin' forever. I thought you'd never get here."

A thoroughly surprised Michael asked, "What the hell are you doing here? What's goin on? Wait! Somethin' happened at graduation?"

"Questions, questions, questions. If you're goin' home, get in the car and let's go. I'll tell ya all about it when we get there."

So, we piled ourselves in the car, and drove the six blocks to Michael's house. When we arrived, Michael's parents were sitting in the kitchen talking. After all the pleasantries were exchanged, and some small talk complete, Michael grabbed a couple of beers, we hurried out of the room, and down to the basement.

I was barely in my seat before Michael started, "Okay, let's hear it. Start from the beginning and don't leave anything out."

"Geeze, okay, but the first thing I gotta know is, can I sleep here tonight? 'Cause if I go home my mother might kill me."

"I knew it, I knew it! Oh shit, somethin' really bad happened. When I didn't see you all this week, I knew the plan was for graduation. Sure, ya can stay here, now what the hell happened?"

"Okay, they did the graduation outside on the field in front of the school. They put up a big stage and everything. All the parents and teachers were in their seats, and then all the big wigs went up on the stage. Then all the guys followed them up, and were standing in front of their seats."

"Okay, so you're up there at your seat..."

"Ummm, no! I said all the guys were up there, but I wasn't one of them."

"What'd ya mean you weren't one of them? Where were you?"

"That's what everyone was wonderin', and then I showed up."

"So, you were a little late, big deal. But wait, this is you. You were wearing somethin' crazy or wearing nothin'." Michael became very agitated, yelling, "What, what! Will ya just tell me!!"

"So, I was standin' on the roof of the school, wearing glider wings, and let out a yell. Everybody turned, and looked up at me. Then I jumped off the roof, glided down, and landed on the side of the stage. It was a perfect landing just like we practiced."

Michael asked incredulously, "What'd ya mean like ya practiced?"

"Well, where'd ya think I've been the last two weeks? We met a guy who does this kind of thing. He supplied the wings, and we've been testin' it out."

"I don't believe you. You are fuckin' nuts! And I say that out of love." Then while laughing added, "What happened then?"

"All the guys were clapping and yelling. Father Hamilton was tryin' really hard not to laugh, and Father Richards was just holdin' his head. Bobby and Kevin came off the stage to help me get the wings off, and my parents ran over to see if I was okay. Well, my father came to see if I was okay, my mother came to strangle me."

"Yeah, and probably woulda, except for all the witnesses, which is why you're not goin' home. And they still gave you the diploma?"

"Well, they don't really give you the diploma at the ceremony. I won't really know till next week, and there's still a question about that after the next thing that happened. But I think it'll be all right."

"Whoa, wait! What else happened?"

"Well, everybody stayed standing through the whole thing, and then when all the commotion was over, Father Hamilton welcomed everyone, said a prayer, and the band played the National Anthem. When all that was done, everybody on the stage sat down. That's when the commotion started again."

"Now, what'd ya do?"

"You're just like everyone else. I didn't do anything. When they sat down, there were tacks on the seats, and everybody started screaming."

Michael started laughing, and placed both hands over his face. "Tacks? Really!"

"Well, that wouldn'tna been so bad, but there was double-sided tape on the chairs, people couldn't get up right away, and chairs were kinda goin' everywhere, and it took a little while for order to be restored."

"I repeat, you are fuckin' nuts!"

"Geeze, my best friend, practically my brother, I thought you would be different. But just like everyone else, you blame me right away. Like I'm the only one who would do somethin' like that."

"Yeah, that's about right!"

I covered my face, and began sobbing, "Gee thanks. It's so sad when your own friends and family don't have faith in you."

"Oh, shut up you idiot, and stop the act. Is the party still on for tomorra?"

THE BEST DRESSED MAN IN ROCKAWAY

I uncovered my face, and answered with a smile, "Sure, sure. She was really pissed today, but she hasta go on with the party. Then I'll probably be safe till we see Father Hamilton next week for the diploma and final grades."

Michael started laughing again, and said, "Man, I wish I coulda seen you flying through the air."

"Michael, it felt so cool! It was even better than being on a wave."

CHAPTER 40

The graduation party was a gala event at the Knights of Columbus Hall. My mother and the Knights outdid themselves. There were relatives galore, in addition to most of Rockaway. However, the graduation day events, and the possible consequences, were only known to a select few. Then the day after the party, my mother packed us up, and we headed to the beach at Keansburg, New Jersey, where Uncle Jimmy and Aunt Mary had summer bungalows with a few other relatives. She wanted to keep me out of Rockaway until after the meeting with Father Hamilton on July 3rd.

A little past eight p.m. that night, I went to the Boardwalk at 96th Street because it was Wednesday night, which meant it was fireworks night, and I knew everybody would be there. When I arrived, everyone was on the beach with cases of beer, and a small barrel of Bash. I was surprised to see Kevin and Bobby standing with Michael and JP. Michael saw me approaching and said, "Well, here he is, and he's upright and walking. That's a good sign."

JP added, "His face looks okay. No black eyes or bandages."

Michael then said, "Wait, wait, Bridget Loof is smart. She'd make sure the bruises were hidden."

I laughed, and lifted my shirt, while tuning completely around saying, "Very funny and true. But see? No beatings.

Michael responded, "No beatings is a good omen."

Then I looked at Kevin and Bobby asking, "I didn't expect to see you guys. What're doin' here?"

Kevin remarked nonchalantly, "Well, we just wanted to be here for fireworks night, ya know'?"

Bobby chimed in, "Why else would we be here?"

The four of them turned their backs on me, and started talking with one another. So, I said, "Okay, ya know what? There's Fourth of July fireworks tomorra, so I'm gonna skip tonight, and I'll catch you all tomorra."

My four friends turned and rushed at me, slapped me around, and poured beer and Bash on me. I yelled out, "Okay, okay! Stop wasting the alcohol! Get me a drink, come on and sit down, and I'll tell ya what happened."

Once we were situated on the Boardwalk steps with our refreshments, I took a sip and began, "There was a lot of haggling about what should happen to me. Father Hamilton reminded me of what my parents kept saying all week. "You could have killed yourself jumping off the roof."

Bobby interrupted, "What about the tacks and the tape?"

"Yeah, he was kinda annoyed at that, but he said one year somebody actually put glue on the seats, which was a lot worse. So, he gave me some credit for being considerate."

Michael asked, "You confessed you did it?"

"Well sure, there was no point denyin' it. Oh, and I told them who helped me too."

Kevin and Bobby stared at me in stunned silence, and I added, "Your parents probably got the call already." Then I took another sip and said, "Boy I hope the fireworks start soon, and wow we'll have more tomorrow for the Fourth!"

Bobby stood up, looked from me to Kevin, and then at Michael, asking, "Ya think he's serious?"

Michael shrugged, and Kevin said to Bobby, "We could feed 'im to the sharks right now!"

They both looked at me with questions stamped all over their faces. I started laughing, pointed at them, and exclaimed, "Nah, Nah! Nah, nah! I had ya for a couple of seconds there, and that's good enough!"

The four of them picked me up, and Kevin shouted, "Let's feed 'im to the sharks anyway!"

Fifteen minutes later I was still pretty wet and sandy, sitting on the lifeguard chair with my Brooklyn Prep brothers, when I proudly announced, "Well, I am officially a graduate of Brooklyn Preparatory School!"

Bobby inquired impatiently, "And what is the rest of the story?"

"Well, like I said, there was a lot of discussion goin' on, and personally, I didn't think it looked good. Then I was asked to wait outside. Ten minutes later, I was called back in, and everybody was smiling, and I got the diploma." After some laughing and back-slapping, I added, "So, I have no idea how I got into the school in the first place, it's a miracle I stayed in, and only three people know how I got the diploma. My entire Brooklyn Prep experience is an enigma, wrapped in a puzzle, that's a complete mystery."

Kevin said, "And the answer is probably better left unknown!"

We toasted to that, and Bobby slapped me on the arm. "Wait, wait, there is one mystery that you can clear up. What was your rank in class? Did you reach your goal!

"That is the most disappointing part of the whole thing. I was 217 out of 218. All that hard work down the drain."

Both of my friends offered their condolences, and Kevin asked, "Do ya know who beat ya?"

"I don't know for sure, but I got it narrowed down to three people. I'm gonna find out, don't worry."

Bobby asked, "I'm sure you will. So, what's gonna happen now?"

"I don't really know for sure. Short term, my mother is gettin' me a job at the restaurant where she works in the city."

Kevin asked, "No college in the discussion?"

"It hasn't really been talked about, but I know she's gotta be planning somethin'. You guys are all set though, right."

Bobby answered first. "I'm goin' to University of Scranton and playin' basketball."

Then it was Kevin's turn. "Me and a couple of other guys are goin' to Iona with the Christian Brothers in New Rochelle."

I said, "Sounds like you're goin' from the frying pan into the fire there, Kev. That's great for you guys. Well, I could always join the Navy." We all laughed and took another drink, and I continued, "I don't know what I'm doin', or where I'm goin', but I know I will never forget my time at Brooklyn Prep, and especially my two best friends. Plus, all the teachers like Mr. Jagger, Mr. Garell, and Mr. Delasalvo. I'll never forget all they did for me, and everything I put them through."

Through our laughter, Kevin asked, "What about Father Richards?"

"Oh my God, without him, Father Knox and Father Hamilton, I never woulda made it." I took a deep breath and said, "But you know, this year with Father McCartney and 4E was really the icing on the cake, and just completed the whole ride. All I know is that whatever the future has in store for me, it is these last four years with the friendships, the knowledge, and the values instilled at Brooklyn Prep, that will help me get wherever I want to go, and overcome any obstacles that get in the way."

Then I got a little chocked up and added, "But ya know, there's somebody missin' here." I looked into the knowing faces of my other musketeers saying, "Yep, Tom Collins! Everything I did the last three years, he was with me. He changed me and opened a whole new world.

I raised my glass, and my two friends joined me in the toast. "Here's to Tom Collins and his lasting influence. Also, to Brooklyn Preparatory School, and its sixty years of turning out young men of character, even me. And may they keep doing it for another sixty years!"

As we put the cups to our lips, we heard the first canisters escape from the barge. Then there was a loud boom, and the sky lit up with color illuminating the ocean, the beach, and the Boardwalk. The three of us watched the show, and I believed that it was a fitting celebration to the end of an important part of my life, and the beginning of a new chapter.

EPILOGUE

My Brooklyn Prep closed its doors for good in 1972. The building is now part of Medgar Evers College of the City University of New York, and is known as the "Carroll Street Building." From 1848 to 1907, some of the land was the location of the Kings County Penitentiary, also known as the Crow Hill Penitentiary. After the school closed, the land was sold to CUNY.

There are two schools today that carry the Brooklyn Prep name. One is a public NYC Department of Education high school in the Williamsburg section of Brooklyn. The other is a fifth through eighth grade middle school operated by the Jesuits in the East Flatbush section of Brooklyn. However, though the original Brooklyn Prep closed its doors almost fifty years ago, The Alumni Association keeps the school's irrepressible spirit and vivid memories alive.

The Alumni Association sponsors an annual dinner, a golf outing, and several other events throughout the year that bring friends together to share stories of our time at Prep and our life's journeys since graduation. Whether it is at these organized events, when we meet by happenstance, or speak on the phone, it is like time stands still, and the camaraderie of our time at Prep is instantly there. However, it is not only with our classmates we find that truth, but the bond of The Prep is also there when we meet alums from any other year.

Many of our teachers are also present at the dinners, and the special relationships that exist between the alumni extend to our instructors. In my case, their long, rich memories have produced some interesting results. At the twenty-fifth anniversary of the Class of '68, it took me a little while to find Father Hamilton. When I finally went over to say hello, before he even answered my greeting, he asked, "Hey Loof, you still got that knife?"

At another dinner, I found out from a classmate whose son was a student at St. Peter's Prep, a Jesuit high school in Jersey City, that now Father Jagger, was telling his students some of the things I did at Prep. Apparently, he had been doing this for years, and one day the son asked his father about me. Their conversation ended when the son asked, "Was that guy really crazy and do all that stuff?"

My friend, classmate, and fellow alum, replied, "Oh yeah he was nuts, and Father Jagger's not lying."

Brooklyn Prep will always be with me. The values instilled by the education, the lasting friendships, and even the antics, were the ignition key that started the ride to becoming The Best Dressed Man in Rockaway. The gas tank was filled, and the trunk was loaded and unloaded many times throughout the journey that added to what was begun at Brooklyn Prep. But without that initial turn of the key, The Best Dressed Man, as we know him today, would not exist.

So, thank you Tom Collins, Bob Atanasio, Kevin Kane, 4E, Father Hamilton, and everyone associated with the school from 1907-1972. It was a great place to grow up, and the only place that could have produced the foundation for my future. If I had the opportunity to go back, I would not change one thing.

Brooklyn Prep Forever!
Sanctitus/Scientia/Sanitas.
Holiness/Knowledge/Health

The next stop on the road to becoming the Best Dressed Man in Rockaway is his relationships with members of the opposite sex. In, *The Best Dressed Man in Rockaway: The Love Stories, Part One* and *Part Two*, read about the women he was involved with before marrying the woman who saved his life. You will learn how he coped with her passing, and how slowly the outfits were added to the personality to complete the Best Dressed Man. With the alter-ego helping in moving forward from the grief, he was happy and not actively searching for romance. Then, meet four women who offer a chance to flirt with love again. Each of these relationships were ended by the women, and the thought of one special person was given up as impossible. However, someone magically comes back into his life, and he unexpectedly finds true love for the second time.

ACKNOWLEDGEMENTS

The Beatles sang, "I get by with a little help from my friends." Well, those words were never truer for me in putting this work together. There are so many people that were instrumental in the finished product that this book represents. I beg the indulgence of anyone I might leave out, but there are people I must especially mention.

Without The Rockaway Times, I would not have been given the title of, The Best Dressed Man in Rockaway. Katie McFadden not only gave me the title, but she was also the first person to read the stories the way they were first written. Her knowledge, expertise, and encouragement were so helpful. I owe her more than she could ever know. Kevin Boyle, the newspaper's Publisher, has become someone I can call a friend of both Owen and The Best Dressed Man. Just as important, it was Mr. Boyle's influence that convinced me to change how the stories were told, which changed the direction of the project for the better. Finally, Kami-Leigh Agard went above and beyond the call of duty in putting on the finishing touches that readied the manuscript for publication. I am extremely lucky to have these intelligent, talented people in my corner.

There are two people who have also been reading the stories and offering insights that made me believe that I was writing something that could touch people in a lot of different ways. Thank you, Rick Campbell and Debra Smith, for your constructive criticism and continued friendship.

The most amazing part of this whole project was reconnecting, and talking with, so many of my classmates. They were all helpful in recalling memories and lending so much to the stories, including their names. In catching up with what happened after Prep, Anton Blackman's story stands out. He joined the Marines in August 1968, and I joined the Army in September 1968. In 1969, he was in Viet Nam, stationed around the city of Da Nang. I was in Viet Nam, stationed around the city of Chu Lai, which was only about one hundred miles South. It is such an amazing coincidence, and talking to him blew me away. I also have to add, he was a much better Marine than I was soldier.

Also, very important for his advice and support was my classmate, friend, and author Alex Avitabile. His two books tell the stories of Al and Mick Forte, two cousins from Brooklyn who stand up against powerful bullies to achieve justice, and are must reads.

Bob Atanasio and Kevin Kane, besides being partners in crime, contributed in many other ways. They were supportive and kept me going with their wit, intelligence, and memory conjuring. I thank them and love them dearly.

I have talked about, and you have read about, the importance of Tom Collins in my life. However, after he left the school, I lost touch with him. Once, while living in Hawaii, I somehow found contact info and we spoke. When I began this project, I searched for my mentor. Miraculously, I was able to find him living just two hours away. Thank you, Tom Collins for being there at Brooklyn Prep and being my friend still.

On page 265, is the original article from our school newspaper, The Blue Jug. It was the April Fool's edition and is printed here just as it appeared then. I thank John Alwill, who was the editor of the paper and supplied the article, and the entire staff who contributed to it.

I also must thank, Melissa Welch. To say she was instrumental in the finished product is a complete understatement. She is a beautiful woman inside and out, and I really believe I would not have started writing or would have continued the project without her support. There is no one, outside of family, that knows me better than she does, and she talked me through so many rough spots.

Finally, I must acknowledge Luminaire Press. I could not have "self-published" this work without the experience and expertise of Patricia Marshall, Kim Harper-Kennedy, Sallie McCann Vandagrift, and Caitlin McCrum. Although, when you work with the talented ladies at Luminaire Press, the term "self-publish" is an exaggeration, as I had no clue how to have this book published and they deserve all the credit.

Made in the USA
Middletown, DE
05 July 2025